# Lovers, Rakes and Rogues

*By the same author*

Love and Drollery
Jest Upon Jest
Demaundes Joyous
Kings, Lords and Wicked Libellers
The Caricatures of George Cruikshank
Juggernaut

# Lovers, Rakes and Rogues

Amatory, merry and bawdy verse
from 1580 to 1830
collected, introduced and annotated
by

John Wardroper

Shelfmark Books
London

*British Library Cataloguing-in-Publication Data*
A catalogue record for this book is
available from the British Library

ISBN 0-9526093-0-4

Shelfmark Books, 60 St Paul's Road, London N1 2QW

Orders to:
Biblios, Star Road, Partridge Green, West Sussex RH13 8LD
Tel 01403 710971 / Fax 01403 711143

Set in Palatino
And printed in Great Britain by The Bath Press, Bath

# Contents

And why not amorous songs,
as well as amorous attires?

*Thomas Campion, 1601*

I propose to cure you without the nauseous and painful discipline of clysters and blisters, of vomits, purges or close-stools. I will set you right in a cleanly way, by merry airs, by the power of numbers and the charms of musick.

*The Merry Musician: or A Cure for the Spleen, 1716*

Lack a day! If that species of composition be the sin against the Haly Ghaist, 'I am the most offending soul alive'.

*Robert Burns (on bawdy songs), 1793*

# INTRODUCTION

These songs and droll verses are not to be found in the usual anthologies. Many now appear in print for the first time in two or three hundred years, and a few have never been printed before. They were sung or recited in taverns and at court, in cottages and in great houses, by street performers and by stars of the theatre; but changing fashions and the advance of moralistic notions pushed them into obscurity. The frolicsome and often ribald offspring of the great Anon or of authors who rarely figure in English syllabuses, they became footnotes at best in the story of our literature. Now here they are to give pleasure again.

An additional reward for many readers will be that these things tell us so much about the language and the life of their day. Social life, that is, for I have avoided directly political items: they need endless explaining, and besides, they would have excessively swelled the collection. The 327 items I have room for range over life high and low, and provide a feast of everyday language from the days of Shakespeare to those of Dickens's youth. You can encounter whores and scoundrels, and learn their slang. You can savour the singing and dancing of poor folk in search of some cheer, and of richer ones purging their melancholy. You can see what qualities men celebrated in a girl, and how they could sing of her seduction.

This collection risks being berated as deplorably male-dominated. Again and again, songs celebrate behaviour that deserves to be frowned on. A girl says no no no and again no no no, but soon the brisk young man has her saying ay ay ay and wanting more. It is not my task, however, to present a sanitized version of what my search uncovers. Note too that the women are well able to speak for themselves. A ballad that was long popular, in which a woman laments that she cannot free her heart of the man who has betrayed her ('I am so deep in love'), ends with this advice to women:

Then if you needs must love,
Love one another.

Women are also quick to be blunt about men's crudeness, vanity or sexual insufficiency. There is no suggestion that women do not desire or deserve sexual pleasure. What haunts them, in a time of minimal or non-existent contraceptive knowledge, is the fear that their belly will swell and the man will be gone. The songs and ballads are often a source of useful counsel, as well as of consolation. Every open-hearted reader will find, I hope, that in all their rakish, amoral, unpolite variety they are not altogether remote from the life of today, when ideals of good behaviour are still sometimes flouted by unruly passions.

This collection has a precursor, published years ago: *Love and Drollery*, the first product of my hunt for unconsidered treasures. In the quarter-century since that appeared, scholars both literary and historical have shown more interest in material that reveals the *mentalité* (to indulge in a fashionable word) of our forebears. There is room for them to do much more, and I hope this new book will help them. My first wish, though, is to reveal delights to general readers and enliven their picture of Britain's past.

*Love and Drollery* was devoted to little more than seven decades of the seventeenth century. This time I have extended the search through the eighteenth century and into the early nineteenth. I was tempted to rove back the other way too, for various merry English themes are found from Chaucer's time onwards, but that might have made the book too sprawling; and besides, the relatively small number of lyrics that survive from those years have been valued and published. So I begin in the 1580s and range over a mere 250 years.

The best pieces in *Love and Drollery* are revived here. It could not be otherwise, for the seventeenth century is especially fruitful. Gentlemen's handwritten collections of songs, merry verse, satire and much else are one good source. The work of wits whose names are lost forever is often found next to privately circulated poems of John Donne, Thomas Carew, John Suckling and others. Young men hoping to pass for wits kept pocket-size hoards. As one satirist wrote:

> Gallo's a pretty man, hath pretty hair,
> A pretty hat, and cloak as one need wear.
> Gallo's a gallant, and as one need use
> Can court his mistress with a sprightly muse.
> Gallo's a dunce, for I supply his wit,
> Which he makes nonsense by his reading it.

A similar mocking point is made by an enterprising man who got hold of a quantity of manuscript verse in 1650 and published it in *The Academy of Complements*. He says in a preface that he is making enemies. A would-be gallant 'takes it very unkindly that I should rob him of his Commonplace Book; he hangs down his head and bites his Lip for indignation... He pursued his Mistress with such Language, writ thus, sung the same songs... This silken Tribe must now of necessity be silent: for if any of their Marmalet Mistresses should catch them at their repetitions again, they may now take this Booke, and turn them to the very page.'

In that great age of English vocal music, collections of songs were kept by musicians in manuscript form, but many composers also published songbooks, no doubt to enhance their earnings as well as their fame. The words were sometimes their own, but more often anonymous. A great deal from these books has been reprinted, but in making my choice from them I have found plenty of scope for bringing out what has been too often ignored, the zestful and robust. The chaste melancholy of John Dowland (whose motto was *Semper Dowland, semper dolens*) has no place here. He did once venture to set a song called 'Finding in fields my Sylvia all alone', for that title got as far as the contents page of his *Second Book of Songs or Ayres* — but then he did not print it.

Other composers of his time set love-songs and psalms with equal readiness (here, after all, were two good markets). The holy and the profane are happily linked, for example, in the subtitle of Thomas Campion's *Two Bookes of Ayres* (about

1613): 'The First Contayning Divine and Morall Songs: The Second, Light Conceits of Lovers'. Campion is notable first of all as a poet. In prefaces to his songbooks he discusses his craft and promotes his theories of syllabic verse. He likes songs 'short and well seasoned', and says, 'Short Ayres, if they be skilfully framed, and naturally exprest, are like quicke and good Epigrammes in Poesie, and breeding as great Difficulty as a larger Poeme.'

After a fine run of songbooks during and just after Shakespeare's time, a sharp falling-off occurs in the 1630s — troubled years leading to the Civil War. Then the long conflict, the destruction of Charles I's court and the closing of the theatres come as sad blows for musicians and songwriters. A pamphlet of 1643, *The Actors' Remonstrance,* says musicians 'now wander with their Instruments under their cloaks, I meane such as have any, into all houses of good fellowship, saluting every room where there is company with *Will you have any musicke, Gentlemen?*' Poets who wrote for the theatre and earned 'annuall stipends and beneficiall second-dayes' are reduced to writing 'contemptible penny-pamphlets'.

But quite soon the upheaval had a positive effect. Music was certainly not silenced (Oliver Cromwell himself loved music). With theatres closed, private music-making and entertainments became more important. Musicians could gain a living by private lessons and performances. A demand for music books arose, and composers formerly employed at court and in noble houses were now ready to publish the songs and dances in their precious handwritten collections.

Chief among those who did so was Henry Lawes, who while at Charles I's court had set lyrics by Herrick, Carew, Suckling, Lovelace, Waller and many others. During the 1650s an enterprising bookseller, John Playford, issued three collections of Lawes's songs, more than 150 in total, as well as hundreds of songs and catches by others. They were sold 'at his shop in the Inner Temple neare the Church doore', together with much else in verse and prose, and 'all sorts of Rul'd Paper for Musick'. Playford's enterprise was much valued. Years later, in some prefatory verses to his *Musical Companion*, 1672, the royalist poet Thomas Jordan says:

I gratefully remember, in those daies,
When pestilential Purity did raise
Rebellion 'gainst the best of Princes, and
Pious Confusiòn untun'd the Land;
When by the Fury of the *Good old Cause*
Will Lawes was slain by such whose Wills were Laws,
And panting Music almost out of Breath,
Thou did'st retrieve its fainting powers from death...

(Will Lawes, Henry's brother, another fine composer of songs, was killed in the war.)

A parallel result of the Civil War was the publication of a cluster of books, often with 'drollery' in their title, bringing out merry and satirical verse that is bawdier and more cynical than what had appeared in print before. Hitherto it had circulated only in manuscript, some of it as far back as James I's time. Now impoverished Cavaliers were willing to sell their verses, or other verses they had gathered on convivial evenings, the work of courtiers, lawyers or university wits who had thought it beneath them to deal with booksellers. The mood was right. Amusement was badly needed, especially by broken royalists. 'Plain Poetry is now dis-esteem'd,' says the publisher Henry Herringman in 1655, launching *Musarum Deliciae*, the earliest collection of this type. 'It must be Drollery or it will not please... Read, laugh and enjoy.' This collection he credits to the Cavalier Sir John Mennes (or Mennis) and his friend the Rev Dr James Smith.

One justification used for going public was to put accurate texts into print before someone brought out false ones. As John Playford says in his introduction to *Wit and Drollery* in 1656: 'These Poems, never before printed, are a collection from the best Wits, of what above 15 years since were begun to be preserved, for mirth and friends; the fear of having some of them imperfectly set forth hath, though unwillingly, made them common. What hath not been extant of Sir J.M., of Ja. S., of Sir W.D., of J.D. and other miraculous muses of the Times, are here at thy Service... Good Drollery is not so loose, or of so late an invention, but that the most serious Wits have thought themselves honoured to own them.' The initials stand for Mennes, Smith, Sir William Davenant and presumably John Donne, whose 'Love's Progress' is in the book.

There was sharp competition for the miraculous muses. When John Phillips, a nephew of Milton, published still more of Mennes's and Smith's verse as *Sportive Wit,* he hit at rival publications 'rak'd from the simple collections of Short-hand prentices'. Another compiler, John Cotgrave, made a point of the pains he took in preparing *Wits Interpreter*, 1655. It is 'a Collection of all that for such a time could be ransackt from the private Papers of the choicest Wits of the three Nations, from which Manuscripts of theirs, if there be any Copies transcribed that are old, it was not the intention, but rather the misfortune of the Insertor, for upon the least intimation whilst I was in Town to attend the Press, I crossed out whatsoever I could hear had been formerly publisht.'

An extra attraction of these once-private funds of wit was that their bawdry, their royalist tone and their ventures into anti-puritan satire angered the authorities. There is a complex irony in the fact that John Phillips, who had undergone his uncle's stern teaching and discipline, was now the compiler of *Sportive Wit.* A dozen years earlier, Milton had published *Areopagitica,* that powerful plea 'for the liberty of unlicensed printing'. Now he held the high post of Latin Secretary in Cromwell's government, which was trying to stamp out hostile pamphlets and news-sheets, whether of defeated royalists or of Cromwell's own disillusioned left wing. On April 25, 1656, the council of state turned its attention to cavalier verse. It declared that *Sportive Wit* contained 'much scandalous, lascivious, scurrilous and profane matter', ordered all copies to be seized and burnt by the hangman, and condemned Phillips, his publisher and printers to be fined. A fortnight later a similar book, *Choyce Drollery,* 'stuffed with profane and obscene matter tending to the corruption of manners', went the same way. (So did a translation of Martial's epigrams.) Copies of these drolleries are therefore extremely rare.

At the Restoration, one Cavalier who returned from exile was the droll Sir John Mennes. 'His company was delightful to all ingenious and witty men,' says Anthony Wood in *Athenae Oxonienses.* Mennes became Charles II's comptroller of the navy — a genial but deplorably inefficient superior to Samuel Pepys, whose diary records many troubled times

('...his folly in his office ... I am sick and weary to speak of it', 1663; '...a report so ridiculous that he hath drawn up ... nothing of it being true', 1664); but also many merry times ('...in the highest pitch of mirth and his mimical tricks that ever I saw... Certainly would have made an excellent actor, and now would be an excellent teacher of actors', 1666).

Charles II's reign was a good time for drolleries — old, new, revised, augmented. Songbooks flourished too, especially those of John Playford. In his *Antidote against Melancholy: Made up in Pills Compounded of Witty Ballads, Jovial Songs, and Merry Catches*, 1661, he extols the healthful power of songs:

Here are Pills of every sort
For the Country, City, Court,
Compounded and made up of sport...

Want'st thou Stomach to thy Meat,
And wouldst fain restore the heat?
This does it more than Choccolet.

Cures the Spleene, revives the blood,
Puts thee in a Merry Mood.
Who can deny such Physick good?

(Soon he has a sideline in physick of less value: 'The excellent Cordial called ELIXIR PROPRIETATIS, a few drops of which drank in a glass of sack or other liquors is admirable for all Coughs and Consumptions of the Lungs and inward Distempers'; and 'The true and right *Sympathetical Powder* ... made by *Sir Kenelm Digby's* own Directions, and Seal'd up in Paper with his Seal, having ever since his death [1665] been choicely preserved in a strong box... A whole Paper is 3s. And half Paper 1s. 6d.' — a good price, as much as a songbook.)

Melancholy had had its vogue earlier in the century, but it is unexpected to see it arise as a selling-point in 1661, less than a full year after Charles II's glorious return. The reign of the so-called merry monarch was often disillusioning and stressful for his subjects. He inspired innumerable lampoons. Here is a taste of one of the mildest:

Silly and sauntering he goes
  From French whore to Italian,
Unlucky in whate'er he does,
  An old ill-favoured stallion.

He was also, it is true, an affable man, fond of rollicking songs, and not royally aloof with commoners who knew how to please him. The songwriter and playwright Thomas Durfey (or D'Urfey, as he restyled himself) proudly recalled how the king rested his hand on D'Urfey's shoulder as they sang together. Beginning in the 1670s, D'Urfey created nearly 500 songs in his long life, often borrowing from or imitating ballad originals. He injects some down-to-earth vigour into collections of 'the Newest Ayres and Songs sung at Court and at the Publick Theatres', which otherwise are often the modish mock dallyings of shepherds and shepherdesses with such names as Strephon and Dorinda. Those tiresome things so nauseated one songwriter that he managed, surprisingly, to slip a protest against 'this Love Maskarade' into one of these books of Newest Ayres:

> Alexis, and Damon, and twenty Swains more,
> Have been sighing and vowing ten thousand times o'er,
> 'Let me dye' and all that's insipid and flat...
> 'O thou charming divine' and 'Oh sweet pretty Creature'
> Is so old, the Amours of a Cobler look greater.

D'Urfey's greatest contribution is to a far from insipid series entitled *Wit and Mirth, or Pills to Purge Melancholy*, issued over many years by Playford and then by his son Henry and others. The *Pills* were aimed at a broad market — a point made in some verses by the facetious writer Thomas Brown in an edition of 1700:

> All conditions and sexes in country and city,
> From the would-be-thought-wise to the really witty,
> From the lady who speaks all her words as in print
> And has eyes which strike fire like steel and a flint,
> To the damsel whose language is coarse as her skin
> And who fain would be dabbling, but starts at the sin
> As she stares at and covets the thing call'd a man,
> And she thinks she could do what Her Ladyship can;
> From the prodigal cit, who's a-settling the nation,
> To the poor country thrasher, who's as great in his station...
> All alike shall be purg'd by your laxative verses,
> Which shall loosen their tongues instead of their arses.

In his old age D'Urfey had a big hand in compiling a six-volume edition of 1719–20, which brought this pharmacopeia of *Pills* to well over a thousand. Though the tone is generally robust, often ballad-like, many of the composers are men of 'the Court and the Publick Theatres'. More than eighty of the settings are by Henry Purcell, whose fame as a composer of higher things has obscured his talent for ribald songs and bawdy catches. (His last creations before his death in 1695 were settings for songs in a D'Urfey play.)

When a vogue for Italian opera invaded the London theatre in the early eighteenth century, the *Pills* and similar collections proved valuable for a pro-English resistance movement. John Gay's *Beggar's Opera* of 1728, which simultaneously mocked the Italian opera and Sir Robert Walpole's corrupt government, found forty of its sixty-nine airs in the *Pills* volumes; and the numerous ballad-opera successors happily went to the same source.

The trade in ballads went back to the sixteenth century. They were published as broadsides: single sheets, often as large as 11x14 inches, printed on one side only, illustrated with simple woodcuts, and headed with titles far more eyecatching than on any other printed wares until the rise of the popular press, far in the future. It was a brisk trade. The Stationers' Register, in which printers began recording their publications in 1557, shows that broadsides far outnumber other printed works for many years. Battles or monsters or the deeds of Robin Hood were frequent themes, but analysis of the register shows that love-songs were by far the most popular. Their amorous freedom alarmed ardent Christians long before the rise of puritanism. One preacher issued in 1561 a counter-ballad, 'Agaynste fylthy wrytinge and suche like Delythynge', of which this is an extract:

> What meane the rimes that run thus large in every shop to sell?
> With wanton sound and filthie sense, me thinke it grees not well.
> ...Tel me is Christ or Cupide Lord? doth God or Venus reigne?

Of the few broadsides that survive from those days, however, the rarest of all are the love-songs. Devout persons no doubt burned some, but the main destroyer was surely their very popularity: passed from hand to hand, they ended in tatters. Telling evidence is provided by 'Greensleeves': it was popular from its first appearance in the 1570s, as frequent references to it show, yet not one broadside copy of it survives from the sixteenth century.

From the mid-seventeenth century on, though, broadside songs survive in their thousands. This is thanks to the fact that gentlemen as well as humbler folk came to delight in them, and a few of these gentlemen valued them enough to give them a place in their libraries. One such was the eminent jurist John Selden (died 1654), who said, 'Take a straw and throw it up into the air: you shall see by that, which way the wind is, which you shall not do by casting up a stone. More solid things do not show the complexion of the times so well as ballads and libels' (the latter meaning such things as political lampoons). Samuel Pepys, an enthusiastic singer, acquired Selden's collection of ballads, kept buying new ones, and brought the total to 1,775 — now a treasured part of the Pepys collection at Cambridge.

The enthusiasm of gentlemen for balladry can be seen as one sign of a loosening of boundaries between high and low. The Civil War was a shaker-up of society. Men and women beneath the gentry made their voices heard. Controversy brought a great increase in printing. Literacy increased: it has been estimated that by the second half of the century 30 per cent of males (rather fewer of females) could read, giving publishers of popular reading-matter a rising market.

Pepys's section-headings for his broadside collection give a good picture of the trade: 'Devotion and Morality; History — True and Fabulous; Tragedy — viz Murders, Executns, Judgmts of God &c; State & Times; Love — Pleasant; Love — Unfortunate; Marriage, Cuckoldry &c; Sea — Love, Gallantry & Actions; Drinking & Good Fellowship; Humour, Frollicks &c.' In their hunt for new topics, the ballad-writers of the Restoration were quick to pick up songs from the theatres or from songbooks. A broadside of the 1670s begins:

> What's here to do? a pretty Modish song
> Turn'd to a Ballad? in troth I think ere long
> A fourth part of the Town will Poets be.
> If that a line of Wit they can but see
> They must be medling and add further still...

And indeed 'modish songs' would sometimes be swelled to twice their length to fill out a broadside.

The borrowing of ideas went the other way too. Many poets were glad to use the ballad form. Gentlemen and peers revelled in ballad-style lampoons on politicians and courtiers, sung to familiar tunes such as 'Old Simon the King' or 'Sellenger's Round'. They were often too libellous to print. A sample from Charles II's time:

Ye Whores of renowne
That ply up and downe
And live upon Gentlemen's Bounties
Will find, I'm afraid,
A Decay in your Trade,
For Stamford's a-bringing his Countess. *Earl of Stamford*

Is Fucking a Crime
When Ballocks divine
Freely scatter their Seed o'er the Nation?
For Burnet's stiff Tarse *Bishop Burnet*
In each pious Arse
Rubs up a devout Meditation...

Lordly balladeering continued in the next century, though perhaps less lewdly. Certainly there was growing pressure for public decorum. The licentiousness of the theatre was denounced and curbed. Songbooks too came under attack. In 1711 one Arthur Bedford, in *The Great Abuse of Musick*, said John Playford's had been bad enough, encouraging drunkenness and lechery, but now 'Son Henry comes up in his Father's stead, and in Publishing of Profaneness and Debauchery excells all that went before him' — naming the *Wit and Mirth* songbooks that Henry had been publishing since 1699. Outward propriety and the deploring of rakishness were part of the self-affirmation of the rising middle class. The words 'elegant' and 'genteel' are seen more and more. A glance at newspapers of, say, the 1750s will reveal not only that the company at Vauxhall Gardens was 'very genteel' and that a dancing master will teach gentlemen to dance 'in a genteel manner', but even that two highwaymen who held up a coach returning from Vauxhall were 'genteelly dressed'. At the same time, more and more people of the ungenteel sort in country and town were being turned into day-labourers and losing what little independence they had.

Changes such as these contributed, in the song trade, to a widening of the divide between the 'genteel' and the lowly. It is harder to find good new pieces. Songs for the polite part of the market are often sadly artificial. Collections of those sung at the Vauxhall, Ranelagh and Marylebone pleasure gardens have titles such as *The Polite Songster* and promise not to bring a blush to maiden cheeks. There is far more tedium than vivacity. This Ranelagh song of 1744 is typical:

When Colin first in yonder Vale
To Celia told his Am'rous Tale
The rising Lark with warbling Strain
Soft'ned her Breast to hear the Swain.
The feather'd Songsters in the Grove — *etc.*

Occasionally there is a teasing hint that Celia or Belinda is a creature of flesh and blood (though not to be rudely touched):

Her lily breasts are like young doves
With innocency blest,
And at each other trembling move
As fearful to be prest —
*As fearful to be prest.*

One of the few places where young ladies could find evidence of a more vital world was in collections of Scottish songs, as if the slight distancing of dialect made the erotic still permissible. The best known was Allan Ramsay's craftily titled *Tea Table Miscellany,* begun in 1724 and often reissued and expanded. Ramsay says in his preface, 'I have kept out all smut and ribaldry, that the modest voice and ear of the fair singer might meet with no affront,' but as a few items that I reprint will show, he allowed his fair singers some freedom.

Printing spread rapidly after the licensing of presses lapsed in 1695. The London song and chapbook trade remained dominant, but provincial rivals arose. Songs originating in York, Newcastle, Glasgow and a dozen other places put some new life into the old stock. One innovation that quickly spread was the 'songster' or 'garland'. These were eight-page collections, measuring no more than six inches by four, often poorly printed, and offering many familiar pieces year after year. Yet a patient searcher is rewarded with lively new things by nameless poets.

The sort of printer/vendor who before long operated in every solid town of Britain and Ireland is nicely conveyed by the advertisements they inserted in these songsters. Here is one from Samuel Harward of Tewkesbury, '...sold also at his Shops in Glocester and Cheltenham; where may be had all Sorts of New and Old Songs, Penny Histories, &c, Wholesale and Retail. Likewise the True Original Daffy's Elixir, Bateman's Drops, Scotch Pills, and all other Medicines of established Reputation'. ('Histories' are chapbooks of perennial stories such as *Jack of Newbury* or *The Seven Champions of Christendom.*) From such printers, songs reached the smallest village. After a process of oral transmission, misremembering, splicing and reinventing, many lived on into the present century, to be collected by scholars and labelled folksong. The delicate question of 'folk' is touched on again in my notes.

Certainly songs were created by people of humble origin. Roving balladmongers bought songs wholesale but some of them also wrote their own and found printers for them. One such was 'the famous Charles Leslie, Ballad-singer, commonly call'd Musle-mow'd Charlie', celebrated in the *Garioch Garland* when he died in 1792 'aged Five Score and Five'.

> He drank and sang five score and five,
>    Bonny Laddie, Highland Laddie.
> Few men so old are now alive,
>    My Bonny Highland Laddie.

The song goes on (skipping the refrain):

> Gang, lads and lasses, to the fair,
> But Charlie ne'er will meet you there.
> Nor in the streets of Aberdeen
> Shall his long spindle shanks be seen.
> For truth he was a canty carle, and
> Many a ballad made and garland.
> The fame of Charlie wander'd far
> Through Angus, Buchan, Mearns and Mar.
> Those songs in the long nights of winter
> He made, and Chalmers was the printer.
> O mourn, good Master Chalmers, mourn,
> For Charlie will no more return...

The printer was James Chalmers of Aberdeen. Charlie, born (perhaps!) in 1687, was still writing and singing when Robert Burns was collecting popular songs, whether new-made or ancient, as part of his poetic inspiration and source-material. Another Scottish songmaker, David Love, born nine years before Burns, told of his early rambling days:

> At length so very bold I grew,
> My songs exposed to public view
> And crowds of people round me drew,
>     I was so funny.
> From side to side I nimbly flew
>     To catch the money.

He roved into and all round England and ended as a noted figure at Nottingham, selling his songs until his death at 77.

In the course of the eighteenth century, the conflict between gentility and free merriment brought some curbing of the bawdry in printed street songs — if one can safely judge by the ones that survive, for these were largely collected by gentlemen and no doubt underwent some weeding. There is strong evidence that in the taverns and alehouses, in raffish pleasure-gardens avoided by ladies, and in the streets, bawdry flourished. A witness to this is Francis Place (born 1771), whose father kept a public house near the Strand in London. Place rose to become a well-to-do master tailor, a campaigner for social reform, and a great collector of facts about the life of his day. Writing his memoirs in 1819, he recalls the songs sold for a halfpenny in his apprentice days:

> Such songs as thirty-five years ago produced applause would now cause the singers to be rolled in the mud... Servant maids used to stop in the markets to hear them sung, and used to purchase them... Two women used to sing a song opposite a public house, the sign of the Crooked Billet, at the back of St Clement's Church in the Strand... The song was a description of a married man who had a lecherous wife. It described his being a hale fellow reduced by her to a skeleton. I can only remember the two last lines:
>
> > And for which I am sure she'll go to hell
> > For she makes me fuck her in church time.
>
> I remember these words in consequence of the shout which was always set up as the song closed.

Being a great pre-Victorian believer in civic betterment, he deplores the songs, but at the same time he is fascinated by them. He sets down page after page of what he and his friends can remember. His notes help to fill out or supply variants of some things in this collection (pages 103, 155, 171, 287). One of his friends, a lawyer called Hayward, adds more remembered verses, and says he has seen a great change in the manners not only of the lower orders 'but the middle classes also'.

> There were for master tradesmen the Dog & Duck — the Temple of Flora — the Apollo Gardens & several other tea gardens & bowling greens. Bagnigge Wells for all sorts — the Bull in the Pound, Merlin's Cave, the Blue Lion, etc, for whores & rogues of all denominations, not forgetting the Cock & Hen clubs. Cutter lads & flash and fancy men with the peculiar dress — rollers at the cheeks, striped silk stockings — numerous knee-strings, long quartered shoes & all en suite. But the great change is in the obscene ballads & the songs in praise of thieving, which were the only ones sung about the streets.

The first three places named were south of the Thames, the next three were in Islington, and the Blue Lion survives as a pub in Gray's Inn Road. He goes on:

> A boy used to get a great collection of servant maids & other listeners on market nights in the vicinity of Clare Market & get a great many halfpence by singing the most bawdy ditties, such as
>
> First he niggled her, then he tiggled her,
> Then with his two balls he began for to batter her.
> At every thrust I thought she'd have burst
> With the terrible size of his Morgan Rattler. *[p171 and notes*

The authorities did take action against street singers in the 1790s, but the overriding aim was to combat radical ideas. Song printers rarely touched on politics, so when they did we can be sure an issue was stirring all classes. When John Wilkes was defying the government in the 1760s, many songs came out in his praise. In one, a girl cries his name while making love — with this climax:

Then with each shove she cried, 'My love!
Wilkes, and a free election!'

During the American Revolution, ballads protested that men

were being sent 'against their own will, their brothers to kill', and girls sang anti-war laments for the loss of their swains. Here are some lines from a song that was often reprinted:

> Kind heavens, bring things to an end
> And peace to Great Britain restore.
> With America join hand in hand
> And then I shall languish no more.
> Then husbands will come to their wives
> And children their fathers will gain.
> 'Twill save many thousands of lives
> And I shall enjoy my dear swain.

In the 1790s the French Revolution aroused in the middling and lower orders something still more threatening to the government: a fervent demand for reform. The most radical printers vended songs praising Thomas Paine, attacking and mocking George III and his ministers, and using 'God Save the King' parodies to suggest sharp revolutionary measures:

> Long live great Guillotine
> Who shaves the head so clean
> Of queen and king.

Some printers were jailed for sedition. And the government hit back another way by using a body of anti-reformers, the Association for Preserving Liberty and Property against Republicans and Levellers, in a subsidized counter-attack. Place's friend Hayward says, 'The association published a large number of what they called loyal songs, and gave them to the ballad-singers. If anyone was found singing any but loyal songs, he or she was carried before a magistrate.'

This campaign served too to get some bawdy songs off the streets; and official measures aimed directly at immorality had begun. In 1787 George III (influenced in part by the blatant dissipation of several of his sons) issued a proclamation 'for preventing and punishing vice'. A Proclamation Society, with William Wilberforce among its leaders, brought prosecutions against such things as John Cleland's *Memoirs of Fanny Hill*. In 1799 the society pursued the publishers of Captain Charles Morris's song 'The Plenipotentiary' (see page 175), but failed to win a conviction. In 1801 a new set of campaigners formed the Society for the Suppression of Vice, which in 1806 got a publisher jailed for two under-the-counter items, *The Frisky Songster* and *The Voluptuarian Museum*.

Hayward goes too far when he says that 'any but loyal songs' were stamped out in the 1790s. Songs in praise of the British tar were vastly promoted, it is true, but the trade still seized on its usual range of other topics. In the early nineteenth century a cockneyish flavour becomes more frequent, complete with the reversal of 'w' and 'v' so merrily picked up later by Dickens. Here is a glimpse of singers in action:

> There's Dolly and I, as ballads we cry
> On a couple of stools see us stand.
> The people flock round as she bawls aloud
> And I takes my fiddle in hand.

*(Spoken)* Come, good customers, here's an entire new song, entitled and called, 'I am a vild and roving boy'... Stop, Dool, let's rosin first...

> *She* — I am a vild and a rambling boy,
> *He* — My lodging's in the Isle of Troy;
> *She* — A rambling boy although I be,
> *He* — I'd leave them all and follow thee.

*(That 'ere man vants a ballad, Dool, vy don't you look about?)*

In the time of the Regency there was a vogue for songs with patter. Here is some with a good London flavour:

> Come, my lucky masters, here's a choice collection of songs that have been sung at Drury Lane, Common Garden, Sadler's Wells, the Uproar House, Fox-Hall and other places, out of the most famoustest roratories. Bless your eyes and limbs, lay out a mag [halfpenny] with poor chirruping Joe. I don't come here every darkey [night]. But come, I'll lip ye a chant. *[He sings 'The Masqueraders', satirizing false-faced lawyers, patriots, methodists, courtiers, clergy.]* What, no copper clinking among you, my hearties? ...It won't do, I say, to stand here for nix — all hearers and no buyers. What, will none of you drop your loose kelter? Crap me, but I must shove my trunk and hop the twig...

One London printer, John Pitts (1765–1844), issued a list in 1836 of more than 1,100 songs; his great rival, James Catnach (1792–1841), offered far more; and in the 1840s Catnach's successor, Ryle & Co, advertised 'upwards of 4,000 different sorts of ballads continually on sale, together with fifty new penny songbooks'. But despite the numbers, by then the trade was struggling, partly owing to competition from an enticing variety of popular matter churned out on steam presses.

What, meanwhile, have the gentlemen been doing? In such eighteenth-century clubs as the Sublime Society of Beef Steaks or the Anacreontic Society, the faster sort of nobleman, banker and merchant joined with actors, writers and artists to enjoy men-only nights at which they sang songs 'not exactly calculated for the entertainment of ladies', as William Parke put it in his *Musical Memoirs*.. Their songbooks are strong in the ribald favourites of the Restoration and the early eighteenth century. They do not seem to have produced much new of note until the Beef Steaks' bard, Charles Morris, rose to fame in the 1780s. It might be rewarding, though, to discover the private collections of such Beef Steaks as Lord Sandwich and John Wilkes, or of Wilkes's friend Thomas Potter, libertine son of an archbishop, or of some witty Anacreontic.

The middling rank of men had their clubs too. A list of 1789 mentions the Bucks, Masons, Albions, True Britons, Sons of Thespis, True Blues, Sons of Comus and Theatrical Geniuses. A generation later the favourite haunts of fast men, in and around Covent Garden, are Offley's, the Cider Cellar, the Coal Hole and the Shades. We can sample the songs in vogue there, for dozens of pocket-size collections from the 1820s and 1830s, with such titles as *The Rambler's Flash Songster* and *The Delicious Chaunter*, survive in the British Library. They have saucy coloured frontispieces and alluring title-page statements. For example: 'A Slashing, Dashing, Leary, Frisky and Delicious Collection of GENTLEMEN'S SONGS, never before printed'. They are very much under-the-counter: other books offered by one of the publishers, Edward Duncombe, are *Every Lover's Book*, 'with beautiful Plates'; *The Lover's Festival, or Melting Moments*; *The Nun in her Shift*; *The Mousetrap of Love*.

I include a few of the 'gentlemen's songs' to bring the amatory story almost as far as the stressful complexities of Victorianism. A few: for they can soon become wearisome in their misogynist doggishness. It is daunting to find songs marketed as 'A capital smutty song' or 'A very capital new smutty parody'. The Society for the Suppression of Vice and its successors can be credited with advancing the sort of nudging trade that goes with anxious concern for propriety. We have come a long way from the hearty merriment of Thomas Campion's time, or of *Pills to Purge Melancholy*.

But now read on, and develop social or literary theories if you will. The original readers and singers needed none.

## A FEW GUIDELINES

The verse is presented in three sections: *Love's pleasures, love's pains; Rakes and wantons; Merriments, mockings, miseries.* (Some of the lovers, it is true, might well be classed as wantons.) Each section runs chronologically, though datings often cannot be precise. Some firm dates are given in the page as useful milestones. Those titles that are not merely first lines are from original sources. About forty examples of music are given. The occasional illustrations are from sources of the time.

### ANNOTATIONS

Old usages and other obscurities are explained in the page, the only helpful way. The endnotes name the sources and also reward readers with a mass of lively additional matter. But I offer no sociolinguistic analysis. I leave to others such insights as this, in a study of eighteenth-century erotic writing: 'A frequent rhetorical epiphenomenon of the nuclear chthonic metaphor is the use of a bellicose lexis to describe the inevitable "amorous combat", especially that of poliorcetics.'

### IN PURSUIT OF TRUE TEXTS

Scholars have problems enough to establish the texts of eminent poets. Here the task is still more fraught. An item may begin in a songbook or broadside, travel from mouth to mouth, acquire sad garblings or clever new stanzas, then be printed again, a creative or a muddled hybrid. Generally I have favoured the earliest coherent text. At times more than one imperfect text must serve to recreate a persuasive whole.

I have corrected misprints and minor bungles. When occasionally I make cuts (indicated by a row of dots), that is never for censorship but only because a passage is irremediably corrupt or is wastefully longwinded.

### BLANKS

Notions varied in the past (as they do still) about words that are best not spelt out. When a word is disguised here with a blank, *that is because the copy used was so written*. If one source of an item has blanks and another does spell the words out, I boldly follow the latter.

### SPELLING

Modernized spelling, capitalization and punctuation are commonly accepted for editions of early verse, and are especially desirable here, as most of the sources are markedly inconsistent. To give a taste of old ways, though, in the introduction I have let quoted passages remain unmodernized.

### PRONUNCIATION

In the seventeenth century and much of the eighteenth, pronunciation was often *less* inconsistent than it is now. For example, these were rhymes: alarm, warm; far, war; have, grave; swear, ear; breast, feast; gone, lone; cow, blow, you. Words such as get and yet were often pronounced git and yit — a usage that survives in dialect, and in everyday words such as 'pretty' and 'England'. Sound-changes must be kept in mind when rhymes seem faulty. Watch too for internal rhymes and assonances that may be lost to the modern ear.

## ACKNOWLEDGMENTS

First of all I must pay tribute to that storehouse of printed and manuscript treasures, the British Library, and thank its staff for their excellent service over many years. My thanks for the use of further material go to the Bodleian Library, Oxford; the Governing Body of Christ Church, Oxford; the President and Fellows of Corpus Christi College, Oxford; Cambridge University Library; the Pepys Library, Magdalene College, Cambridge; Nottingham University Library; the library of the English Folk Dance and Song Society; and the British Museum department of prints and drawings for the illustrations on pages 282 and 284.

# 1

# *Love's pleasures, love's pains*

## Thirsis to die desired

Thirsis to die desirèd,
Marking her eyes that to his heart was nearest,
And she that with his flame no less was firèd
Said to him, Oh heart's love dearest, oh heart's love dearest,
Alas, forbear to die now!
By thee I live, with thee I wish to die too,
To die too.
By thee I live, with thee I wish to die too,
To die too.

Thirsis that heat refrainèd
Wherewith in haste to die he did betake him,
Thinking it death yet,
And while his look full fixèd he retainèd
On her eyes full of pleasure,
And lovely nectar sweet from them he tasted,
His dainty nymph, that now at hand espièd
The harvest of love's treasure,
Said thus, with eyes all trembling, faint and wasted,
I die now,
I die now.
The shepherd then repliècd,
And I sweet life do die too,
And I sweet life too,
And I sweet life do die too.

NICHOLAS YONGE, *1583*

## Cruel, you pull away too soon

Cruel, you pull away too soon
Your dainty lips whenas you kiss me.
O, but you should hold them still
And then, then should you bliss me.
Now or ere I taste them
Straight away they haste them.
But you perhaps retire them
To move my thoughts thereby the more to fire them.
Alas, such baits you need to find out never.
If you would let me I would kiss you ever.

THOMAS MORLEY, *1593*

## I go before, my darling

I go before, my darling.
Follow thou to the bower in the close alley.
There we will together
Sweetly kiss each other
And like two wantons dally,
Dally dally dally dally dally dally dally dally dally dally dally
dally dally .

MORLEY, *1595*

## What saith my dainty darling?

What saith my dainty darling?
Shall I now your love obtain? *Fa la la la.*
Long time I sued for grace,
And grace you granted me
When time should serve and place.
Can any fitter be? *Fa la la la.*

This crystal running fountain
In his language saith, 'Come, love.' *Fa la la la.*
The birds, the trees, the fields,
Else none can us behold.
This bank soft lying yields
And saith 'Nice fools, be bold.' *Fa la la la.*

MORLEY, *1595*

## My lovely wanton jewel

My lovely wanton jewel,
To me at once both kind, alas, and cruel, *fa la,*
With hopeless words torments me
And with her lips again straightway contents me. *Fa la la.*

If this you do to kill me,
Say, cruel nymph, why kiss not you then still me? *Fa la.*
So shall you ease my crying,
And I could never wish a sweeter dying. *Fa la la.*

MORLEY, *1595*

From an Italian madrigal, 'La bella ninfa mia', and strictly matching its seven- and eleven-syllable lines (below, one all of seven-syllable lines)

## Lady, you think you spite me

Lady, you think you spite me
When by the lip you bite me,
But if you think it trouble
Then let my pain be double –
Aye, triple! – but you bliss me,
For though you bite, you kiss me
And with sour sweet delight me.

MORLEY, *1597*

## Fie fie fie, what a coil is here!

Fie fie fie, what a coil is here!
Why strive you so to get a kiss?
Do do do what you will,
You shall be ne'er the near. *no nearer*
Had I been willing
Thus to be billing
You had prevailed long ere this.
Sweet, stand away, let me alone,
Or else in faith I'll get me gone.

Come come come, do you not perceive
I am not yet disposed to yield?
Stay stay stay but a while,

My love will give you leave.
  This my denial
  Is but a trial
If faint desire will fly the field.
Whoop! Look you now! I pray be still.
Nay then, in faith, do what you will.

*1600*

## I care not for these ladies

I care not for these ladies
That must be wooed and prayed.
Give me kind Amarillis,
The wanton country maid.
Nature art disdaineth;
Her beauty is her own —

  Who when we court and kiss,
  She cries, 'Forsooth, let go!'
  But when we come where comfort is
  She never will say no.

If I love Amarillis
She gives me fruit and flowers,
But if we love these ladies
We must give golden showers.
Give them gold that sell love;
Give me the nutbrown lass,

  *Who when we court, etc —*

These ladies must have pillows
And beds by strangers wrought.
Give me a bed of willows,
Of moss and leaves unbought,
And fresh Amarillis
With milk and honey fed,

  Who when we court and kiss,
  She cries, 'Forsooth, let go!'
  But when we come where comfort is
  She never will say no.

THOMAS CAMPION, *1601*

## Are lovers full of fire?

Are lovers full of fire?
How comes it then my verses are so cold?
And how, when I am nigh her
And fit occasion wills me to be bold,
The more I burn, the more I do desire,
The less I dare require?

Ah love, this is thy wondrous art,
To freeze the tongue and fire the heart.

FRANCIS DAVISON, *1602*

## What is beauty but a breath?

What is beauty but a breath?
Fancy's twin at birth and death,
The colour of a damask rose
That fadeth when the north wind blows.
'Tis such that though all sorts do crave it,
They know not what it is that have it;
A thing that sometimes stoops not to a king
And yet most open to the common'st thing,
For she that is most fair
Is open to the air.

*1604*

## When from my love I looked for love

When from my love I looked for love
And kind affection's due,
Too well I found her vows to prove
Most faithless and untrue.
For when I did ask her why,
Most sharply she did reply
That she with me
Did ne'er agree
To love but jokingly.

Mark but the subtle policies
That female lovers find,
Who love to fix their constancies

Like feathers in the wind.
Though they swear, vow and protest
That they love you chiefly best,
Yet by and by
They'll all deny
And say 'twas but in jest.

## Think'st thou, Kate, to put me down

Think'st thou, Kate, to put me down
With a no or with a frown?
Since love holds my heart in bands
I must do as love commands.

Love commands the hands to dare
When the tongue of speech is spare.
Chiefest lesson in love's school:
Put it in adventure, fool!

Fools are they that fainting flinch
For a squeak, a scratch, a pinch.
Women's words have double sense:
Stand away, a simple fence.

If thy mistress swear she'll cry,
Fear her not, she'll swear and lie.
Such sweet oaths no sorrow bring
Till the prick of conscience sting.

## What if I sped where I least expected

What if I sped where I least expected, what shall I say? Shall I lie?
What if I missed where I most affected, what shall I do? Shall I die?
No, no, I'll have at all.
'Tis as my game doth fall.
If I keep my meaning close
I may hit, howe'er it goes,
For time and I
Do mean to try
What hope doth lie
In youth, *fa la la.*

The minds that doubt
Are in and out,
And women flout
At truth, *fa la la.*

She whom above the skies I renownèd, she whom I lovèd, she,
Can she leave all in Lethe drownèd? Can she be coy to me?
Her passions are but cold.
She stands and doth behold.
She retains her looks estranged
As if heaven and earth were changed.
I speak, she hears;
I touch, she fears.
Herein appears
Her wit, *fa la la.*
I catch, she flies;
I hold, she cries
And still denies,
And yet —*fa la la.*

May not a wanton look like a woman, tell me the reason why?
And if a blind man chance of a bird's nest, must he be prating? Fie!
What mortal strength can keep
That's got as in a sleep?
The felony is his
That brags of a stolen kiss:
For when we met
Both in a net
That Vulcan set,
Were hid, *fa la la.*
And so, God wot,
We did it not,
Or else forgot
We did, *fa la la.*

## Four arms, two necks, one wreathing

Four arms, two necks, one wreathing;
Two pair of lips, one breathing, *[his girl with another man*
*Fa la la.*
Two hearts that multiply
Sighs interchangeably,
*Fa la la.*

The thought of this confounds me,
And as I speak it wounds me,
*Fa la la.*
It cannot be expressed.
Good help me whilst I rest,
*Fa la la.*

Bad stomachs have their loathing, *[accounting for her betrayal*
And oh! this all is no thing,
*Fa la la.*
This 'no' with griefs doth prove
Report oft turns in love,
*Fa la la.*

## Though my carriage be but careless

Though my carriage be but careless,
Though my looks be of the sternest,
Yet my passions are compareless:
When I love, I love in earnest.

No, my wits are not so wild
But a gentle soul may yoke me,
Nor my heart so hard compiled
But it melts, if love provoke me.

*1608*

## Love not me for comely grace

Love not me for comely grace,
For my pleasing eye or face,
Nor for any outward part,
No, nor for my constant heart,
For those may fail or turn to ill,

So thou and I shall sever.
Keep therefore a true woman's eye
And love me still but know not why:
So hast thou the same reason still
To dote upon me ever.

## Young and simple though I am

Young and simple though I am,
I have heard of Cupid's name.
Guess I can what thing it is
Men desire when they do kiss.
Smoke can never burn, they say,
But the flames that follow may.

I am not so foul or fair
To be proud or to despair,
Yet my lips have oft observed,
Men that kiss them press them hard
As glad lovers use to do — *usually do*
When their new-met loves they woo.

Faith, 'tis but a foolish mind,
Yet methinks a heat I find
Like thirst-longing, that doth bide
Ever on my weaker side
Where they say my heart doth move.
Venus grant it be not love!

If it be, alas — what then?
Were not women made for men?
As good 'tis a thing were past
That must needs be done at last.
Roses that are overblown
Grow less sweet, then fall alone.

Yet nor churl nor silken gull
Shall my maiden blossom pull.
Who shall not, I soon can tell.
Who shall, would I could as well!
This I know: whoe'er he be,
Love he must, or flatter me.

THOMAS CAMPION, *1609*

Every line seven syllables: by a syllabic enthusiast

## Sweet Cupid, ripen her desire

Sweet Cupid, ripen her desire,
Thy joyful harvest may begin.
If age approach a little nigher
'Twill be too late to get it in.

Cold winter storms lay standing corn,
Which once too ripe will never rise;
And lovers wish themselves unborn
When all their joys lie in their eyes.

Then sweet, let us embrace and kiss.
Shall beauty shale upon the ground? *[like grain from the ear*
If age bereave us of this bliss
Then will no more such sport be found.

## Lais now old, that erst attempting lass

Lais now old, that erst attempting lass
To goddess Venus consecrates her glass,
For she herself hath now no use of one;
No dimpled cheeks hath she to gaze upon.
She cannot see her springtime damask grace,
Nor dare she look upon her winter face.

## Come hither, you that love

Come hither, you that love, and hear me sing
    Of joys still growing,
Green, fresh and lusty as the pride of spring,
    And ever blowing.
Come hither, youths that blush and dare not know
    What is desire,
And old men worse than you, that cannot blow
    One spark of fire,
And with the power of my enchanting song
Boys shall be able men, and old men young.

Come hither, you that hope and you that cry,
    Leave off complaining.
Youth, strength and beauty that shall never die
    Are here remaining.

Come hither, fools, and blush you stay so long
From being blessed,
And mad men, worse than you, that suffer wrong
Yet seek no rest,
And in an hour with my enchanting song
You shall be ever pleased, and young maids long.

JOHN FLETCHER, *1612*

## Away, away, call back what you have said

Away, away, call back what you have said
When you did vow to live and die a maid.
O if you knew what shame to them befell
That dance about with bobtail apes in hell *
You'd break your oath, and for a world of gain
From Hymen's pleasing sports no more abstain.
Yourself your virgin girdle would divide
And put aside
The maiden veil that hides the chiefest gem
Of nature, and would lie
Prostrate to every peasant that goes by,
Rather than undergo such shame.
No tongue can tell
What injury is done to maids in hell.

* It was a familiar saying that a woman who died a maid would 'lead apes in hell'; it seems they had a lewd role

## Dear, why do you say you love

Dear, why do you say you love
When indeed you careless prove?
Reason better can digest
Earnest hate than love in jest.

Wherefore do your smiling eyes
Help your tongue to make sweet lies?
Leave to statesmen tricks of state.
Love doth politicians hate.

You perchance presume to find
Love of some chameleon kind,

But be not deceived, my fair:
Love will not be fed on air.

Love's a glutton of his food,
Surfeits make his stomach good.
Love whose diet grows precise
Sick of some consumption dies.

Then, dear love, let me obtain
That which may true love maintain;
Or if kind you cannot prove,
Prove true, say you cannot love.

SIR ROBERT AYTOUN

## To His Forsaken Mistress

I do confess th'art smooth and fair
And I might ha' gone near to love thee
Had I not found the slightest prayer
That lip could move had power to move thee.
    But I can let thee now alone
    As worthy to be loved by none.

I do confess th'art sweet, yet find
Thee such an unthrift of thy sweets
Thy favours are but like the wind
Which kisseth every thing it meets.
    And since thou canst with more than one
    Th'art worthy to be kissed by none.

The morning rose that untouched stands,
Armed with her briers, how sweet she smells!
But plucked, and strained through ruder hands,
Her sweets no longer with her dwells,
    But scent and beauty both are gone
    And leaves fall from her one by one.

Such fate ere long will thee betide,
When thou hast handled been a while
With sere flowers to be thrown aside.
And I shall sigh when some shall smile
    To see thy love to everyone
    Hath brought thee to be loved by none.

SIR ROBERT AYTOUN

## Have I found her? O rich finding!

Have I found her? O rich finding!
Goddess-like for to behold,
Her fair tresses seemly binding
In a chain of pearl and gold.

Chain me, chain me, O most fair,
Chain me to thee with that hair.

*1613*

## O when I think what a paltry thing

O when I think what a paltry thing
Is a glove, or a ring,
Or a top of a fan to brag of,
And how much a noddy will triùmph
In a busk-point with the tag off, *a corset lace*
Then I say,
Well fare him that hath ever used close play. *real lovemaking*

## See the building

See the building
Which whilst my mistress lived in
Was pleasure's essence.
See how it droopeth
And how nakedly it looketh
Without her presence.
Hark how the hollow winds do blow
And seem to murmur
In every corner
For her being absent, from whence doth chiefly grow
The cause that I do now this grief and sorrow show.

See that garden
Where oft I had reward in
For my true love.
See the places
Where I enjoyed those graces
The gods might move.
Oft in that arbour, while that she

With melting kisses
Distilling blisses
From her free lips for joy did ravish me,
The pretty nightingale did sing melodiously.

Hail to those groves
Where we enjoyed our loves
So many days!
May the trees be springing
And the pretty birds be singing
Their roundelays!
Oh, may the grass grow ever green
Whereon we lying
Have oft been trying
More several ways of pleasure than love's queen
Which once in bed with Mars by all the gods was seen!

## Art thou that she than whom no fairer is?

Art thou that she than whom no fairer is?
Art thou that she desire so strives to kiss?
Say I am, how then?
Maids may not kiss such wanton-humoured men.

Art thou that she the world commends for wit?
Art thou so wise and mak'st no use of it?
Say I am, how then?
My wit doth teach me shun such foolish men.

## As on a day Sabina fell asleep

As on a day Sabina fell asleep,
Into her bower I by stealth did creep,
And first spake soft, then loud unto my dear,
And still Sabina heard, but would not hear.

Then to myself more courage I did take
When I perceived she did both wink and wake. *wink = close her eyes*
Then down I laid me by her on the ground,
And still awake-asleep Sabina found.

Then showed her sights more strange to her than me,
Yet still Sabina saw but would not see.
Now whenas I had tried all ways but one
I looked about, and found myself alone.

Then thought it best the best way for to woo,
And still Sabina did but would not do.
Then did I touch each part from head to heel,
Yet still Sabina felt but would not feel.

Now, from the doer why should she have hid it
If it be true that 'twas Sabina did it?
But she says nay. I swear and say so too,
She did both hear, and see, and feel, and do.

See endnotes for more on this theme

## Down lay the shepherd swain

Down lay the shepherd swain
So sober and demure,
Wishing for his wench again,
So bonny and so pure,
With his head on hillock low
And his arms akimbo,
And all for the loss of her hi-nonny-nonny-no.

His tears they fell as thin
As water from a still.
His hair upon his chin
Grew like thyme upon a hill.
His cherry cheeks as pale as snow
Testified his mickle woe *great*
And all for the loss of her hi-nonny-nonny-no.

'Sweet she was, as kind a love
As ever fettered swain.
Never such a dainty one
Shall I enjoy again.
Set a thousand on a row,
I'll forbid that any show
Ever the like of her hi-nonny-nonny-no.

'Faced she was of filbert hue
    And breasted like a swan.
Backed she was of bended yew
    And waisted by a span.
Hair she had as black as crow
From the head unto the toe,
Down, down all over her hi-nonny-nonny-no.

'With her mantle tucked up high
    She foddered her flock.
So buxom and alluringly
    Her knee upheld her smock.
So nimbly did she use to go,
So smooth she danced a-tiptoe,
That all men were mad on her hi-nonny-nonny-no.

'She smiled like a holiday
    And simpered like the spring.
She pranked like a popinjay
    And like a swallow sing.
She tripped like a barren doe
And strutted like a gorcrow,
That all men were fond of her hi-nonny-nonny-no.

'To sport it on the merry down,
    To dance the lively hay, *country dance*
To wrestle for a green gown *make love in the fields*
    In heat of all the day,
Never would she say me no,
Yet methought I had though
Never enough of her hi-nonny-nonny-no.

'But gone she is, the bravest lass
    That ever trod on plain.
Whatever hath betided her
    Blame not the shepherd swain.
For why? She was her own foe
And gave herself the overthrow
By being too frank of her hi-nonny-nonny-no.'

## Why were we maids made wives

Why were we maids made wives
But for to change our lives
And unknown joys to know?
Yet is my hap so strange
To wed and find no change.
O Love! Why should men woo
That know not how to do
The rites that 'long thereto?
Ay me!

We wives that have such men,
Let's all turn maids again
And married state forgo.
And prayers to Cupid make
That he would undertake
That no such man may woo
That know s not how to do
The rites that 'long thereto.
Ay me!

## Lovers rejoice, your pains shall be rewarded

Lovers rejoice, your pains shall be rewarded.
The god of love himself grieves at your crying.
No more shall frozen honour be regarded
Nor the coy faces of a maid's denying.
No more shall virgins sigh and say, 'We dare not,
For men are false, and what they do they care not.'
All shall be well again; then do not grieve.
Men shall be true, and women shall believe.

Lovers rejoice: what you shall say henceforth
When you have caught your sweethearts in your arms,
It shall be accounted oracle and worth.
No more fainthearted girls shall dream of harms
And cry they are too young. The god hath said
Fifteen shall make a mother of a maid.
Then, wise men, pull your roses yet unblown.
Love hates the too ripe fruit that falls alone.

JOHN FLETCHER, *1615*

## Beauty, since you so much desire

Beauty, since you so much desire
To know the place of Cupid's fire:
About you somewhere doth it rest,
Yet never harboured in your breast,
Nor gout-like in your heel or toe.
What fool would seek love's flame so low?
    But a little higher, but a little higher,
    There, there, oh there lies Cupid's fire.

Think not when Cupid most you scorn
Men judge that you of ice were born,
For though you cast love at your heel,
His fury yet sometime you feel,
And whereabouts if you would know,
I tell you still, not in your toe,
    But a little higher, but a little higher,
    There, there, oh there lies Cupid's fire.

THOMAS CAMPION

## Cupid is Venus' only joy

Cupid is Venus' only joy
But he is a wanton boy,
A very, very wanton boy.
He shoots at ladies' naked breasts.
He is the cause of most men's crests:
    I mean upon the forehead,
    Invisible but horrid. *cuckolds' horns*
'Twas he first thought upon the way
To keep a lady's lips in play.

Why should not Venus chide her son
For the tricks that he hath done?
He shoots his fiery darts so thick
They wound poor ladies to the quick,
    Ay me, with cruel wounding!
    His darts are so confounding
That life and strength would soon decay,
But that it keeps their lips in play.

THOMAS MIDDLETON

## Hark, ye virgins that so prize

Hark, ye virgins that so prize
    That sweet flower we beauty call,
Shall I tell you what the wise
    Think of it and of you all?

'Tis a pretty glass combining
    White and red in their due places.
'Tis a dainty varnish shining
    Brightest in the female faces.
Do not prize it more than meet
For it is as short as sweet.

Tell me where is now the spark *Helen*
    That sent Troy up to the skies.
Now she's mouldered in the dark
    And raked up in ashes lies.

Where are now those Grecian dames,
    Flowers still sweet in poets' posies?
What remains now but their fames?
    Think upon these withered roses.
Roses of the brightest hue,
They are withered: so must you.

## When meadow grounds are fresh and gay

When meadow grounds are fresh and gay
    And on each shrub a bird doth sing,
Upon a welcome holiday
    When young men's spirits freely spring,
        Their needless work forsaking
They took the maids from their haymaking.
'Twas not to dance but tumble tumble tumble tumble tumble tumble
        Up and down the meadow.

A tabor and a shepherd's reed,
    A bagpipe trimly hugged and dandled,
A carter's whistle, and for a need
    A fiddle by a tailor handled,
        All in a hubbub sounding,
The maidens' hearts for joy abounding,
*Who did not dance but tumble, etc —*

Their head and arms about they flung
With all the might and force they had.
Their legs like flails but loosely hung
Did kick their breech as they were mad.
Their jolly feats did kindle
The maids, who turned like any spindle,
*And did not dance but tumble, etc —*

In steeple hats and cypress bands — *oldfashioned black collars*
Came old men of an age before.
Behind their backs they bore their hands,
Whose gloves their girdles for them wore.*
They blamed the young men's footing
And chid the times that left off shooting,*
*And not to dance but tumble, etc —*

The middle men did there resort
And gently walking o'er the plain
They brought their wives to see the sport,
Each wishing other young again,
That both together tripping
Might mend the younglings' ruder skipping,
*Who did not dance but tumble, etc —*

Yet all their pishing, stamps and quips
Their jolly sport could nothing let. — *could not hinder*
Their feet none minded, so their lips
In time and measure fully met.
When they were out, they wist not.
He was not in that likewise missed not.
*They did not dance but tumble, etc —*

When sweat had changed the scent of hay
And tumbling joys had spent the light,
They had no power to go away.
'Twas better tumbling in the night.
Each courting there his sweeting
Requested for a further meeting,
*And not to dance but tumble tumble tumble tumble tumble tumble tumble*
*Up and down the meadow.*

*They thrust their hands into their girdles

*They criticized the young men's dancing and grumbled that they were not practising archery

# When Phoebus addressed his course to the west

When Phoebus addressed his course to the west
To take up his rest below,
Cynthia agreed in her glittering weed
Her light in his stead to bestow.
I travelled alone, attended by none,
Till suddenly one did cry,
'O do not, do not kill me yet,
For I am not prepared to die!'

With that I drew near to see and to hear
And there did appear a show!
The moon was so bright that I saw such a sight
Not fit that each wight should know.
A man and a maid together were laid,
And ever she said, 'Nay fie!
O do not, do not kill me yet,
For I am not prepared to die!'

The young man was rough and he took up her stuff
And to blindman's buff did go.
Though she cried 'Fie fie' yet still she did lie
And put him but by with 'No'.
For she was so young and he was so strong,
She rested not long to cry,
'O do not, do not kill me yet,
For I am not prepared to die!'

Thus striving in vain, well pleasèd with pain,
She vowed to remain his foe.
She kept such a coil when he gave her the foil
That greater the broil did grow.
He was so prepared, he did not regard
Her words when he heard her cry,

*coil = fuss, strife*

'O do not, do not kill me yet,
    For I am not prepared to die!'

He said to the maid, 'Sweet, be not afraid.
    Thy physician I will be.
An I find but the place, I'll handle the case — *an = if*
    And give thee thy physic free.'
He went to it again and found out the vein
    Wherein her pain did lie.
'O kill me, kill me,' then she said,
    'For now I am prepared to die!'

At length he gave o'er and solemnly swore
    He would kill her no more that night.
Full little he knew when he bid her adieu
    She would tempt him to new delight.
But when he did part, it went to her heart
    And taught her more art to cry,
'O kill me, kill me once again,
    For now I am prepared to die!'

In each of the surviving versions a few of the triple internal rhymes have been lost. Conflating these versions has restored all but two triples in the penultimate stanza (one could be mended with 'Thy physician unpaid I'll be')

## Walking in a meadow green

Walking in a meadow green
    Fair flowers for to gather,
Where primrose ranks did stand on banks
    To welcome comers thither,
I heard a voice that made a noise
    Which caused me to attend it.
I heard a lass say to a lad,
    'Once more, and none can mend it.'

They two did lie so close together
    They made me much to wonder.
I thought he would this nymph quite smother
    Whenas I saw her under.
Then off he came and blushed for shame
    That he so soon had ended.
Yet still she lies and to him cries,
    'Once more, and none can mend it.'

His looks were dull and very sad;
His courage she had tamèd.
She bade him play the lusty lad
Or else he quite was shamèd.
'Then stiffly thrust and hit me just.
Fear not, but freely spend it,
And play a bout at in and out
Once more, and none can mend it.'

Then in her arms she did him fold
And oftentimes she kissed him,
Yet still his courage was but cold
For all the good she wished him.
Then with her hand she made it stand
So stiff she could not bend it,
And then anon she cries, 'Come on!
Once more, and none can mend it.'

And then he thought to venture her,
Thinking the fit was on him,
But when he came to enter her
The point turned back upon him.
Yet she said, 'Stay! Go not away
Although the point be bended,
But to't again and hit the vein!
Once more, and none can mend it.'

'Adieu, adieu, sweetheart,' quoth he,
'For in faith I must be gone.'
'Nay then, you do me wrong,' quoth she,

'To leave me thus alone.'
Away he went when all was spent,
Whereat she was offended.
Like a Trojan true she made a vow
She would have one should mend it.

## The Indifferent Lover

Is it true I am derided
And you please to laugh at me?
Know, I am not unprovided
Every way to answer thee:
With love or hate, whate'er it be.

Never twins so nearly met
As thou and I in our affection.
When thou weep'st my eyes are wet;
What thou lik'st is my election.
We are in the same subjection.

In one centre are we both,
Both our lives the same way tending.
Do thou refuse, and I shall loathe.
As thine eye, so mine is bending,
Either storm or calm portending.

I am careless if despisèd
For I can contemn again.
How can I be then surprisèd
Or with comfort, or with pain,
When I can love or else disdain?

## Men that more to the yard nor the church

Men that more to the yard nor the church*
Are oft inclined
Take young maids now and then at lurch
To try their mind.
But young maids nowadays are so coy they will not show
When they're in love,
But for fear oft say no
When perhaps they would fain do
If 'twould not prove. *if they would not become pregnant*

If for a time for fear they be wily
    And seem coy
There is one that perhaps may beguile ye:
    The blind boy. *Cupid*
He'll strike home when he please, to the quick he'll shoot his dart
    Without delay.
  Then they'll sigh and lament
  When alas! their own kind heart
    Cannot say nay.

The small fly that playeth with the candle
    Oft doth burn.
Such young maids as do love for to dandle
    Once may mourn.
Let flies burn and maids mourn, for in vain you do persuade
    Them from their folly.
  Nature binds all their kinds
  Now and then to play the jade
    Though they seem holy.

* *yard*: churchyard (young folk were frequently denounced for dancing and dallying in the churchyard, even during service); *nor*: than (still dialect usage)

## Great and proud, if she deride me

Great and proud, if she deride me
Let her walk, I'll not despair.
Ere tomorrow I'll provide me
One as great, less proud, more fair.
  They that seek love to constrain
  Have their labour for their pain.

Those so wise that none can win them,
Those coy, stately, saintlike dames,
Have their raging fires within them
But they closely hide the flames —
  Flames which we for others blow
  Whilst our loves we so bestow.

He that stiff in loving duty
And blind faith doth fondly err
To adore a scornful beauty
Is a mere idolater
  And a powerful idol serves
  Which never grants what he deserves.

They that strongly can importune
And will never yield nor tire,
Gain they may in spite of fortune,
But such game I'll not desire.
  Where the prize is shame or sin
  Winners lose and losers win.

Look upon the faithful lover:
Grief stands painted in his face.
Groans and tears and sighs discover *show*
That they are his only grace.
  He must weep as children do
  That will in the fashion woo.

Can that man a man be stylèd
That without his credit's care
Weeps like to a babe beguilèd
Of its apple, nut or pear?
  Were't not better him to term
  A kind fool that means no harm?

I who fly those idle fancies
Which my dearest rest betray,
Warned by others' harmful chances
Use my freedom as I may.
  When the world says all it can,
  'Tis but, 'Oh, unconstant man!'

## A man and a young maid

A man and a young maid that loved a long time
Were ta'en in a frenzy i' the midsummer prime.
  *The maid she lay drooping hye,*
  *The man he lay whopping hey, the man lay whopping ho.*

Thus talking and walking they came to a place
Environed about with trees and with grass.
  *The maid she, etc —*

He shifted his hand whereas he had placed;
He handled her knees instead of her waist. *[here 'knees' should be legs*
  *The maid, etc —*

He shifted his hand till he came to her knees.
He tickled her and she opened her thighs,
  *Yet still she, etc —*

He hottered and tottered, and there was a lane
That drew him on forward. He went on amain,
*Yet still she, etc —*

The lane it was strait; he had not gone far,
He lit in a hole ere he was aware.
*But she fell a-kissing hye,*
*And he lay drooping ho, and he lay drooping ho.*

'My Billy, my pilly! How now?' quoth she.
'Get up again, Billy, if that thou lovest me.'
*Yet still he lay, etc —*

He thought mickle shame to lie so long.
He got up again and grew very strong.
*The maid she lay, etc —*

The trees and the woods did wring about
And every leaf began to shout,
*And there was such whopping hye,*
*And there was such whopping hey, there was such whopping ho.*

## Two Kisses

'Once and no more,' so said my love
When in my arms enchained.
She unto mine her lips did move,
And so my heart had gained.

This done, she said, 'Away I must
For fear of being missed.
Your heart's made over but in trust.'
And so again she kissed.

## A Lady's Complaint

When I was young, unapt for use of man,
I wedded was unto a champion,
Youthful and full of vigour as of blood,
Who unto Hymen's rites full stiffly stood.
But see the luck: this gallant youngster dies,
And in his place an aged father lies,
Weak, pithless, dry, who suffers me all night
To lie untouched, now full of years and might,

Whereas my former man, God rest his sprite,
Girl as I was, tired me with sweet delight.
For when he would, then was I coy and cold,
Yet what I then refused, now fain I would
But cannot have. O Hymen, if you can,
Give me those years again, or such a man!

## How great delight from those sweet lips

How great delight from those sweet lips I taste
Whether I hear them speak, or feel them kiss!
Only this want I have, that being graced
With one of them, the other straight I miss.

Love, since thou canst do wonders, heap my blisses
And grant her kissing words, or speaking kisses.

## My days, my months, my years I spend

My days, my months, my years I spend
  About a moment's gain,
A joy that in th'enjoying ends,
  A fury quickly slain.

A frail delight, like that wasp's life
  Which now both frisks and flies
And in a moment's wanton strife
  It faints, it pants, it dies.

And when I charge, my lance in rest,*
  I triumph in delight,
And when I have the ring transpierced
  I languish in despite,

Or like one in a lukewarm bath,
  Light-wounded in a vein,
Spurts out the spirits of his life*
  And fainteth without pain.

*1622*

* An image from tournaments – a rider had to pierce a ring with his lance
* *spirits*: a word used for both life-blood and semen

## On a Virgin not yet Ripe

Why should passion lead thee blind
Because thy Lydia proves unkind?
She's yet too young to know delight
And is not plumed for Cupid's flight.

She cannot yet in height of pleasure
Pay her love with equal measure,
But like a rose new-blown, doth feed
The eye alone, but yields no seed.

She is yet but in her spring,
Cold in love till Cupid bring
A hotter season with his fire
Which soon will ripen her desire.

Autumn will shortly come and greet her,
Making her taste and colour sweeter,
And then her ripeness will be such
That she will fall even with a touch.

## Stay, lovely wanton, stay

Stay, lovely wanton, stay.
    Fly not away.
Here is a place most fit.
    Love framèd it
To crown desire with joy.
    Then be not coy,
Nor strive not thus, dear life,
    But let our strife
Be which of thee or I
    Can soonest die.
Secured by love's dread night
    Then let us fight:
Whilst thy fair eyes give fire
    To my desire,
Volleys of kisses send
    My life to end.

## Young Thirsis lay in Phillis' lap

Young Thirsis lay in Phillis' lap
And gazing on her eye
Thought life too mean for such good hap
And fain the boy would die.

When Phillis, who the force did prove
Of love as well as he
Cried to him, 'Stay a while, my love,
And I will die with thee.'

So did these happy lovers die,
But with so little pain
That both to life immediately
Returned to die again.

*1632*

## Come, lovers, all to me

Come, lovers, all to me
And cease your mourning:
Love hath no shafts to shoot,
No more brands burning.

He means my pains shall you
From pains deliver,
For in my breast h'as emptied
All his quiver.

Had he not been a child
He would have known
H'as lost a thousand servants
To kill one.

## Since all things love, why should not we

Since all things love, why should not we,
The best of creatures, be as free?
The pearl-eyed fish in every water
Pursues his love, being taught by nature.
The seely worm, the lamb and harmless dove, *innocent*
Which knoweth nothing, yet know how to love.

All senseless things love's passions feel;
The stone attracts th'unyielding steel. *loadstone*
The ivy twines on every tree
And loves it more than you love me,
And in the cold of winter fresh is seen,
For heat of love is it that keeps it green.

Then learn by seeing what they do.
If they want eyes, hands, tongues, yet woo,
Can you that have of each the best,
Apt for that use, yet use them least?
'Twere sin to think the world did ne'er yet show
So unkind a breast graced with so mild a brow.

The lass that loved the Idaean swain *Helen; Paris*
Thought it not base nor found it vain.
Adon was loved, though proud and coy; *Adonis*
Endymion too, that drowsy boy,
Whom for to please, such care fair Cynthia took
That ever since that time she pale doth look.

Then let us love whilst we're in youth,
You fraught with beauty, I with truth.
We'll make the world, being in our prime,
Wrinkled with envy more than time,
And when too old to live the fate draws nigh,
Our love shall make us too too young to die.

*1632*

## Cupid's Holiday

Ladies whose marble hearts despise
Love's soft embraces; whose chaste eyes
Ne'er shot a glance, but might beseem
Diana and her maiden team
Of icy virgins: hence away!
Disturb not our licentious play,
For now 'tis Cupid's holiday.

Go glory in that empty name
Of virgin. Let your idle flame
Consume itself, while we enjoy
Those pleasures which fair Venus' boy
Grants to those whose mingled thighs

Are trophies of his victories,
From whence new pleasures still arise.

Those only are admitted here
Whose looser thoughts ne'er knew a fear
Of men's embraces; whose fair face
Can give enjoyment such a grace
As wipes away the hated name
Of lust, and calls their amorous flame
A virtue free from fear or shame.

With them we'll number kisses till
We pose arithmetic, and fill
Our hearts with pleasure till it swells
Beyond those bounds where blushing dwells.
Then will we ourselves entomb
In those joys which fill the womb
Till sleep possesses Cupid's room.

At waking no repentance shall
With our past sweetness mingle gall.
We'll kiss again till we restore
Our strength again to venture more.
Then we'll renew again our play
Admitting of no long delay
Till we end our holiday.

## Invitation to Dalliance

Be not thou so foolish-nice *foolishly coy*
As to be invited twice.
What should women more incite
Than their own sweet appetite?
Shall savage things more freedom have
Than nature unto women gave?
The swan, the turtle and the sparrow
Bill a while, then take the marrow.
They bill and kiss; what then they do
Come bill and kiss, and I'll show you.

## Now in the sad declension of thy time

Now in the sad declension of thy time
When all the world forsakes and lays thee by,
I but unveil my love, masked in the prime
Of thy transcendent glories, for mine eye
Judged thee not woman but a deity.

And till those roses blushing on thy cheek,
Those lilies and those violets were seen
To wither thus; till all those sweets we seek
In ruin lay, I could ne'er begin
To court thee without hazard of a sin.

Freed from all rival doubts and jealous fears
By time's rude hand, those relics I adore.
My flames increase although thy beauty wears;
And in this temperate season love thee more
Than in that scorching heat that went before.

## A Motive to Love

Faith, be no longer coy,
  But let's enjoy
What's by the world confessed
  Women love best.
Thy beauty fresh as May
  Will soon decay.
Besides, within a year or two
I shall be old, and cannot do.

Dost think that nature can
    For every man
(Had she more skill) provide
    So fair a bride?
Who ever had a feast
    For a single guest?
No, without doubt she did intend
To serve the husband and his friend.

To be a little nice
    Sets better price
On virgins, and improves
    Their servants' loves,
But on the riper years
    It ill appears.
After a while you'll find this true:
I need provoking more than you.

## Disdain me not, sweet love

Disdain me not, sweet love, though I am old.
Green is my love, although my hairs be gray.
        Nor am I cold,
    No matter what these young men say.
I have my blood as red and as fresh as they.
I am not wavering; constant is my love.
Young in desires I am, though old in years.
        Sabina, prove: *put me to the proof*
    My chest that always virtue bears *
Shall turn both mine and thine to golden hairs.

Thy youth will make me young; then, fair, be mine.
My hairs will leave their snowy livery
        By being thine.
    Therefore now pledge thyself and me,
So mine shall not be white, thine gold shall be.
I am in nature's debt and thou must pay.
O pass thy word or thou wilt do me wrong.
        Send age away
    And wipe off with thy sugared tongue
Old scores of years to make an old man young.

* *chest*: perhaps a chest of magical potions; the song seems to be from a play

## Fond lovers, what d'ye mean

Fond lovers, what d'ye mean
    To court an idle folly?
Platonic love is nothing else
    But merely melancholy.
'Tis active love that makes us jolly.

To dote upon a face
    Or court a sparkling eye
Or to conceive a dimpled cheek
    Complete felicity
Is to betray your liberty.

Then pray be not so fond.
    Think you that women can
Rest satisfied with compliment,
    The frothy part of man?
No no, they hate a Puritan.

They care not for your sighs
    Nor your erected eyes. *[like a hypocritical Puritan's*
They hate to hear a man complain
    Alas, he dies, he dies!
Oh no, they love a close surprise. *sudden attack*

Then venture to embrace:
    'Tis but a squeak or two.
I'm confident no woman lives
    But sometimes she will do.
The fault lies not in them, but you.

On the fashion for platonic love, see endnote

## Do not delay me

Do not delay me
Though you have the power
Ages to stay me:
O do't in an hour.

Then do not slight me,
O do not reject me.
Say not what might be,
Since thus I affect thee.

Nobody's stirring,
O none that can hear thee,
Then leave demurring
Now I am so near thee.

This is the season
Each bird is a-billing.
You that have reason,
O be not unwilling.

## Cupid is an idle toy

Cupid is an idle toy.
Never was there such a boy.
If there were, let any show
Or his quiver, or his bow,
Or a wound by him they got,
Or a broken arrow shot.
Money, money makes us bow:
There is no other Cupid now.

While the world continued good
People loved for flesh and blood.
Men about them bore the dart
That would catch a woman's heart,
And the women great and small
With a pretty thing they call
Cunny, cunny won the men,
And this was all the Cupid then.

## I swear by muscadell

I swear by muscadell
That I do love thee well
And more than I can tell.
By the white, claret and sack
I do love thy black, black, black. *her private parts*

So lovely and so fair,
O'ershadowed with thy hair,
So nimble just like air —
All these set me on love's rack
For thy sweeter black, black, black.

No goddess 'mongst them all
So slender and so tall
And graceful too withal,
Which makes my sinews to crack
For thy dainty black, black, black.

Thy kind and loving eye
When first I did espy,
Our loves it did descry,
Dumb-speaking, 'What d'ye lack?'
Mine answered, 'Thy black, black, black.'

## 'Tis not your virtues make you to refuse me

'Tis not your virtues make you to refuse me.
Women are often coy, though seldom chaste.
Howe'er you use me
And seem straitlaced,
The fruit in the midst of the garden placed
You long to taste.

Think not to cheat me then with seeming coldness.
You do but counterfeit when you seem nice.
A little boldness
Will thaw that ice.
He spoils his market, sets too high a price
On your device.

## Inconstancy in Woman

I am confirmed a woman can
Love this, or that, or any man.
This day her love is melting hot;
Tomorrow swears she knows you not.
Let her but a new object find
And she is of another mind.
Then hang me, ladies, at your door
If e'er I dote upon you more.

Yet still I'll love the fair ones. Why?
For nothing but to please mine eye.

And so the fat and soft-skinned dame *[plumpness was liked*
I'll flatter to appease my flame.
For her that's musical I long
When I am sad, to sing a song,
But hang me, ladies, at your door
If e'er I dote upon you more.

I'll give my fancy leave to range
Through every face to find out change:
The black, the brown, the fair shall be
But objects of variety.
I'll court you all to serve my turn
But with such flames as shall not burn,
For hang me, ladies, at your door
If e'er I dote upon you more.

## All the materials are the same

All the materials are the same
Of beauty and desire.
In a fair woman's goodly frame
No brightness is without a flame,
No flame without a fire.
Then tell me what those creatures are
That would be thought both chaste and fair.

If modesty itself appear
With blushes in her face,
Think'st thou the blood that dances there
Can revel it no other-where
Nor warm no other place?
Then tell me what those creatures are
That would be thought both chaste and fair.

If on her neck her hair be spread
In many a curious ring,
Why sure, the heat that curls her head
Will make her mad to be in bed
And do the other thing.
Then tell me what those creatures are
That would be thought both chaste and fair.

Go ask but thy philosophy *natural philosophy = science*
What gives her lips the balm,
What spirit gives motion to her eye,
What makes her breast to swell so high
And gives moisture to her palm.
Then tell me what those creatures are
That would be thought both chaste and fair.

## Ill tide the cruel peace

Ill tide the cruel peace that hath gained a war on me.
I never fancied laddy till I kenned mine enemy.
Sic another bonny and blithe a one
Never yet I set mine eyes upon.
Weel he might'a fooled a wiser one
As he did me.
He talked so witty and wooed so pretty
None could deny,
But needs must yield the fort up. Gude faith, and so did I.

Tantara! went the trumpets and straight we were in arms.
We dreaded no invasions; embraces were our charms.
Near we clasped until each other knit
And according to our mother wit,
And there's nothing now can smother it:
It will be known.
Alack and welly! Sic a back and belly
Never was made.
A soldier is a-coming, though young, makes me afraid. *a baby*

To England bear this sonnet: direct it unto none
But to the cavalerie, to sigh and me bemoan.
Some of them may happen take my part.
Be content and do not ache, my heart.
At his bosom, Cupid, shake thy dart,
Who is mine own,
Or mayst thou never wear bow or quiver
Till that I see
Once more the happy feature of my loved enemy.

The song probably dates from Charles I's campaign against the Scots in 1639, in which the poets Suckling and Lovelace served; might one of them claim it?

## Fine young folly

Fine young folly, though you were
That fair beauty I did swear
    Yet you ne'er could reach my heart,
For we courtiers learn at school
Only with your sex to fool.
    Y'are not worth the serious part.

When I sigh and kiss your hand,
Cross my arms and wondering stand,
    Holding parley with your eye,
Then dilate on your desires,
Swear the sun ne'er shot such fires,
    All is but a handsome lie.

When I eye your curl or lace,
Gentle soul, you think your face
    Straight some murder does commit,
And your virtue doth begin
To grow scrupulous of my sin
    When I talk to show my wit.

Therefore, madam, wear no cloud,
Nor to check my love grow proud,
    For, in sooth, I much do doubt
'Tis the powder in your hair,
Not your breath, perfumes the air
    And your clothes that set you out.

Yet though truth hath this confessed
And I vow I loved in jest,
    When I next begin to court
And protest an amorous flame
You'll swear I in earnest am.
    Bedlam! this is pretty sport.

WILLIAM HABINGTON, *1640*

## Love's Flattery

I can love for an hour
When I'm at leisure.
He that loves half a day
Fools without measure.

Cupid then tell me
What art had thy mother
To make men love one face
More than another?

Some to be thought more wise
Daily endeavour
To make the world believe
They can love ever.
Ladies, believe them not,
They'll but deceive you,
For when they have their ends
Then they will leave you.

Men cannot tire themselves
On your sweet features.
They'll have variety
Of loving creatures.
Too much of any thing
Sets them a-cooling.
Though they can never do't
Yet they'll be fooling.

## Though Cupid be a god

Though Cupid be a god,
Alas, he's but a boy,
And Venus whom he mother calls
We all know for a toy. *a trivial thing*

There's no such thing as love
That dares now to appear.
Great Mars himself hath gi'n it o'er
And is turned Cavalier.

What wonder is it then
If ladies here below
Are left alone to make their moan
And sing hey-nonny-no?

See how they ride and run
To lay hold on a man.
Some pull, some cry, some swear they'll die,
Yet not a thing will stand.

Well, in a rage they swear
They all will Roundheads be,
For then the Cavaliers again
Will at them furiously.

The poet Edmund Waller found a happier amatory effect of the Civil War:

Cloris, since first our calm of peace
Was frighted hence, this good we find:
Your favours with your fears increase
And growing mischief makes you kind.

## O smother me to death

O smother me to death
With thy sweet balmy breath,
While thy dear mouth affords
Whole kisses, and half words.

And, cruel, long be trying
The pleasure thus in dying,
That I so slain may pardon thee
And all the world may envy me.

## If thou dost love me as thou say'st

If thou dost love me as thou say'st
Then do what I desire.
That love is sickly and doth waste
Which yields not equal fire.
'Tis but a languishing delight
That does in kisses die!
Come, let us triumph in the height
Of all that's thou and I.

What? shall the tyrant conscience awe?
Or goblin honour fear? *make fearful*
Let us be one another's law;
No sprite but ours appear.
Our love has zeal enough to make
Religion of our own
And thine eyes light enough to shake
The other devil home.

Then in the pride of all our joy
Let's fix Elysium here.
The only hell is to be coy
And only shame to fear.
Our hearts for conscience shall not break
Nor fames from honour go.
All is religion that we speak
And honour that we do.

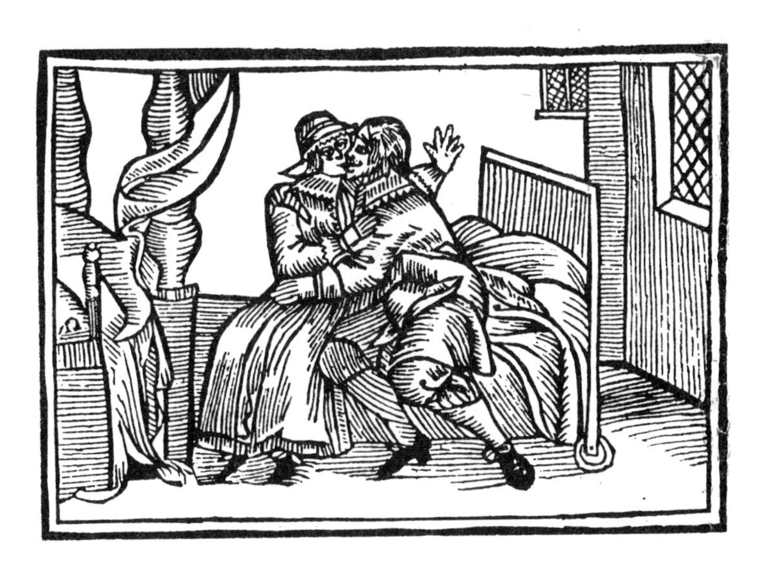

## Whenas I do record

Whenas I do record
The pleasures I have had
At yonder slidethrift board *shove-halfpenny*
With many a lively lad
It makes me merry and glad,
Though it puts me to mickle pain:
I would give mine old white jade
That Jinny were here again.

She baked and brewed to sell
To those that passèd by.
Good fellows loved her well,

In faith and so did I,
For ever when I was dry
Of drink I would have ta'en.
I would tread both shoes awry
That Jinny were here again.

Full oft have she and I
Within the buttery played
At trey-trip with a die*
And sent away the maid,
For she's of the dealing trade,
She'll give you three for one.
She is no sullen jade.
If Jinny were here again!

A man might for his money
Have had a pot of ale
And tasted of a coney, *coney/cunny*
Of either leg or tail,
For she would never fail
If she were in the vein.
Alas! all flesh is frail.
If Jinny were here again!

Full oft I have been her man
Her market for to make,
And after I have ridden
A journey for her sake.
Her panel I could take*
And gallop all amain.
I'd make both bedsides crack.
That Jinny were here again!

You hostesses that mean
For to live by your trade,
If you scorn to kiss
Then keep a pretty maid,
For drink is not worth a louse
If lasses there be nane.
I would drink a whole carouse
That Jinny were here again.

* *trey-trip*: a dice-game, but here a sexual jest: he plays to win with his three, testicles+penis (another song has, 'I'll clap my trey unto your ace')

* *panel*: saddle cushion or makeshift saddle; or a softer place to ride

## Love's Drollery

I love thee for thy fickleness
And great inconstancy,
For hadst thou been a constant lass
Then thou hadst ne'er loved me.

I love thee for thy wantonness
And for thy drollery,
For if thou hadst not loved to sport
Then thou hadst ne'er loved me.

I love thee for thy poverty
And for thy want of coin,
For if thou hadst been worth a groat
Then thou hadst ne'er been mine.

I love thee for thy ugliness
And for thy foolery,
For if thou hadst been fair and wise
Then thou hadst ne'er loved me.

Then let me have thy heart a while
And thou shalt have my money.
I'll part with all the wealth I have
T'enjoy a lass so bonny.

## What would any man desire?

What would any man desire?
Is he cold? Then here's a fire.
Is he hot? She'll gently school him
Till he find that heat does cool him.
Is he sad? Then here's a pleasure.
Is he poor? Then here's a treasure.
Loves he music? Here's the choice
Of all sweet sounds in her sweet voice.
Does he hunger? Here's a feast
To which a god might be a guest.
And to these viands, if he thirst
Here's nectar for him: since the first
Of men that was for sin a debtor
Never any tasted better.
Here's all complete from head to heel
To hear, to see, taste, smell or feel.

## Note of me was never took

Note of me was never took
For my woman-like perfections,
But so like a man I look
It hath gained me best affections.

Though some lord it over me
They in vain thereof have braved,
For their lusts my servants be
Whereunto their minds are slaved.

A subtle boast from a woman: printed in 1654

## If my lady bid begin

If my lady bid begin
Shall I say, 'No, 'tis a sin'?
If she bid me kiss and play
Shall I shrink, cold fool, away?
If she clap my cheeks and spy
Little Cupids in my eye,
Gripe my hand and stroke my hair,
Shall I like a faintheart fear?
No no no, let those that lie
In dismal dungeons and would die
Despair and fear. Let those that cry
They are forsaken and would fly
Quit their fortunes: mine are free.
Hope makes me hardy; so does she. *bold*

## Prethee die and set me free

Prethee die and set me free
Or else be
Kind and brisk and gay like me.
I pretend not to the wise ones,
To the grave,
To the grave or the precise ones.

Prethee, why those bolts and locks,
Coats and smocks?
And those drawers? With a pox!

I would wish, could nature make it,
    Nakedness,
Nakedness itself more naked.

Prethee, why the room so dark?
    Not a spark
Left to light me to the mark.
I love daylight or a candle,
    And to see,
And to see as well as handle.

There is neither art nor itch
    In thy breech,
Nor provoking hand or speech.
And when I expect thy motion,
    Fall'st asleep,
Fall'st asleep, or to devotion.

But if a mistress I must have
    Wise and grave,
Let her so herself behave:
By daylight a Susan Civil,
    Nell by night,
Nell by night, or such a devil.

SIR JOHN DENHAM

## The Threading of the Needle

Oh that I durst but thread your needle, lady,
There would I work till I had made a baby.
Or stop your floodgates, on condition I
Did at the jointer in the river lie. *where the lock-gates meet*

Oh that I durst but shoot a gulf I know,
Or in the Lower Countries my seed sow,
Or plough the bottom of that Netherland
Until my plough did fall, and I not stand.

Oh that I durst but play at in-and-in. *a dice game*
If I were out, I would again begin;
Or fast-or-loose, I care not whether much. *a trickster's game*
Yet should I lose at both, my play is such.

Oh that I durst tread the grass that grows
About your river, where perfect nectar flows,

Or that my smaller current might distil
His moisture into yours, till yours it fill.

Oh that I durst monopolize a thing,
I mean that curious black-enamelled ring
Whose virtue's such in durance that it has
Worn out a world of stones that did surpass. *testicles*
  Yet I care not: for all that I will venture,
  If you'll give leave, within your ring to enter.

## Maids they are grown so coy of late

Maids they are grown so coy of late,
Forsooth, they will not marry!
Though they be in their teens and past
They say they yet can tarry.
But if they knew how sweet a thing
It were in youth to marry
They'd sell their petticoats, smocks and all
Ere they so long would tarry.

The lass that is most coy of all,
If she had time and leisure
Would lay by all her several thoughts
And turn to love and pleasure.
Winter nights are long, you know,
And bitter cold the weather.
Then who's so fond to lie alone *foolish*
When two may lie together?

## If thou wilt love me, I'll love again

  If thou wilt love me, I'll love again.
  If my grief move thee, I'll love my pain.
  If love disdain me, I'll die for woe,
  And if thou fly me, I'll fly thee too,
For love my breast hath filled with such a fire
That whatsoe'er thou wilt, 'tis my desire.

  Thy sighs so burning, I'll cool with mine,
  And at thy mourning, my heart shall pine.
  But one kiss give me, I'll kissing die,
  And if thou leave me, adieu say I,
*For love, etc —*

If melancholy possess thy heart,
Then of thy sadness I'll bear a part.
If to be merry be pleasing to thee
I'll leave off sadness, and merry be,
*For love, etc —*

If griefs perplex thee, my heart shall mourn,
And if sighs vex me, I'll sigh my turn.
If tears do please thee, mine eyes shall weep
Till sorrow works my heart asleep,
*For love, etc —*

If thou love music, I'll love it too.
If courtship please thee, I'll learn to woo.
If thou bid'st 'Leave me,' I'll fly away.
If thou command'st, I'll longer stay,
For love my breast hath filled with such a fire
That whatsoe'er thou wilt, 'tis my desire.

## Thy love is yet asleep

Thy love is yet asleep, cannot be waked.
An oven's heat, and yet thy love not baked.

Not taste sweet nectar's love though still renewing —
One dies of thirst to have it still a-brewing.

Ambrosia love not eat, but still a-dishing:
Thus we shall starve. Love cannot live with wishing.

Thus we shall famish both. Love faints, it lingers.
They're ill love's cooks that cannot lick their fingers.

Th'art love's ill husband thus. Be provident, *poor manager*
Let nature teach us what sweet nature meant.

JOHN GAMBLE

## Prithee, oh prithee, prithee

Prithee, oh prithee, prithee — 'Tis not well
To pray thee do that which I cannot tell.

Something I'd have thee do, not this or that,
And then I find it is I know not what.

When thou dost love me, 'tis an overjoy;
That's trouble. When I love thee, thou art coy.

That's trouble too. When with thee, I'm so fain
And yet am troubled; absent, full of pain.

Long for to speak, imprisoned words release.
When speak, more grieved than when I hold my peace.

When I'm awake, thoughts strive against love's stream.
When I'm asleep, thou troublest every dream.

Love's never quiet until lovers dead.
Yes, faith, they're quiet when they are abed.

JOHN GAMBLE

## Great sums of love

Great sums of love now thou dost owe me,
Like bankrupt debtors, will not know me.

Ten thousand pounds of sighs at least,
Groans full as much out of my breast,

Millions of tears out of mine eyes;
Great store of paleness, my heart dries.

From love's exchequer you had store —
Forget love's debts, still ask for more.

I prethee pay me what's my due
Or else I swear I will pay you.

JOHN GAMBLE

## Love is a sickness and a strange disease

Love is a sickness and a strange disease.
Love's heart's grief's joy, a sadness that doth please,*

At love's eyes kindled, fed with thoughts' desire
And so inflamed into love's fever's fire.

Taken by love, I long cannot endure.
'Tis only one and one only the cure:

That's thee. Prithee tell me, what wilt thou do?
For thou'rt the doctor, physic, patient too.

Like the magnetic cure—thou givest the wound;*
Love's medicine laid on thee doth make me sound.

JOHN GAMBLE

* A lover's heart's grief is a joy, a pleasing pain (Gamble is fond of the 's)
* *magnetic cure*: a saucy play on the claim of Sir Kenelm Digby (1603–65), one of the 'magnetic cure' theorists of the time, that he had a powder that would cure a wound by being rubbed on whatever had *caused* the wound

## As thou dost look in love of me

As thou dost look in love of me
Love's climate alters love's degree,

For if a kinder look obtain
I'm then in Italy or Spain.

If but a sweeter love's look glance,
In fruitful Germany or France.

If frown, Moscova; thou dost make
Me a furred Russian for thy sake.

Nay, more: thou freezest up my soul
In darkness at love's six-months pole.

JOHN GAMBLE

## What a thin, fine, cool, airy love at first

What a thin, fine, cool, airy love at first
We had, now swelled as if our loves would burst,

And trembling earthquakes in us still do move.
At last burst forth in boisterous sighs our love,

Which being fanned with our hearts' heat's desire
Inflamed the world into a loving fire.

You and I made one love's sun, fixèd still;
The rest love's waiting stars upon our will.

JOHN GAMBLE

## Love should be gentle sweet delight

Love should be gentle sweet delight.
Thou look'st so hard, put'st out my sight.

Love's softer whisper in each ear —
Thy louder love that sense doth tear.

Each tender touch, thou wring'st my hand:
My fingers dislocated stand.

When I would gently touch thy lip
Thou smack'st a crack like coachman's whip,

And tread'st so hard upon my foot
My corns cry out, Oh do not do't!

Cupid's lame soldier, I must beg
At love's town's-end with a lame leg,

Thus overlaid in love; nay, worse,
Like a child killed with a fat nurse.

Be not so boisterous, pray be mild.
I swear you'll get me else with child.

JOHN GAMBLE

## Love's actual sins I did commit

Love's actual sins I did commit
And to confess them think it fit.

Looking's no pleasure to my sight;
Did kiss thy lips without delight.

And when I touched thy softer skin,
So rough, methought it was a sin.

Thy sweeter language to my ear
As if impertinent it were.

Adorned as if thyself wouldst sell,
And yet methought not dressed so well,

Traduced thus by a friend of mine:
But I will swear she's none of thine.

JOHN GAMBLE

## I saw myself on shipboard lie

I saw myself on shipboard lie,
Sailing in thy kind watery eye.

Down thy salt tears sailed in love's ship,
Anchored in the Red Sea, thy lip.

Love's anchor weighed, I would not stay.
A loving sigh blew me away

Between breasts' rocks; and did not stick —
Sailed down love's strait, that narrow crick.

Then down thy belly's ocean fine
To pass thy navel, called love's Line. *equator*

Hoist sail, touched love's each finer rope; *her pubic hair*
The heaven gained, Cape of Good Hope.

Thus gained the port — though safe in it,
Love's tossing waves did make me split.

JOHN GAMBLE

## The Concealment

I loved a maid, she loved not me,
But that was a maid's infirmity.
She wore a garter above her knee,
But that was a secret bravery.
I played with her paps, she gave me some raps.
*But what did you else beside?*
Nay, that were a folly: the fox is unholy *[folly/unholy rhyme*
And yet he hath grace to hide.

Her feet were little, her fingers small,
Her hips did wear no farthingale;
Her body straight, her belly round,
The whalebone use there was not found. *she wore no corset*
I haled her, I pulled her, I kissed her, I culled her. *cuddled*
*But what did you, etc —*

I wrung her hands, she wrung mine again.
God bless such wringing as breeds no pain!
I looked on her face and I gave her a dance.

She dimmed my sight with a coloured glance.
I hung on her neck, she gave me a check.
*But what did you, etc –*

When each man had danced with his maid,
Then down behind a tree we stayed.
My knees against her knees I thrust.
She cried, 'Sweetheart, let be!' and blushed,
But yet at last I grasped her fast.
*But what did you, etc –*

Behind my ear I wear her lock,
And she my favour next her smock.
She loves me more, if more you mark,
Since last we tumbled in the dark.
She was so kindhearted, she wept when we parted.
*But what did you else beside?*
Nay, that were a folly: the fox is unholy
And yet he hath grace to hide.

## Poor Jenny and I, we toiled

Poor Jenny and I, we toiled
A long, long summer's day
Till we were almost spoiled
With making of the hay.
Her kerchief was of holland clear
Bound low upon her brow.
Ise whispered something in her ear,*
But what's that to you?

Her stockings were of kersey green, *coarse woollen*
Well stitched with yellow silk.
Oh, sic a leg was never seen!
Her skin as white as milk,
Her hair was black as any crow,
And sweet her mouth was too.
Oh! Jenny daintily could mow,
But what's that to you?

Her petticoats were not so low
As ladies now do wear 'em.
She needed not a page, I trow,
For I was by to bear 'em.

Iz took 'em up all in my hand
And I think her linen too,
Which made a friend of mine to stand,
But what's that to you?

King Solomon had wives enough
And concubines a number,*
Yet Iz possess more happiness
And he had more of cumber.
My joy surmounts a wedded life.
With fear she lets me mow.
A wench is better than a wife,
But what's that to you?

The lily and the rose combine
To make my Jenny fair.
There's no contentment like as mine.
I'm almost void of care.
But yet I fear my Jenny's face
Will cause more men to woo,
Which I shall take for a disgrace.
But what's that to you?

* *Ise* or *Iz:* dialect, chiefly northern (compare Ich in German)

*Robert Burns, a great collector of old songs, instances Solomon's concubines in 'The Bonniest Lass' (*Merry Muses of Caledonia*):

King Solomon, prince o' divines,
Wha proverbs made, an' a' that,
Baith mistresses an' concubines
In hundreds had, for a' that.

## Instructions to his Mistress how to behave herself at Supper before her Husband

Since to restrain our joy, that ill-bred, rude,
Familiar thing your husband will intrude,
For a just judgment may th'unwelcome guest
At this night's lucky supper eat his last.
O how shall I with patience e'er stand by
While my Corinna gives another joy —
His wanton hands in her soft bosom warms
And folds about her neck his clasping arms?
Oh! torturing sight, but since it must be so,
Be kind and learn what 'tis I'd have you do:

Come first, be sure, for though the place may prove
Unfit for all we wish, 'twill show your love.
When called to table you demurely go,
Gently in passing touch my hand, or so.
Mark all my actions well, observe my eye,
My speaking signs, and to each sign reply.
If I do aught of which you would complain,
Upon your elbow languishingly lean,
But if you're pleased with what I do or say,
Steal me a smile, then snatch your eyes away.
When you reflect on our past secret joys,
Hold modestly your fan before your eyes,
And when the nauseous husband tedious grows,
Your lifted hands with scornful anger close
As if you called for vengeance from above
Upon that dull impediment of love.
A thousand skilful ways we'll find to show
Our mutual love, which none but we shall know.
I'll watch the parting glass whene'er you drink
And where your lips have touched it, kiss the brink;
Like still the dish that in your reach does stand — *still = always*
Taking the plate, I so may feel your hand.
But what he recommends to you to eat,
Coyly refuse as if you loathed the meat.
Nor let his matrimonial right appear
By any ill-timed household freedom there:
Let not his fulsome arms embrace your waist,
Nor lolling head upon your bosom rest.
One kiss would straight make all my passion known
And my fierce eyes with rage would claim their own.

Yet what thus passes will be done i' th' light.
But oh! the joys that may be kept from sight:
Legs locked in legs, thighs pressing thighs, and all
The wanton spells that up love's fury call.
Those cunning arts that I so oft have used*
Make me now fear to be myself abused.
To clear my doubts, so far your chair remove
As may prevent th'intelligence of love.
Put him in mind of pledging every health
And let the tutored page add wine by stealth.
The sot, grown drunk, more easier may retire
And do as the occasion will require.

But after all, alas! how small the gains
Will be for which we take such mighty pains.
Torn from my arms, you must go home to bed
And leave your poor forsaken lover dead.
Cruel divorce! enough to break my heart,
Without you promise this before we part:
When my blessed rival goes to reap his joy,
Receive him so as may the bliss destroy.
Let not the least kind mark of love escape,
But all be duty, and a lawful rape;
So deadly cold and void of all desire
That, like a charm, it may put out the fire.
But if, compelled, you should at last comply,
When we meet next, be sure you all deny.

*One manuscript reads '...which you so oft have used'; but it is subtler to have his jealous anxiety arise from his having instructed and aroused her

## As I walked in the woods

As I walked in the woods one evening of late
A lass was deploring her hapless estate.
In a languishing posture, poor maid, she appears,
All swelled with her sighs and blubbed with her tears.
She sighed and she sobbed, and I found it was all
For a little of that which Harry gave Doll.

At last she broke out, 'Wretched!' she said,
'Will no youth come succour a languishing maid
With what he with ease and with pleasure may give?
Without which, alas! poor I cannot live.
Shall I never leave sighing and crying and all
For a little of that which Harry gave Doll?

'At first when I saw a young man in the place
My colour would fade and then flush in my face.
My breath would grow short, and I shivered all o'er.
My breasts never popped up and down so before.
I scarce knew for what, but now find it was all
For a little of that which Harry gave Doll.'

THOMAS SHADWELL, *1672*

## Of all the brisk dames

Of all the brisk dames, my Selina for me,
For I love not a woman unless she be free.
The affection that I to my mistress do pay
Grows weary unless she does meet it half-way.
There can be no pleasure till humours do hit,
And jumping's as good in affection as wit.

No sooner I came, but she liked me as soon;
No sooner I asked, but she granted my boon,
And without a preamble, a portion or jointure
She promised to meet me where'er I'd appoint her.
So we struck up a match, and embracèd each other
Without the consent of father or mother.

Then away with a lady that's modest and coy.
Let her ends be the pleasures that we do enjoy.
Let her tickle her fancy with secret delight
And refuse all the day what she longs for at night.
I believe my Selina, who shows they're all mad
To feed on dry bones when flesh may be had.

## The Maiden's Complaint against Young Men's Unkindness

I am so deep in love
    I cannot hide it.
It breaks me of my rest
    And of my quiet,
For when I see his face
    It so inflames me
That I must love him still
    Though the world blames me.

O fie upon this love,
  It will undo me.
I'll ne'er love man again,
  Should the gods woo me.
Now if that once I can
  Shake off this passion
I'll ne'er love man again
  Only for fashion.

There's no belief in men
  Though they seem civil,
For when they sit like saints
  They think most evil.
Therefore be ruled by me:
  Never trust no man,
But if you needs must love,
  Pray love a woman.

I wish blind Cupid had
  Been soundly sleeping
When like a crafty lad
  He came so creeping
To wound my tender heart
  And pierce my marrow.
I felt his fatal dart,
  To my great sorrow.

Never poor virgin was
  In such a taking.
I oft looked in my glass,
  Pleasure forsaking.
My cheeks are pale and wan,
  My lips do tremble
Because I loved a man
  That did dissemble.

O what a simple girl
  I was for certain!
For to love lord or earl
  I will not hearken.
Not one in twenty score
  But is deceitful,
Therefore I'll love no more.
  Men are ungrateful.

It is their constant trade
    To cog and flatter, *cheat*
Or to delude a maid,
    Her fort to batter.
But if they pray and lie
    I'll not believe them.
Such love I'll never try,
    Although it grieve them.

They profess and pretend
    Much of affection
Until they make you bend
    To love's subjection.
Of your hearts craftily
    They will bereave you,
Till a new face they spy;
    Then they will leave you.

Their words they are but wind,
    Like winter weather,
Unconstant and unkind,
    Light as a feather.
I tell you short and plain,
    I'll not abide it
To love a man again,
    Once having tried it.

Blame me not, though I be
    Something in passion,
For now I plainly see
    It is the fashion
For such false-hearted men
    Are grown so common
That when I love again
    I'll love a woman.

Why should a woman dote
    On such a bubble
That's good for nothing but
    To procure trouble?
Every day I will pray
    For to live single,
That my affections may
    With no man's mingle.

Ladies, take my advice.
　You have rare features.
Always be coy and nice
　To such false creatures.
No man will constant prove,
　No, not my brother.
Then if you needs must love,
　Love one another.

## Sawney was tall and of noble race

Sawney was tall and of noble race
　And loved me better than any eane,
But now he liggs by another lass, *lies*
　And Sawney will ne'er be my love agen.
I gave him a fine Scotch sark and band, *shirt and collar*
I put 'um on with mine awn hand;
I gave him house and I gave him land,
　Yet Sawney will ne'er be my love agen.

I robbed the groves of all their store
　And nosegays made to give Sawney yen.
He kissed my breast and fain would do more.
　Gude feth methought he was a bonny yen. *good faith*
He squeezed my fingers, grasped my knee,
And carved my name on each green tree,
And sighed and languished to ligg by me,
　But now he will ne'er be my love agen.

My bongrace and my sunburnt face *broadbrimmed hat, or its veil*
　He praised, and also my russet gown,
But now he dotes on the copper lace
　Of some lewd quean of London town. *whore*
He gangs and gives her curds and cream
Whilst I, poor saule, sit sighing at heam *soul; home*
And ne'er joy Sawney unless in a dream,
　For now he will ne'er be my love agen.

THOMAS D'URFEY, *1680*

An early London-made 'Scotch' song, used by D'Urfey in his play *The Virtuous Wife*

## Cupid's Trapan, or Up the Green Forest

Once did I love a bonny bonny bird,
Thinking that he had been mine own,
But he loved another far better than I,
And he has taken his flight and is flown, brave boys,
*And he has taken his flight and is flown.*

Up the green forest and down the green forest
Like one much distressed in mind
I whooped and I whooped, and I flung up my hood
But my bonny bird I could not find, brave boys,
*But my bonny bird I could not find.*

But she that hath gotten my bonny bonny bird,
Would the devil had had her, for me.
It was not a crown nor a noble so round *[her rival had money*
That should have bought my bonny bird from me, brave boys,
*That should have bought my bonny bird from me.*

He set me upon his dissembling knee
And looked me all in the face.
He gave unto me a Judas kiss
But his heart was in another place, brave boys,
*But his heart was in another place.*

But she that hath gotten my bonny bonny bird,
Let her make as much on't as she can.
For whether I have him or I have him not,
I will quaff with him now and then, brave boys,
*I will quaff with him now and then.*

These five stanzas make a self-contained song with a spirited ending, and later variants end in a similar insouciant way. I see this as the song's original form. But the broadside where they are found follows on illogically with 14 more stanzas – no doubt added by the printer to fill out his space – in which the girl suddenly takes a high moral line and vows to preserve her virginity:

Those virgins that take him I think are stark mad,
For he that proves false unto one
That loved him as life will be false to his wife.
I have cause to be glad that he's gone, brave boys...

I vow to be jolly, brisk, bonny and free
And march under chastity's banners.
I'll sing and I'll dance and my spirits advance
In spite of all Cupid's trapanners, brave boys...

'Cupid's Trapan' inspired a male riposte so vaunting that it belongs with 'Rakes and Wantons', but for convenience I offer nine of its 20 stanzas next —

## A Young Man put to his Shifts
### or The Ranting Young Man's Resolution

*To the tune of 'Cupid's Trapan'*

Of late did I hear a young damsel complain
    And rail much against a young man.
His cause and his state I'll now vindicate,
    *And hold battle with Cupid's Trapan, brave boys,*
    *And hold battle with Cupid's Trapan.*

Surely she thinks that I am stark mad,
    To wed every girl I do see.
No, let her stay a while, for I can make a fool
    *Of twenty far better than she, brave boys, &c.*

For if I court a maid she will get nothing by't,
    For so soon as her money is gone
And I have got her rings and other fine things,
    *Then the devil may take her for John, &c.*

. . . . . .

I count him a noddy that can't win a maid
    To buckle, to bow and to bend,
And if he stands in need, to do a good deed
    *And to give him some money in hand, brave boys, &c.*

. . . . . .

I'll never be bound when I may live free,
    Nor I'll never be tied to a wife.
There's soap, fire and candle, a child for to dandle,
    *Which makes a man weary on's life, &c.*

So I get but the child, let who will it keep.
    For my part I do not mean to keep none.
So I have but the sport, let them provide for't,
    *For so soon as I've done I am gone, &c.*

For if I should keep all the children I get
    I should have a great many lives.
I will take a halter and cut my own throat
    *Before I'll have so many wives, &c.*

. . . . . .

So young men, I'll leave you. Make use of your time.
    For so long as my codpiece do hold
I am sure of this, let it hit or miss,
    *I shall want neither silver nor gold, brave boys,*
    *I shall want neither silver nor gold.*

# The Enjoyment
## or No no changed to Ay ay

When the kine had given a pailful
And the sheep came bleating home,
Doll that knew it would be healthful
Went a-walking with young Tom.
Hand in hand, sir,
O'er the land, sir,
As they wandered to and fro
Tom made jolly love to Dolly
But was dashed with No no no,
No no no, no no no.

Faith, says Tom, the time's so fitting,
We shall never get the like.
You can never stir from knitting
When I'm digging in the dyke.
Now we're gone too,
And alone too,
No one by to see or know.
Prithee, Dolly, shall I, shall I?
Still she answered, No no no,
No no no, no no no.

Fie upon you men, cries Dolly.
In what snares you make us fall!
You get nothing but the folly
But I should get the devil and all.

Tom with sobs
And some dry-bobs
Cried, You're a fool to argue so.
Come come, shall I? Prithee, Dolly.
Still she answered, No no no, &c.

To the tavern then he took her.
Wine to love's a friend confessed.
By the hand he often shook her
And drank brimmers of the best.
She grew warm,
And thought no harm,
Till after a brisk pint or two
To what he said the silly jade
Could hardly get out No no no, &c.

She swore he was the prettiest fellow
In the country or the town
And began to be so mellow,
On the couch she laid her down.
Tom to woo her
Then came to her,
Thinking this the time to try,
And something passed, so kind at last,
The note was changed to Ay ay ay,
Ay ay ay, ay ay ay.

Closely now were joined their faces.
Lovers, you know what I mean.
Nor could she hinder his embraces —
Love was now too far got in.
Both now lying,
Panting, dying,
Calm succeeds to stormy joy.
Tom would fain renew again
And Doll consents with Ay ay ay,
Ay ay ay, ay ay ay.

Tom, you did me overpower
In this pleasant shady grove,
But it was the sweetest hour
As I e'er enjoyed of love.
Therefore ever
My endeavour
Shall be Tommy to enjoy.
Do but crave it, you shall have it
Granted with an Ay ay ay,
Ay ay ay, ay ay ay.

THOMAS D'URFEY, *1684*

## Tell me, Mother, Pray now Do

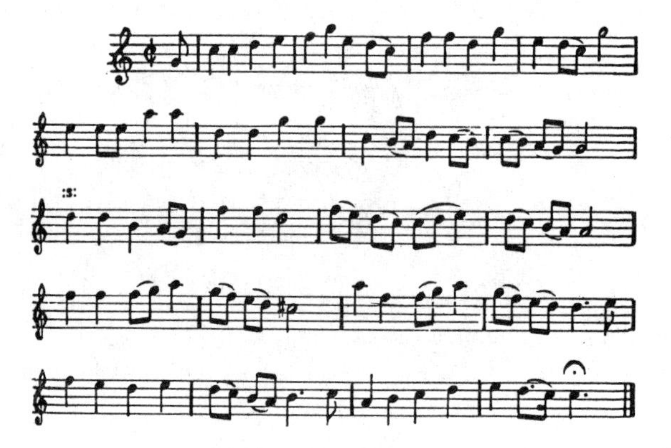

Oh mother! Roger with his kisses
Almost stops my breath, I vow!
Why does he gripe my hand to pieces
And yet says he loves me too?
Tell me, mother, pray now do,
Pray now do, pray now do,
What Roger means when he does so,
For never stir, I long to know.

Nay more, the naughty man beside it
Something in my mouth did put.*
I called him beast and tried to bite it,
But for my life, I cannot do't.
Tell me, mother, pray now do,
Pray now do, pray now do,
For never stir, I long to know.

He sets me in his lap whole hours,
Where I feel I know not what:
Something I never felt in yours.
Pray tell me, mother, what is that?
Tell me, mother, what is that?
What is that? What is that?
For never stir, I long to know.

*1685*

*Nothing more daring than his tongue, as the last stanza shows

## The Frightened Yorkshire Damsel
### or Fears Dispersed by Pleasure

When first I began to court
And pretty young maidens to woo,
I could not win the virgin fort
But by the Bogulmaroo.

I kissed her in summer time
And in the cold winter too;
At last I took her in the prime, *the spring*
But by the Bogulmaroo.

My love she was going one night
To bed as she used to do *as she usually did*
When on the stairs she saw a spright:
It was the Bogulmaroo.

She came to my chamber-door
And could not tell what to do,
But straight began to weep full sore
For fear of Bogulmaroo.

At last she came boldly in,
Though still her poor heart did rue,
For looking back, the spright did grin.
O cruel Bogulmaroo!

She started and run in haste
And close to my bedside drew.
Her eyes she durst not backward cast
For fear of Bogulmaroo.

But into my bed she crept,
And did her sorrows renew:
She wrung her hands and sadly wept
For fear of Bogulmaroo.

I turned about to the maid,
As lovers are wont to do,
And bid her be no more afraid
Of th'ugly Bogulmaroo.

I kissed and embraced her then.
Our pleasures they were not few.
We lay abed next day till ten
For fear of the Bogulmaroo.

My love she was all dismayed
To think of what she had done.
Arise, said I, be not afraid,
The Bogulmaroo is gone.

I married her the next day
And did her pleasures renew.
Each night we spend in charming play,
For all the Bogulmaroo.

I ne'er said a word of the thing
Nor never intend to do,
But every time she smiles on me
I think of Bogulmaroo.

Here, from a broadside dated 1689, is the original of that much-loved but muddled song, 'The Foggy Dew' (a phrase that makes no sense). 'Bogulmaroo' combines 'boggle' (bogle), a spectre, and 'mare', a demon (as in 'nightmare'). Now we see the story: thwarted in his wooing, the man sets up a bogulmaroo on the dark stairs leading to the girl's room, sending her scurrying – perhaps welcoming the excuse – to his bed . (And see endnote)

## I gave her cakes, I gave her ale

I gave her cakes, I gave her ale
And I gave her sack and sherry.
I kissed her once and I kissed her twice
And we were wondrous merry.

I gave her beads and bracelets fine
And I gave her gold down-derry.

I thought she was a-feared
Till she stroked my beard,
And we were wondrous merry.

Merry my hearts, merry my cocks, merry my sprights,
Merry, merry, merry, merry, merry,
My hey-down-derry!
I kissed her once and I kissed her twice
And we were wondrous merry.

*set by* HENRY PURCELL

## Phillis at first seemed much afraid

Phillis at first seemed much afraid,
Much afraid, much afraid,
Yet when I kissed she soon repaid.
Could you but see, could you but see
What I did more, you'd envy me,
What I did more, you'd envy me,
You'd envy me.

We then so sweetly were employed,
Were employed, were employed,
The height of pleasure we enjoyed.
Could you but see, could you but see,
You'd say so too, if you saw me,
You'd say so too, if you saw me,
If you saw me.

She was so charming, kind and free,
Kind and free, kind and free,
None ever could more happy be.
  Could you but see, could you but see
  Where I was then you'd wish to be,
  Where I was then you'd wish to be,
    You'd wish to be.

All the delights we did express,
Did express, did express,
Yet craving more still to possess.
  Could you but see, could you but see
  You'd curse, and say, Why was't not me?
  Why was't not me, why was't not me?
    Why was't not me?

Ladies, if how to love you'd know,
Love you'd know, love you'd know,
She can inform what we did do.
  But could you see, but could you see,
  You'd cry aloud, The next is me.
  You'd cry aloud, The next is me,
    The next is me!

## A Dialogue Sung in Oroonoko by the Boy and Girl

*Boy* Celemena, pray tell me,
When those pretty eyes I see,
Why my heart beats in my breast,
Why it will not let me rest.
Why this trembling too all o'er,
Pains I never felt before,
And when thus I touch your hand,
Why I wish I was a man.

*Girl* How should I know more than you?
Yet would be a woman too.
When you wash yourself and play
I methinks could look all day.
Nay, just now am pleased so well,
Should you kiss me I won't tell,
Though I could do that all day
And desire no better play.

Sure in love there's something more,
Which makes Mamma so big before.
Once by chance I heard it named:
Don't ask what, for I'm ashamed.
Stay but till you're past fifteen,
Then you'll know what 'tis I mean.
However, lose not present bliss,
But now we're alone, let's kiss.

My breasts do so heave. My heart does so pant.
There's something something something more we want.

*Both* There's something something something more we want.
There's something something something more we want.

THOMAS D'URFEY; *set by* PURCELL

Thomas Southerne's play *Oroonoko* (1695), based on Aphra Behn's novel about a 'noble savage', had a Caribbean setting but was gingered up with songs such as this (see endnote for another erotic boy-and-girl song)

## Young Coridon and Phillis

Young Coridon and Phillis
Sat in a lovely grove
Contriving crowns of lilies,
Repeating tales of love,
And something else, but what I dare not name.

But as they were a-playing
She ogled so the swain
It saved her plainly saying,
Let's kiss to ease our pain,
*And something else, &c –*

A thousand times he kissed her,
    Laying her on the green,
But as he farther pressed her
    A pretty leg was seen,
*And something else, &c –*

So many beauties viewing
    His ardour still increased,
And greater joys pursuing,
    He wandered o'er her breast,
*And something else, &c –*

A last effort she trying
    His passion to withstand,
Cried, but 'twas faintly crying,
    Pray take away your hand,
*And something else, &c –*

Young Coridon grown bolder,
    The minute would improve:
This is the time, he told her,
    To show you that I love,
*And something else, &c –*

The nymph seemed almost dying,
    Dissolved in amorous heat.
She kissed, and told him sighing,
    My dear, your love is great,
*And something else, &c –*

But Phillis did recover
    Much sooner than the swain.
She blushing asked her lover,
    Shall we not kiss again?
*And something else, &c –*

Thus love his revels keeping
    Till nature at a stand,
From talk they fell a-sleeping,
    Holding each other's hand,
*And something else, but what I dare not name.*

? SIR CHARLES SEDLEY; *set by* JEREMIAH CLARKE

# The Scotch Parson's Daughter

Peggy, in devotion
Bred from tender years,
From my loving motion
Still was called to prayers. *always*
I made muckle bustle
Love's dear fort to win
But the kirk apostle
Told her 'twas a sin.

Fasting and repentance
And such whining cant
With the doomsday sentence
Frightened my young saint.
He taught her the duty
Heavenly joys to know;
I that liked her beauty
Taught her those below.

Nature took my part still,
Sense did reason blind,
That for all his art, still
She to me inclined.
Strange delights hereafter
Did so dull appear,
She, as I had taught her,
Vowed to share 'em here.

Faith, 'tis worth your laughter.
'Mongst the canting race
Neither son nor daughter
Ever yet had grace.
Peggy on the Sunday
With her daddy vexed
Came to me on Monday
And forgot his text.

*1700*

## The Comical Dreamer

Last night a dream came into my head,
Thou wert a fine white loaf of bread.
Then if May butter I could be,
How I would spread,
Oh, how I would spread myself on thee!
This morning too my thoughts run hard
That you were made a cool tankard.
Then could I but a lemon be,
How I would squeeze,
Oh, how I would squeeze my juice in thee!

Lately when fancy too did roam
Thou wert, my dear, a honeycomb,
And had I been a pretty bee
How I would suck,

Oh, how I would creep, creep into thee!
A vision too I had of old
That thou a mortar wert of gold.
    Then could I but a pestle be,
        How I would pound,
Oh, how I would pound my spice in thee!

Once too my dream did humour take
Thou wert a bowl of Hefford's rack. *arrack punch*
    Zoons, could I then the ladle be,
        How would I pour,
Oh, how would I pour out joys from thee!
Another time, by charm divine,
I dreamt thou wert an orchard fine.
    Then could I but thy farmer be,
        How I would plant,
Oh, how I would plant my fruit in thee!

Soon after, whims came in my pate
Thou wert a pot of chocolate,
    And could I but the rowler be,
        How would I rub,
Oh, how would I twirl and froth up thee!
But since all dreams are vain, my dear,
Let now some solid joy appear.
    My soul still thine is proved to be,
        Let body now,
Let body now with soul agree.

*1714*

# Slighted Nancy

'Tis I have seven braw new gowns
    And ither seven better to mak,
And yet for a' my new gowns
    My wooer has turned his back.
Besides I have seven milk-ky, *dairy cows*
    And Sandy he has but three,
And yet for a' my good ky
    The laddie winna hae me. *will not have*

My daddy's a delver of dikes,
    My mither can card and spin,

And I am a fine fodgel lass *plump and goodhumoured*
And the siller comes linkin' in. *money flows in*
The siller comes linkin' in
And it is fou fair to see,
And fifty times wow! O wow!
What ails the lads at me?

Whenever our Bauty does bark,
Then fast to the door I rin
To see gin ony young spark *if any*
Will 'light and venture but in,
But never a ane will come in,
Though mony a ane gaes by.
Syne far ben the house I rin, *Then far within*
And a weary wight am I.

When I was at my first prayers
I prayed but anes i'the year. *once*
I wished for a handsome young lad,
And a lad with muckle gear. *plenty of possessions*
When I was at my neist prayers *next*
I prayed but now and then.
I fashed na my head about gear *troubled not*
If I got a handsome young man.

Now when I'm at my last prayers
I pray on baith night and day,
And O! if a beggar wad come,
With that same beggar I'd gae.
And O! what 'ill come o' me!
And O! what 'ill I do?
That sic a braw lassie as I
Should die for a wooer, I trow!

## Nanny's Reply to Robin's Complaint

Ungrateful Robin, to complain!
Why say'st thou Nanny is unkind?
How can we help a bashful swain
When maidens may not tell their mind?
Sure if thou loved'st me thou wouldst try.
How canst thou tell that I'd deny?

Whene'er I called thou ne'er didst stay,
　Nor loitered when I bid thee run.
Yet naught of love thou ne'er didst say.
　How then could all I wished be done?
What though thou always thought of me?
It was thoughts, and thoughts are free.

What though my cows thy clover cropped,
　What though my heifers chewed thy hay?
Know'st thou what tears thy Nanny dropped
　When Robin rose by break of day?
Robin would ne'er a welcome feared
Had he his Nanny overheard.

What though whene'er I lost my sheep
　Thou didst most freely give me two?
Love's secret thou didst from me keep
　Although I'd lost ten sheep for you.
Why then dost think thy Nanny cold?
What should she do unless she's told?

Granted I to the well did come
　And that thou didst my pitchers fill.
Granted thou brought'st them for me home,
　And bore my corn unto the mill.
Had but my Robin known the joke,
One of my pitchers he'd have broke.*

My cocks and hens had all their shares
　Of Robin's oats, the very best;
My pigeons fed on Robin's tares,
　He grudged them nothing he possessed.
Then why of me, as pigeons bill,
Did Robin never take his fill?

Ah Robin! wouldst thou once but woo
　No longer would I on thee frown.
I'd find thee work enough to do,
　As much as any girl in town.
Don't hang thee in my apron-string.
I'll give thee far a better thing.

*For the pitcher joke, and for the Complaint to which this is a reply, see endnote

# The Damsel's Complaint

I laid my head on a lonesome pillow,
Thinking indeed it had been my own,
But I, poor girl, must wear the willow,*
For by experience 'tis well known.

Why should we submit to folly,
Or why should I so silly be
To settle my love and affections
Upon the man that loves not me?

My father grieves, my mother chides me.
All my friends do me scorn.
Heaven knows what will betide me
When the baby I have borne.

All you that bear goodwill unto me,
Come tell me and tell me true
If this green garland does become me,
For I am forced to wear it now.

I laid my head on a young man's pillow,
Thinking that old love would renew.

But I at last must wear the willow,
Changing my old love for a new.

The ripest apple is soonest rotten,
The hottest love is soonest cold.
Young men's words are soon forgotten.
Maids, you must not be too bold.

You east and west winds that blow,
That blow the green leaf off the tree—
Come death and strike a fatal blow,
For of my life I'm quite weary.

**willow*: the willow garland traditionally worn by a person betrayed in love
An example of the charming disorder of oral transmission appearing already in a cheap songbook of the early 18th century (see endnote commentary)

## A Dialogue in the Comedy called The Boarding School*

Hey ho! Who's there?
*Nobody here but I, my dear.*
Hey ho! Who's above?
*Nobody here but I, my love.*
Shall I come up and see how you do?
*Ay, marry and thank you too.* [*catch-phrase from popular ballad*

Where's your governess? *She's abed.*
Where are the keys, my love? *Under her head.*
Go, go, fetch them hither,
That you and I may be merry together.
*The dog it will bark, and I dare not, I swear.*
Take a halter and hang up the cur.

*Oh no!* Why, why?
*I'd not for a guinea my dog should die.*
Then farewell my dearest, for I must be gone.
*Tarry, sweet John, I'll be with you anon.*
Oh no! *Why, why?*
Your dog is much better beloved than I.

*Indeed and indeed, now you do not say true.*
Give me a kiss, then I'll stay here with you.
*Oh fie!* Don't deny.
*My mother will whip me should I comply.*
Your mother's not here, love, then lose no more time.
*Oh Law! But indeed now, I've heard it's a crime.*
No, no. *Yes, yes.*
*Indeed I do love you, but must not kiss.*

CHORUS

Indeed if you loved me you'd give me a kiss.
*Indeed I do love you, but must not kiss.*

CHARLES COFFEY

* At Drury Lane, 1733 – a duet for a dancing-master, Coupée, and Jenny, aged 15, played by the brilliant Catherine Raftor (Kitty Clive), then aged 21

## The Cruel Nymph

I am as brown as brown can be, *dark-complexioned*
My eyes as black as a sloe.
I am as brisk as a nightingale
And as wild as any doe.

My love sent me a letter,
Not far, from yonder town,
That he could not fancy me
Because I was so brown.

I sent his letter back again
For his love I valued not,
Whether he could fancy me
Or whether he could not.

My love sent me another letter
That he lay dangerous sick,
And I must needs go presently *at once*
And give my love physick.

But now you shall hear what a love I had
And a love for that sick man:
That I was a whole summer's day
One mile a-going on.

When I came to my love's bedside
Where he lay dangerous sick,
I could not then for laughing stand
Upright upon my feet.

I sat me down by his bedside
And laid a white wand on his breast,
And then cried I, 'Since you are well*
I hope your soul's at rest.'

No sooner had I spoke these words,
He lifted up his eyes:
'But since you see how bad I am,
'Tis you your love denies.'

'I'll do as much for my true love
As any pretty maiden may:
I'll dance and sing upon your grave
For a twelvemonth and a day.

'When I have done what I can do
I'll sit me down and cry,
And every tear that I do shed,
I''ll hang them up to dry.'

*This evidently should read, 'Since you must die' (and see endnote)

## Fiddle and Flora

My fiddle and Flora
Begins with a letter.
My fiddle I love
But my Flora much better.
Could I play on my Flora
As I do on my fiddle,
I'd begin at her neck
And play down to her middle,
Her middle, her middle, her middle.
I'd begin at her neck and play down to her middle.

There briskly I'd play
Pricked notes sweet and mellow
Till my Flora should say,
'Play on, my kind fellow.

You charm me for ever,
    Your touch gives me pleasure.
Such a man sure I never
    Did find out so clever.'

Then with my long bow
    I'd play a sonata    [*pronounced sonayta*
Till my Flora should say,
    'Play on, my sweet creature.    [*pronounced crayt'r*
Your music is taking.
    I love such sweet shaking.
I fear you will leave me.
    O! my heart is breaking,
    Is breaking, is breaking, is breaking.
I fear you will leave me. O! my heart is breaking.'

## The Lover's Litany

By that mole on your bosom so soft and so white,
By that mole on your neck where my arms would delight,
By whatever mole else thou hast got out of sight,
    I beseech thee to hear me, dear Molly, dear Molly, dear Molly.
    I beseech thee to hear me, dear Molly.

By that kiss just a-starting from off thy moist lips,
By the tip of thy tongue, which all tongues far out-tips,
By the delicate motion and spring of thy hips,
    I beseech thee, &c —

By thy soft downy bosom on which my soul dies,
By the down of all downs which I love as my eyes,
By your last thoughts at night and the first when you rise,
I beseech thee, &c —

By all the soft pleasures a virgin can share,
By the critical minute no virgin can bear,
By the joy which I languish to ask, but don't dare,
I beseech thee to hear me, dear Molly, dear Molly, dear Molly.
I beseech thee to hear me, dear Molly.

## Davy and Kate

A loving couple met one day,
Kate and Davy, Kate and Davy.
A loving couple met one day,
Bonny Kate and Davy.
A loving couple met one day,
And as they did together play,
'Come, let us pass the day away,'
And he whips in little Davy.

He wee'd her o'er the Curled Pole, *[dialect: meaning lost*
O my Davy, dainty Davy.
He wee'd her o'er the Curled Pole
Because he was her Davy.
He was her love both late and soon,
And on her fiddle he played a tune
*With her fiddle diddle —*
<And he whipped in little Davy.>

He took her o'er the water wide,
O my Davy, dainty Davy.
He took her o'er the water wide
Because he was her Davy.
He took her from the water wide
And there he laid her legs aside
And on her belly he did ride,
And he whipped in little Davy.

He took her in her father's land,
O my Davy, dainty Davy.

He took her in her father's land,
Because he was her Davy,
And there he made her a bed of sand.
He put a stiff thing in her hand
And whipped in little Davy.

He took her on her father's pease,
O my Davy, dainty Davy.
He took her into her father's pease
Because he was her Davy.
He took her into her father's pease
And down among the cherry trees,
And there he crept between her knees
And whipped in little Davy.

He took her in her father's barn,
O my Davy, dainty Davy.
He took her into her father's barn
Because he was her Davy.
He took her into her father's barn
And vowed he would do her no harm.
There he mowed o'er the corn
And whipped in little Davy.

He took her on her father's rye,
O my Davy, dainty Davy.
He took her on her father's rye
Because he was her Davy.
He took her on her father's rye
And there he got a little boy,
And then what needed she to cry?
<He whipped in little Davy.>

The boy began to kick and jump,
O my Davy, dainty Davy.
The boy began to kick and jump,
Because he was her Davy.
The boy began to kick and jump,
And she began to curse her rump
For playing with her Davy.

This version of a much-loved song was printed in Sheffield in 1753; see endnote for more

## Dick and Kate

I made love to Kate,
Long I sighed for she,
Till I heard of late
She had a mind to me.
I met her on the green
In her best array.
So pretty she did seem
She stole my heart away.

*Oh, then we kissed and pressed.*
*Were we much to blame?*
*Had you been in my place*
*You'd have done the same.*

As I fonder grew
She began to prate.
Quoth she, I'll marry you
If you will marry Kate.
But then I laughed and swore
I loved her more than so,
For tied each to a rope's end,
'Tis tugging to and fro.

*Again we kissed and pressed.*
*Were we much to blame?*
*Had you been there yourself*
*You'd have done the same.*

Then she sighed, and said
She was wondrous sick.
Dicky Katy led,
Katy she led Dick.
Long we toyed and played
Under yonder oak.
Katy lost the game
Though she played in joke.

*For there we did, alas!*
*What I dare not name.*
*Had you been in my place*
*You'd have done the same.*

A song loved high and low: during George III's madness of 1788–9, in his merry phases this was one thing he sang

# Let Me Alone

## Sung by Mr Cooke, at Sadler's Wells

As I was a-walking to Chelsea one day
I met with a pretty young girl by the way.
I asked to salute her, but this was her tone:
'Why can't you be easy, and let me alone?'

I told her my name was young amorous James
And I called her a thousand fine delicate names.
I told her her heart was as cold as a stone.
'No matter,' says she, 'can't you let me alone?'

'My dear child,' says I, 'I am not on my fun.
If you'll go to the Bun House I'll give you a bun.' *
Quoth she, 'I've got money enough of my own
To buy half a hundred, so let me alone.'

'Sweet creature,' says I, 'with me you shall dine
At Pinchbeck's: I hear he sells excellent wine.
Besides, there's the waxwork and dwarf to be shown.'
'Maybe so, sir,' says she, 'but pray let me alone.'

However, I followed her field after field
Till by my persuasions I brought her to yield.
Next day we were wed and she altered her tone,
And she teases me now if I let her alone.

*The Chelsea Bun House, an imposing establishment in the fields of Pimlico, famous from the 1740s, demolished 1839

## The Black's Lamentation

I am a poor black, 'tis true.
  Love does invade me.
It hath proved my overthrow
  And distracted made me.
    O Cupid, kinder be
    And wound that fairer she
    That now confineth me
      Here in New Bedlam.

Ye gods in nature great,
  To die I'd rather,
Unless you pity take—
  Make me a white creature.
    For here I'm confined in chains
    While my jewel doth me disdain.
    O come death and ease my pain
      Now in New Bedlam.

Why do I here complain?
  My chains, I'll rend them
And in my passion great
  To her I'll send them.
    I'll fly unto my dear
    Unless you bring her here
    That she may ease my care
      Now in New Bedlam.

I'll make me a ring of straw,
  None shall be neater.
I'll send it to my dear
  For to complete her.
    Who knows but she may prove kind
    And be to love inclined
    And ease my troubled mind
      Now in New Bedlam.

Hark how the pretty birds
  Sing their pleasant ditty,
Methinks in my behalf,
  To make her pity.
    Their pretty fluttering wings
    The joyful tidings brings

She'll free me from these chains
Now in New Bedlam.

When first I placed my love
With pure affection
I little thought 'twould prove
My sad distraction.
If she'd but wed with me
How happy should I be
And gain my liberty
Out of New Bedlam.

Venus, thou queen of love,
Send Cupid to her
And let her for to know
It is in thy power
To wound her stubborn heart
That acts this tragic part,
That she may feel the smart
Of her true lover.

How happy are young men
That keep their freedom
And never in love do trust
A perjured woman!
For if they find you prize
Their handsome shape and eyes,
O how they tyrannize!
Young men, ne'er heed them.

See endnote for the girl's reply

## When jolly Dick and Jane were wedded

When jolly Dick and Jane were wedded,
At e'en when they first were bedded
Cries Dick, If you had not denied
Before you were confirmed my bride
To let me taste the fruits of love
I ne'er had married you, by Jove.
Why, truly, Dick, I thought as much
And therefore would not let you touch.
I'd been so often flung before,
I swore I'd not be flung no more.

# Blood-an-Ouns! Och, dear, dear! What can the Matter be?

At sixteen years old you could get little good of me,
Then I saw Norah, who soon understood of me.
I was in love, but myself for the blood of me
    Could not tell what I did ail.
'Twas dear, dear! what can the matter be?
Och, blood-an-ouns! what can the matter be?*
Och, gramachree! what can the matter be?
    Bothered from head to the tail.

I went to confess me to Father O'Flannagan,
Told him my case, made an end, then began again.
Father, says I, make me soon my own man again
    If you find out what I ail.
Dear, dear! says he, what can the matter be?
Och, blood-an-ouns! can you tell what can the matter be?
Both cried, what can the matter be?
    Bothered from head to the tail.

Soon I fell sick, I did holloa and curse again.
Norah took pity to see me at nurse again,
Gave me a kiss—oh zounds! that threw me worse again.
    Well she knew what I did ail.
But dear, dear, says she, what can the matter be?
Och, blood-an-ouns! what can the matter be?
Both cried, what can the matter be?
    Bothered from head to the tail.

'Tis long now since I left Tipperary.
How strange, growing older, our nature should vary.
All symptoms are gone of my ancient quandary.
    I cannot tell now what I ail.
But dear, dear! what can the matter be?
Och, blood-an-ouns! what can the matter be?
Och, gramachree! what can the matter be?
    Bothered from head to the tail.

**blood-an-ouns:* from 'Christ's blood and wounds'

# When We Went out a-Shooting

## A rummy parody on 'When we went out a-gipsying'

When we went out a-shooting
    A long time ago
Our flash girls in their best
    Were togged from top to toe.
We went among the haycocks
    Where we could not be seen,
But now we does it other vays
    Because we're not so green.

*And thus we passed the merry time,*
    *Nor thought of care or woe*
*In the days when we went shooting*
    *A long time ago.*

All hearts were light and eyes were bright,
    We never knew much strife.
The girls they were so pleasant
    And full of buxom life.
'Twas there we rolled and rolled again
    So easy on the ground.
It seemed indeed as if the world
    Was going round and round.
    *And thus, &c —*

We filled a glass to every lass
    And got dead-drunk with swipes, *cheap beer*
But though we drunk so much of it
    We never got the gripes.
No Braithwait then was known to us. *a brand of beer*
    We drunk strong ale and gin
Until we could not see to shoot
    And then we all pigged in.

*And thus we passed the merry time,*
    *Nor thought of care or woe*
*In the days when we went shooting*
    *A long time ago.*

# 2

# *Rakes and wantons*

## John, you're my husband's man, you know

John, you're my husband's man, you know.
Why should you use your mistress so?
You make me breathless. Here's good gear!
What if your master now were here?
But good John, leave off and be gone,
For yet, for yet, for yet, for yet, for yet, for yet, for yet, for yet, for yet,
for yet, for yet
You're an honest man, John.

God's body, what do you go about?
What woman's able to hold out?
You put me to my shifts so fast
That long I fear I cannot last.
But now be quiet and be gone,
*For yet, etc —*
You are an honest man, John.

Will you not leave? Alas, I faint!
This is enough to undo a saint.
Your master comes! For shame, away!
What should I do, what should I say?
Aye me, my breath and all is gone
And now, and now, and now, and now, and now!
You're no honest man, John.

*about 1610*

## A Servingman and his Mistress

My mistress loves no woodcocks *simpletons*
Yet loves to pick the bones.
My mistress loves no jewels
Yet loves the precious stones. *testicles*

My mistress loves no hunting
Yet she loves the horn. *erection*
My mistress loves no babies
Yet loves to see men borne.

My mistress loves no wrestling
Yet loves to take a fall.
My mistress loves not some things
And yet she loveth all.

My mistress loves a spender *to spend = to ejaculate*
Yet loves she not a waster. *premature ejaculator*
My mistress loves no cuckolds—no cuckolds—
And yet she loves my master,
And yet and yet and yet and yet and yet she loves my
master.

## The man that hath a handsome wife

The man that hath a handsome wife
And keeps her as a treasure,
It is my chiefest joy of life
To have her to my pleasure.

But if that man regardless were
As if he cared not for her,
Though she were like to Venus fair
In faith I would abhor her.

If to do good I were restrained
And to do evil bidden
I would be Puritan, I swear,
For I love the thing forbidden.

It is the care that makes the theft.
None loves the thing forsaken.
The bold and willing whore is left
When the modest wench is taken.

She's dull that is too forward bent.
Not good what but is reason.
Fish at a feast and flesh in Lent
Are never out of season.

## My mistress is in music passing skilful

My mistress is in music passing skilful
And plays and sings her part at the first sight,
But in her play she is exceeding wilful
And will not play but for her own delight,
Nor touch one string nor play one pleasing strain
Unless you catch her in a merry vein.

Also she hath a sweet delicious touch
Upon the instrument whereon she plays,
And thinks that she doth never do too much,
Her pleasure is dispersed so many ways.
She hath such judgment both in time and mood
That for to play with her, 'twill do you good.

And then you win her heart. But here's the spite:
You cannot get her for to play alone,
But play you with her, and she plays all night,
And next day too, or else 'tis ten to one,
And runs division with you in such sort,
Run ne'er so swift, she'll make you come too short.

One day she called me for to come and play
And I did hold it an exceedng grace,
But she so tired me ere I went away
I wished I had been in another place.
She knew the tune, where prick and rest both stood,*
Yet would she keep no time for life nor blood.

I love my mistress, and I love to play,
So she will let me play with intermission,
But when she ties me to it all the day
I hate and loathe her greedy disposition.
Let her keep time as nature doth require
And I will play as long as she desire.

**prick*: old term for a note in music

## The birds flew over the green, boys

The birds flew over the green, boys,
The birds flew over the green.
The birds flew into the poor man's corn
A little way over the green,
A little way over the green.

Up starts the little boy
Full early in the morn.
He looked about and he spied his dame — *his master's wife*
In the middle of the corn,
In the middle of the corn.

And straight he stepped unto her
And he kissed her cheek and chin.
'O fie away thou naughty boy!
It's a part of deadly sin,
It's a part of deadly sin.'

He took her about the neck
And he kissed her ten times more.
'It's enough to tempt a woman,' quoth she,
'That never knew man before,
That never knew man before.'

He took her about the middle
And he laid her upon the ground.
'Condition thy master could do so much
I'd give thee five hundred pound,
I'd give thee five hundred pound.'

Up starts the old man
And looks out of his ween, — *window*
And there he spied his wife's legs abroad
And the little boy laid between,
And the little boy laid between

'O fie away, thou naughty boy!
God send thee grief and sorrow.
Since my wife and thee hath served me so
I'll keep birds myself tomorrow,
I'll keep birds myself tomorrow.'

Away went the little boy
As fast as he could hie.
He called his master old cuckold
And a cuckold he should die,
And a cuckold he should die.

## A Maid's Denial

Nay pish, nay phew, in faith and will you? Fie!
A gent and use me thus? In truth, I'll cry.
God's body, what means this? Nay fie, for shame!
Nay nay, come come, indeed you are to blame.
Hark hark, somebody comes. Hands off, I pray!
I'll pinch, I'll scratch, I'll spurn, I'll run away.
In faith, you strive in vain, you shall not speed.
You mar my ruff, you hurt my back, I bleed.
Look how the door stands open, somebody sees.
What will they say? Leave off, you hurt my knees.
Your buttons scratch. O what a coil is here! *struggle, fuss*
You make me sweat. In faith, here's goodly gear!
Nay, faith, let me entreat you if you list,
You mar my bed, my smock. But had I wist *known*
So much before, I would have kept you out.
It is a pretty thing you go about!

I did not think you would have done me this,
But now I see I took my mark amiss.
A little thing would make us not be friends.
You've used me well, I hope you'll make amends.
Hold still, I'll wipe your face, you sweat amain.
You've got a goodly thing with all this pain.
O God, how hot I am! What will you drink?
If you go sweating down, what will they think?
Remember, sir, how you have used me now.
I doubt not but ere long I'll meet with you.
If any man but you had used me so
Would I have put it up? In faith, sir, no. *put up with it*
Nay, go not yet: stay supper here with me.
Come, let's to cards. I hope we shall agree.

For more on this early dramatic monologue, see endnote

# Sweet, do not stay, but come away

Sweet, do not stay, but come away, come away, come away,
come away.
Sweet, do not stay, but come away.
Stand a helpless maiden's friend
That does you affection lend
And ready is, poor heart, to ——
*Come away, come away, come away !*
And ready is, poor heart, to meet you.

Why do you trifle? Fie upon't, fie upon't, fie upon't, fie upon't!
Why do you trifle? Fie upon't!
Those are not men but idle drones
That stay till ladies make their moans.
'Tis pity, but they lost their ——
*Fie upon't, fie upon't, fie upon't!*
Tis pity, but they lost their labour.

He shall not do so that I love, that I love, *etc* –
He shall not do so that I love,
But so soon as I am sick
Shall never fail me in the nick
To give me proof of his good ——
*That I love, that I love, that I love!*
To give me proof of his good meaning.

Nor can it be too thick and long, thick and long, *etc* –
Nor can it be too thick and long.
If any of you chance to fear
That I am too young, pray look you here.

Few maids can show you so much ——
*Thick and long, etc* –
Few maids can show you so much favour.

Fain would I go both up and down, up and down, *etc* –
Fain would I go both up and down.
No child is fonder of the gig *a top*
Than I to dance a merry jig.
Fain would I try how I could ——
*Up and down, etc* –
Fain would I try how I could caper.

Come let us do then you know what, you know what, *etc* –
Come let us do then you know what.
Why should not I endure the brunt
As well as other maids have done't?
I'm sure I have as good a ——
*You know what, etc* –
I'm sure I have as good a courage.

Sweet, if you love me there and then, there and then, *etc* —
Sweet, if you love me there and then,
Had ever maiden that good luck
For to encounter, the first pluck?
O 'twould invite a maid to ——
*There and then, etc* –
O 'twould invite a maid to marry.

The trick of dodging an expected rude rhyme goes back long before this. Some readers may need help with missing words: stanza 1, *spend* (it was thought that women as well as men 'spent' seed in orgasm); stanza 2, *stones* (testicles); stanza 4, *gear;* stanza 5, *frig* (and see endnote)

## Fie, away, fie! What mean you by this?

Fie, away, fie! What mean you by this?
Did you not love me when you did kiss?
Wherein could I offend you so soon,
*Oh tell me, tell me,*
That you so roughly tumble me down
As if you meant to kill me?

What do you mean thus on me to lie,
Closing my lips with yours when I cry?

Was ever man so false as thou art,
*Oh tell me, tell me,*
To kiss when murder is in your heart?
For now thou mean'st to kill me.

Do you not blush, me thus to unclothe?
Methinks the sight you rather should loathe.
Heaven defend me, what do you call,
*Oh tell me, tell me,*
The weapon in your hand wherewithal
You go about to kill me?

I fear 'tis a thing will breed my shame.
Mercy shield me! Are you not to blame
To press a woman that's like to die?
*Oh tell me, tell me,*
Why do you give me cause to cry?
God's body, man, you kill me!

## I am a knight's lady and lately decayed

I am a knight's lady and lately decayed,
And now am enforced to maintain the old trade.
If I may get custom and frankly be paid
'Twill raise up my honour again.

If any fair lasses in city or town
Will leave off their russet and wear a silk gown
Their labour shall be but hey-down-a-down-down
To raise up my honour again.

If any such wenches of Windsor there be,
At Staines or at Chertsey or in the country,
That want entertainment, pray send them to me
To raise up my honour again.

I will have no female but from the fresh air,
That's free from infection and from the plague scare,
And they must be handsome and have wholesome ware
To raise up my honour again.

Knights that are English and Scottish at court
Have promised already to me they'll resort.
I vow for their money they shall have good sport
To raise up my honour again.

Besides, there are some noblemen too
That love a thing well, yet nothing can do,
But they are most willing with hand for to woo
To raise up my honour again.

I'll not dwell at Lambeth nor yet at Bankside,
Nor Turnball or Shoreditch where everyone ride,*
But near the court always I still will abide
To raise up my honour again.

Four brave panders I will have in store
To give their attendance to usher a whore.
Myself will be constant to porter the door
To raise up my honour again.

If any knights' ladies do take this in scorn,
Let them understand that I'm as well-born
As some other ladies that will give the horn *cuckold their husbands*
To raise up their honour again.

The place where I dwell is the sign of the Fiddle
And the thing which men love is below women's middle,
And so I conclude with hey-down-down-diddle
To raise up my honour again.

*All notorious for bawdy-houses; Turnball a corruption of Turnmill, still a street in Clerkenwell

## Her for a mistress would I fain enjoy

Her for a mistress would I fain enjoy
That hangs the lip and pouts for every toy;
Speaks like a wag; is fair; dare boldly stand
And rear love's standard with a wanton hand;
That in love's fight for one blow gives me three
And being stabbed, falls straight a-kissing me.
For if she want those tricks of venery
Were't Venus' self, I could not love her, I.
    If she be modest, wise and chaste of life,
    Hang her! she's fit for nothing but a wife.

## The Loose Wooer

Thou dost deny me 'cause thou art a wife.
Know, she that's married lives a single life
That loves but one. Abhor the nuptial curse,
Tied thee to him for better and for worse.
Variety delights the active blood,
And women the more common, the more good,
As all goods are. There's no adultery,
And marriage is the worst monopoly.
The learned Roman clergy admits none
Of theirs to marry; they love all, not one.
And every nun can teach you, 'tis as meet
To change your bedfellow as smock or sheet.
Say, would you be content only to eat
Mutton or beef and taste no other meat?
    It would grow loathsome to you, and I know
    You have two palates, and the best below.

## The Ladies' Fort Besieged

Full forty time over I have strived to win,
Full forty times over repulsèd have been,
But 'tis forty to one I shall 'tempt her again,
        For he's a dull lover
        That so will give over
Since thus runs the sport, since thus runs the sport:

Assault her but often, you'll carry the fort.
Since thus runs the sport.
Assault her but often, you'll carry the fort.

There's a breach ready made which still open hath been,
With thousands of thoughts to betray it within.
If you once but approach you are sure to get in.
Then stand not off coldly
But venture on boldly
With weapon in hand, with weapon in hand.
If you charge her but home she's not able to stand.
With weapon in hand
If you charge her but home she's not able to stand.

Some lady-birds when down before them you sit *[as in a siege*
Do strive to maintain it with fireballs of wit,
But alas! they're but crackers and seldom do hit.
You'll vanquish them after
In 'larums of laughter.
Their forces being broke, their forces being broke,
And the fire quite spent, you may enter in smoke.
Their forces being broke
And the fire quite spent, you may enter in smoke.

With pride and with state some outworks they'll make
And with volleys of frowns drive the enemy back.
If you mine them discreetly they're easy to take.
Then to it, ne'er fear her
But boldly come near her
By working about, by working about.
If you once but approach she can ne'er hold it out.
By working about
If you once but approach she can ne'er hold it out.

Some ladies with blushes and modesty fight,
And with their own fears the rude foe do affright,
But they're easily surprised if you come in the night.
For this you must drive at,
To parley in private,
And then they're o'erthrown, and then they're o'erthrown.
If you promise them fairly they'll soon be your own,
And then they're o'erthrown.
If you promise them fairly they'll soon be your own.

A song of Samuel Pepys's student days: see endnote

*Cavalier in the height of fashion, 1646*

# Though Oxford be yielded

Though Oxford be yielded and Reading be taken *
I'll put in for quarter at thy Maidenhead.
There while I'm ensconced, my standard unshaken,
Lie thou in my arms, and I in thy bed.

Let the young zealots march with their wenches,
Mounting their tools to edify trenches,
While thou and I do make it our pleasure
To dig in thy mine for the purest treasure,
  Where nobody else shall plunder but I.

And when we together in battle do join
We scorn to wear arms but what are our own.
Strike thou at my body and I'll thrust at thine.
By nakedness best the truth is made known.
Cannons may roar and bullets keep flying;
While we are in battle we never fear dying.
Isaac and's wenches are busy a-digging*
But all our delight is in japing and jigging, *japing = making love*
  And nobody else shall plunder but I.

And when at the last our bodies are weary
We'll straight to the tavern our strength to recruit,
Where when we've refreshed our hearts with canary
We shall be the fitter again to go to't.
We'll tipple and drink until we do stagger,
For then is the time for soldiers to swagger.
Thus night and day we'll thump it and knock it,
And when we've no money, then look to your pocket,
  For nobody else shall plunder but I.

ALEX BROME

*Oxford surrendered to the parliamentary forces in 1646

*When Isaac Pennington, Lord Mayor of London, organized outworks against the king's army, women joined in the digging

## He that will court a wench that is coy

He that will court a wench that is coy,
That is proud, that is peevish and antic,
Let him be as careless to sport and to toy
And as wild as she can be frantic.
      Tickle her and spite her,
      Flatter her and slight her,
   Rail and commend her again.
      'Tis the way to woo her
      If you mean to do her.
   Such girls love such men.

He that will court a wench that is mild,
That is sweet and kind of behaviour,
Let him gently woo her, not roughly come unto her.
'Tis the way to gain her favour.
Give her kisses plenty,
She'll take them were they twenty.
Stroke her and kiss her again.
'Tis the way to woo her
If you mean to do her.
Soft girls love mild men.

He that will court a wench that is mad,
That will squeak and cry out if you hand her,
Let him frisk and fling and make the house to ring.
'Tis the only way to command her.
Take her up and touze her,
Tickle her and rouse her,
Kick her and please her again.
'Tis the way to woo her
If you mean to do her.
Mad girls love wild men.

He that will court a wench that is pure,
That has zeal to account him a sinner,
If he will affect her let him meet her at a lecture, *Puritan sermon*
Take notes, and repeat after dinner. *[as the Puritans did*
Preach unto her diet
And privily apply it,
Yea verily, apply it o'er again.
'Tis the way to woo her
If you mean to do her.
Pure girls love strict men.

## The Merry Man's Resolution

### or, His last farewell to his former acquaintance

Now farewell to Saint Giles's
That standeth in the fields
And farewell to Turnbull-street, *Turnmill-street, Clerkenwell*
For that no comfort yields.
Farewell to the Greyhound
And farewell to the Bell,
And farewell my landlady

Whom I do love so well.
*With a come love,*
*Stay love,*
*Go not from me,*
*For all the world I'll forsake for thee.*

. . . . .

Farewell to Cross-lane,
Where live some babes-of-graces.
Farewell to Common-garden — *Covent Garden*
And all her wanton places.
Farewell unto Westminster
And farewell to the Strand
Where I had choice of mopsies
Even at my own command.
*Sing come love,*
*Stay love,*
*Go along with me,*
*For all the world I'll forsake for thee.*

. . . . .

Now farewell unto Wapping
And farewell to Blackwall.
Farewell to Ratcliffe Highway, — *now The Highway, E1*
Rosemary-lane and all, — *now Royal Mint Street, E1*
And farewell unto Shoreditch,
And Moorfields eke also,
Where mobs to pick up cullies — *mopsies cruising for men*
A-nightwalking do go.
*Then come love, &c —*

In Whitecross-street and Golden-lane
Do strapping lasses dwell,
And so they do in every street
'Twixt that and Clerkenwell.
At Cowcross and Smithfield
I have much pleasure found,
Where wenches like to fairies
Did often trace the round.
*Yet come love, &c —*

. . . . .

To all the country mopsies
Wherever they do dwell,
In this my last conclusion
I likewise bid farewell.

Though they were used in former time
To come when I did call,
I take thee for the boldest
And best among them all.
*Then come love, &c —*

. . . . . .

Farewell black patches
And farewell powdered locks,
And farewell Luthner's ladies,*
For they have got the pox.
Farewell to Cherry-garden, *in Rotherhithe*
Forevermore adieu,
And farewell to Spur-alley
And all that wanton crew.
*And come love,*
*Stay love,*
*Go not from me,*
*For all those girls I'll forsake for thee.*

* Luthner's-lane (or Lewknor's, Lukenor's), now Macklin-street, off Drury-lane, was notorious for its bawdy houses

## The Hector's Farewell

'Farewell Three Kings, where I have spent
Full many an idle hour,
Where oft I won, but ne'er did lose
If it were within my power;

'Where the raw gallants I did chouse *cheat*
Like any ragamuffin. *ragged scoundrel*
But now I'm sick and cannot play.
Who'll trust me for a coffin?

'Farewell my dearest Piccadilly,
Notorious for great dinners.
Oh what a tennis court was there!
Alas! too good for sinners.

'Farewell Spring Garden where I used — *[adjoining St James's Park*
To piss before the ladies.
Poor souls, who'll be their hector now — *a swaggering scapegrace*
To get 'em pretty babies?

'Farewell the glory of Hyde Park
Which was to me so dear.
Now since I can't enjoy it more,
Would I were buried there!

'Farewell tormenting creditors
Whose scores did so perplex me. — *bills*
Well! Death, I see, for something's good
For now you'll cease to vex me.

'Farewell true brethren of the sword,
All martial men and stout.
Farewell dear drawer at the Fleece, — *rakish Covent Garden tavern*
I cannot leave thee out.

'My time draws on, I now must go
From this beloved light.
Remember me to pretty Sue,
And so dear friends goodnight.'

With that, on pillow low he laid
His pale and drooping head:
And straight, e'er cat could lick her ear,
Poor hector he was dead.

Now God bless all that will be blessed,
God bless the Inns of Courts
And God bless Davenant's opera *
Which is the sport of sports.

*Sir William Davenant put on his opera *The Cruelty of the Spaniards in Peru* at the Cockpit, Drury Lane, in 1658, the year this was published

## Insatiate Desire

O that I could by any chemic art
To sperm convert my spirit and my heart,
That at one thrust I might my soul translate
And in her womb myself degenerate.
There steeped in lust nine months I would remain,
Then boldly —— my passage back again.

## Moll Medlar's Song

Soldiers fight and hectors rant on
    Whilst poor wenches go to rack.
Who would be a wicked wanton
    Only for suppers, songs and sack?
To endure the alteration
    Of these times that are so dead—
Thus to lead a long vacation    *[the law vacation robs her of custom*
    Without money, beer or bread.

Farewell Bloomsbury and Sodom,
    Lukeners-lane and Turnbull-street.
Woe was me when first I trod 'em
    With my wild unwary feet!
I was bred a gentlewoman
    But our family did fall
When the gentry's coin grew common    *[during the Civil War*
    And the soldiers shared it all.

THOMAS JORDAN, *1664*

## The Ranting Whore's Resolution

*To the tune of General Monk's March*

    Oh, fie upon care!
    Why should we despair?
Give me the lad that will frolic.
    There is no disease
    But music will please,
If it were the stone of the colic.
    The lad that drinks wine
    Shall only be mine:
He that calls for a cup of canary,
    That will tipple and sing,
    Kiss, caper and spring
*And calls for his Mab and his Mary.*

    Such sinners as these
    My palate will please,
For this is a lad that will knock it,
    Provided he be
    Not niggard to me
But carry good gilt in his pocket.

    I care not from whence<br>
    He gets his expense<br>
Nor how he comes by his treasure,<br>
    So I have the sweets<br>
    When he and I meets,<br>
*For I am a lady of pleasure.*

    I love a young heir<br>
    Whose fortune is fair<br>
And frolics in Fish-street dinners;<br>
    Who boldly doth call<br>
    And in private pays all.<br>
These boys are the noble beginners.<br>
    For what the old father<br>
    In long time did gather,<br>
He topes it away without measure.<br>
    He'll lie in my lap<br>
    Like a bird in a trap<br>
*And call me his lady of pleasure.*

    He wears gallant clothes<br>
    And studies new oaths<br>
And gets pretty words from the players.<br>
    He swaggers and roars,<br>
    He calls the next oars     *summons a Thames boatman*<br>
And cries, Here's a piece for your fairs.     *he tips them well*<br>
    Thus we in delight<br>
    From morning till night<br>
Do study to cast away treasure.<br>
    At night in my arms<br>
    I secure him from harms,<br>
*For I am a lady of pleasure.*

    When this gallant's broke<br>
    I've another bespoke,<br>
And he hath my protestation.<br>
    I call him my love,<br>
    My jewel, my dove,<br>
And swear by my reputation<br>
    That I never did know<br>
    What love was till now,<br>
Though I have had men beyond measure.<br>
    With such tricks as these<br>
    All coxcombs I please<br>
*For I am a lady of pleasure.*

When they're in the jail
They wretchedly rail
And at me they cast all their curses.
Let them laugh that win:
I care not a pin
When I have confounded their purses.
While they have disgraces
I know not their faces,
When warriors of Wood-street make seizure. *debtors' jail*
But when they're whole men
I'll know them again
*For I am a lady of pleasure.*

I live by the quick
And not by the sick
Or such whose estates lie a-bleeding.
My waist must be bound
By men that are sound
For I am a lass of high feeding.
If once they grow poor,
No money, no whore,
And yet they shall wait on my leisure.
I only fulfil
My fancy and will,
*Which shows me a lady of pleasure.*

I laugh when they tell
Me stories of hell.
I think there is no such cavern.
If heaven there be
(As some will tell me)
I am sure it must be in the tavern.
Where there is no wine
There's nothing divine.
We'll think of a grave at more leisure.
Boy, fill t'other glass,
For I am a lass
*That will be a lady of pleasure.*

In freedom and joys
I'll spend all my days,
For there is no greater blessing
Than music and meat,
Good wine and the feat,
And nothing to pay for the dressing.

Let sisters precise
Go turn up their eyes
And speak words by line and by leisure.
If death come at last
And take me in haste,
*Then there lies a lady of pleasure.*

*puritans*

## Pox on 'um all!

Pox on 'um all! These mistresses must be
Prayed (with a devil to 'um), courted, treated.
They must deride their servants' misery;
Coy to permit what, O! they hug repeated.
Mad things these men, to stoop to women thus
Who otherwise unasked would fall to us.

Must we invent fine names to please 'um too?
Mogg must be Phyllis and Jugg called Gloria,
And every trull must for a Daphne go.
O but the raptures on my Julia!
Strange mad conceits. He that but calls her jade,
Swears stiffly he'll upon her: that's your blade.

Then comes a letter to love's paragon
Swearing with complement all oaths and vows,
With many a lying protestatiòn,
As heaven, and man's deluded self, well knows.
What aim we at at last? Troth, this is all:
To do as bulls with cows, as Dick with Doll.

Lips all of rubies, diamond eyes, a nose
Of ivory sure, and hairs like threads of gold,
Studs of bright pearl for teeth, each cheek a rose—
Damned lies (by Jove) as ever mortal told.
We make 'um proud by praising such a brood.
Hang't, there's but one small spot about 'um good.

## Like Mother, Like Daughter

O had you been there to have seen it!
It was a most pleasant sight
When Jenny stayed out till morning
And she should have been home at night.

O how she was touzled and rouzled
That used to look trim and tight!
For Jenny stayed out till morning
And she should have been home at night.

Her mother flew into a passion
For fear that all was not right,
'Cause Jenny stayed out till morning
And she should have been home at night.

'O huzzy, where have you been flirting?
I fear you are ruined quite.
How dare you stay out till morning
And you should have been home at night?'

'Dear mother, be not so angry.
I'm sure I got no harm by't.
Did you never stay out till morning
And you should have been home at night?

'But now I am quit with my mother
And i'faith she should pay for her slight.
I know where she stayed out till morning
And she should have been home at night.'

## The cocks may crow in the day

'The cocks may crow in the day
And the cats may miaule in the night,
And why may not Churchill and I,*
My joy and my heart's delight?'

She first began for to feague
With Harry and with Hodge.
With a lackey she had an intrigue
Which did end in the porter's lodge.

She needed no knight to betray her.
She cared not who did know it.
Since His Majesty —— with a player  *with Nell Gwynn*
She swore she would with a poet.*

The number can never be reckoned.
She —— both with great and small
From our good King Charles the Second
To honest Jacob Hall.*

But if his love be not gone *[the king's love*
She deceives his subjects' hopes,
And she'll leave him as poor on the throne
As Jacob upon the ropes.

*The speaker at the start is Barbara Villiers, Lady Castlemaine, Charles II's exorbitantly rewarded mistress early in his reign; Churchill is John Churchill, later 1st Duke of Marlborough—credited with a daughter born to her in 1672

**poet*: William Wycherley, with whom Lady C began an amour by shouting from her coach, 'Sir, you are a rascal! you are a villain! you are the son of a whore!'—wittily alluding to a song in Wycherley's play *Love in a Wood*:

Great wits and great braves
Have always a punk to their mother

**Hall*: a rope-dancer at Bartholomew Fair in Smithfield, spotted by Lady C and employed by her in a more private athletic role

## I'll have no serving-man

I'll have no serving-man, footman or cooks
For they can afford a maid nothing but looks,
But I'll have Tom-Tinker, and he'll be my dear,
And he and no other shall tickle my gear
*This way, that way, which way you will.*
*I'm sure I say nothing that you can take ill.*

I met with a footman was bound to the spring.
He told me his errand was water to bring.
He laid me down on the grass, and gave me no money,
Therefore he shall never play with my coney
*This way, that way, &c —*

The cook in the kitchen doth so swear and broil.
He spends all his strength with his sweat and his toil:
Yet would he be fumbling as he was wont,
But faith, he shall never more play with my c—t
*This way, that way, &c —*

The serving-man though he be bonny and brave,
Yet small satisfaction a woman can have.

But jovial Tom-Tinker, oh he's the brave man
For he can do that which few other men can
*This way, that way, &c —*

But Tom he will travel, I greatly do fear.
And I will go with him his budget to bear.
In stopping of holes he hath the best luck.
All day he will tipple, all night he will f—k
*This way, that way, which way you will.*
*I'm sure I say nothing that you can take ill.*

## I'd have you, quoth he

I'd have you, quoth he.
Would you have me? quoth she.
O where, sir?

In my chamber, quoth he.
In your chamber? quoth she.
Why there, sir?

To kiss you, quoth he.
To kiss me? quoth she.
O why, sir?

'Cause I love it, quoth he.
Do you love it? quoth she.
So do I, sir.

## A maid, I dare not tell her name

A maid, I dare not tell her name
For fear I should disgrace her,
Tempted a young man for to come
One night, and to embrace her,
But at the door he made a stop,
He made a stop, he made a stop.
But she lay still, and snoring said,
*The latch pull up, the latch pull up.*

This young man, hearing of her words,
Pulled up the latch and entered,

And in the place unfortunately
To her mother's bed he ventured.
The poor maid was sore afraid
And almost dead, and almost dead,
But she lay still, and snoring said,
*The truckle-bed, the truckle-bed.*

Unto the truckle-bed he went,
But as the youth was going
Th'unlucky cradle stood in's way
And almost spoiled his wooing.
After that, the maid he spied,
The maid he spied, the maid he spied,
But she lay still, and snoring said,
*The other side, the other side.*

Unto the other side he went
To show the love he meant her;
Pulled off his clothes courageously
And fell to the work he was sent for.
But the poor maid made no reply,
Made no reply, made no reply,
But she lay still, and snoring said,
*A little too high, a little too high.*

This lusty lover was half ashamed
Of her gentle admonition.
He thought to charge her home as well
As any girl could wish him.
O now, my love, I'm right I know,
I'm right I know, I'm right I know.
But she lay still, and snoring said,
*A little too low, a little too low.*

Though by mistakes, at length this youth
His business so well tended,
He hit the mark so cunningly
He defied the world to mend it.
O now, my love, I'm right I swear,
I'm right I swear, I'm right I swear.
But she lay still, and snoring said,
*O there, O there, O there, O there!*

## Was ever mortal man like me

Was ever mortal man like me
Continually in jeopardy,
And always, saucy p—, by thee!

Have I not fed your fond desire
Till I have set myself on fire
With poxes horrid and most dire?

'Tis strange you should be still so stout.
Have you forgot the double clout *bandaging*
That lately swathed your dropping snout?

But why should I at that admire
When ulcers filled with liquid fire
Could not from c—t make you retire?

But in those hot and rigid pains,
When venom runs through all thy veins
(The product of thy tainted reins),

Then, even then, thou didst essay
To lead my timorous flesh astray,
Still pushing, though you made no way.

There's not a petticoat goes by
But from my codpiece out you fly,
Not to be held 'twixt hand and thigh.

I never feel a soft white hand
But hector-like you strutting stand
As if the world you would command.

Then must I never rest till she
Chafe and squeeze out my lechery,
Which is the very strength of me.

For all these crying sins of thine
The suffering part is always mine.
'Tis I am crammed with turpentine.*

For my sake and your own, beware.
Remember that you mortal are
And liable to scald and scar.

But if audaciously you still
Will fucking be against my will,
Know thus your lechery I'll chill:

Cakes of ice shall wall thee in
Till thou appear'st nought else but skin —
Not like a prick, but chitterlin. *pork tripe, fried*

If what I've said will nothing do,
But snivelling c—t you still pursue,
Loving in filth and stench to stew,

My sentence I'll in action put
Which shall so tame thy will to rut
That thou shalt rivel like a gut.

For know, in snow I'd rather lie
Than still in Etna's flames to fry.
Thus, p—ck, I'll tame thy lechery.

* *turpentine*: one of the potions that pox victims had optimistically to swallow

## Advice to a C--tmonger *(extract)*

Whitehall c--ts are grown so common,*
Foul, and wide, and fit for no man:
Torn and teased, from prince to carmen, *wagoners*
Ruffled by porters, rammed by chairmen, *sedan-chair men*
Fr-gged in chapel, f-cked in th'entries
By the singing-boys and sentries,
Peppered as they come from prayers
By the next oars at water-stairs;*
Tail turned up to all men now,
From Dr Crew to coachman Crow.*

**Whitehall*: Charles II's palace, noted for debauchery
* *next oars*: next in the line of Thames boatmen waiting for fares (like taxis)
* *Dr Crew*: Nathaniel Crew (1633-1721), Bishop of Durham, Clerk of the Closet to Charles II, satirized as The Pious Prelate

## Daniel Cooper, or the Highland Laddy

There's ne'er a lad in our town that's worth an ounce of powder
But will have his beaver hat and ribbons to his shoulder.
There's ne'er a lass in our town that's worth a bunch of leeks–a
But she'll have a sarsnet hood and ribbons tull her cheeks–a. *to*

Daniel Cooper and his man, they went tull a fair, Jo,
And all to seek a bonny lass, but the de'il a girl was there, Jo.

The fiddler kissed the piper's wife, the blind-man sat and saw her.
She lifted up her holland smock and Daniel Cooper clawed her.

There's four-and-twenty Highland lads went to a Highland market,
And twelve of them had hose and shoon and twelve of them went
barefoot.
And they went tull a widow's house and she was dancing naked,
And all the tune the piper played was 'Prithee widow, take it.'

'Some do call me shentleman, and some do call me trooper,
But when I am at mine own house my name is Daniel Cooper.
Cooper, Cooper, canst thou hoop? Canst thou hoop a kin-
a-kin? *cannikin*
I've forty shillings in my purse, and that will serve us drinking.

'And I can hoop a kin-a-kin, and I can hoop a cogie, *bowl or tub*
And I can stop the water-gap that lets out all the gravy.'*
Daniel Cooper was his name, all others far exceeding;
He might have been a lord of fame, for worthy birth and breeding.

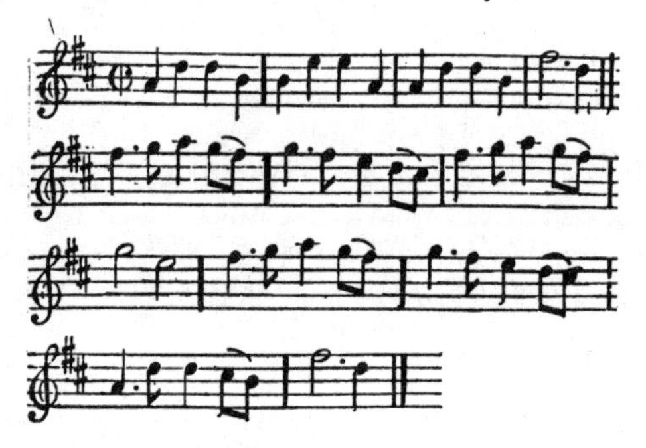

Daniel Cooper he did gang to the town of Pauling Coddle.
There he lent the Parson John a sound clank o'er the noddle.
He brust his costard till the blood ran streaming down his hair, sir,*
'Cause it was said the parson played with Daniel's tickling gear, sir.

Daniel Cooper met, forsooth, a lass was clothed in grey, Jo,
And she was going to Edinburgh with buttermilk and whey, Jo.
He laid her down upon the green, for he was a lusty fellow,
And there he tied her garter green upon her stocking yellow.

Such tying of a garter fair I think was never seen, Jo,
For she that came a maiden there did ne'er return again so.
Daniel skipped away with joy, the maid was well contented.
Though in a while she had a boy, and then she sore repented.

Daniel Coooper he could fight and he a horn could blow well
To hawk or hunt for his delight; and Daniel he could mow well,
Which made him gang full oft and soon unto the Lady Cardle,
Who said he was the bonniest loon that e'er was girt in girdle.

*In Scotland gravy was a *white* sauce; and in a ballad from the same shop as this one ('You'll Never Get Her Up', about a soldier making love to a girl against a tree) there is a further clue–'Though you i'th' gravy gap will play...'

**brust his costard*: broke his head

## The Captain's Courtship to a Town Miss

*To the tune of a minuet*

*Captain* Dear pickaninny,*
If half a guinea
To love will win ye,
Lay it here down. *[he is holding out the coin*
We must be thrifty.
'Twill serve to shift ye,
And I know fifty
Will do't for a crown. *[half as much*

Duns come so boldly,
And money so slowly,
That by all things holy,
'Tis all I can say.
Yet I am so rapt in
The snares that I'm trapped in,
As I'm a true captain,
It's more than my pay.

*Miss* Good Captain Thunder,
Go mind your plunder.
Odzooks! I wonder
You dare be so bold
Thus to be making
A treaty so sneaking,
Or dream of the taking
My fort without gold.

Other town misses
May gape at half-pieces,
But who me possesses
A guinea shall pay.

To all poor rogues in buff *military coat*
Thus, thus I strut and huff;
So Captain Kick and Cuff,
    March on your way.

*Captain* Come come, leave slighting
And take delight in
One that loves fighting,
    Yet you does love more.
Do but once try me,
You'll ne'er more deny me.
Then prithee lie by me,
    Thou little damned w——.

Here, my dear honey,
Ne'er refuse money.
Thou'rt brisk and bonny
    And live by the trade.
It's but a folly
To stand shilly-shally,
For I'll no more dally
    With thee like a maid.

*Miss* As for my ware, sir,
You must forbear, sir,
And come not there, sir,
    Although you scold.
'Tis not your huffing
Nor yet your puffing
Nor kick-and-cuffing
    Shall do, without gold.

I'll not deceive ye,
Therefore believe me,
You must now give me
    A guinea or more.
Without the yellow, *gold*
You are no fellow,
And if you bellow,
    Sir, there is the door.

THOMAS D'URFEY, *1696*

**pickaninny*: in those days a general term of endearment, also spelt pinkaninny, pickninny

# The Jolly Miller

The old wife she sent to the miller her daughter
To grind her grist quickly and so return back.
The miller so worked it that in eight months after
Her belly was filled as full as her sack.
Young Robin so pleased her that when she came home
She gaped like a stuck pig and stared like a mome, *a fool*
She hoydened, she scampered, she hollowed and whooped,
And all the day long
This was her song,
Hoy, was ever maiden so lericompooped!

'Oh Nelly!' cried Celie. 'Thy clothes are all mealy.
Both backside and belly are rumpled all o'er.
You mop, mow and slubber. Why, what a pox ail ye?
I'll go to the miller and know all, ye whore.'
She went, and the miller did grinding so ply,
She came cutting capers a foot and half high.
She waddled, she straddled, she hollowed, she whooped,
And all the day long
This, this was her song,
Hoy, were ever two sisters so lericompooped!

Then Mary o' th' dairy, a third of the number,
Would fain know the cause they so jigged it about.
The miller her wishes long would not encumber,
But in the old manner the secret found out.
Thus Celie and Nelly and Mary the mild
Were just about harvest-time all big with child.

They danced in a hay, they hallowed and whooped,
And all the day long
This, this was their song,
Hoy, were ever three sisters so lericompooped!

And when they were big they did stare at each other
Crying, 'Oh sisters! what shall we now do?
For all our young bantlings we have but one father,
And they in one month will come to town, too.
O why did we run in such haste to the mill,
To Robin who always the toll-dish would fill?*
He bumped up our bellies, then hallowed and whooped.'
And all the day long
This, this was their song,
Hoy, were ever three sisters so lericompooped!

THOMAS D'URFEY, *1696*

* *toll-dish*: people who had grain ground for their own use gave part of the flour as a toll; but Robin takes his reward another way (and see page 155)

## The Town Rake

What life can compare with the jolly town rake's
When in his full swing of all pleasure he takes!
At noon he gets up for a whet and to dine,
And wings the swift hours with mirth, music and wine,
Then jogs to the playhouse and chats with the masques,
And thence to the Rose, where he takes his three flasks.*
There great as a Caesar he revels when drunk,
And scours all he meets as he reels — as he reels to his punk,
And finds the dear girl in his arms when he wakes.
What life can compare with the jol——ly, the jolly town rake's?
The jol——ly, the jolly town rake's?

He like the Great Turk has his favourite she,
But the town's his seraglio and still he lives free.
Sometimes she's a lady, but as he must range
Black Betty or Oyster Moll serve for a change.
As he varies his sports, his whole life is a feast.
He thinks him that is sob'rest the most like a beast.
At houses of pleasure breaks windows and doors,
Kicks bullies and cullies, then lies with their whores.
Rare work for the surgeon and midwife he makes.
What life can compare with the jolly town rake's?

Thus in Covent Garden he makes his campaigns,
And no coffee-house haunts but to settle his brains.
He laughs at dry morals, and never does think
Unless 'tis to get the best wenches and drink.
He dwells in a tavern, and lives everywhere,
And improving his hours, lives an age in a year.
For as life is uncertain, he loves to make haste,
And thus he lives longest because he lives fast,
Then leaps in the dark, and his exit he makes.
What death can compare with the jolly town rake's?

PETER MOTTEUX, *1696*

**Rose*: tavern in Russell Street, haunt of rakes and whores (see Hogarth's *Rake's Progress*, plate 3) and a reliable source of condoms (see p 352–3)

## 'Tis sultry weather, pretty maid

*Gent* 'Tis sultry weather, pretty maid.
Come, let's retire to yonder shade.
Pray, why so shy? Why thus do you stand?
Sure 'tis no crime to touch your hand.
Oh let me take a civil kiss. (*Kisses her*)
What harm is there in doing this?
Fy fy fy! Why d'you cover thus your breast?
One favour more and then you're blessed.

*Lass* Oh pray sir! Nay nay sir!
Oh fy sir! Oh why sir,
Why d'you pull me thus to you?
(*Aside*) Oh what shall I, what shall I, what shall I say?
When a gentleman's suitor, 'tis hard to say nay.
I'm e'en out of breath. Oh dear, what do you do?
Good La—! Is it thus that you gentlefolks woo?
Good sir, do not hold me.

*Gent* Good lass, do not fly.
*Lass* What good can I do you?
*Gent* Come yonder, we'll try.
*Lass* I vow I can't find in my heart to deny.
*Gent* Oh come to the grove!
*Lass* Oh I dare not, I swear.
I'm afraid of the serpents that sting women there.
One stung my poor sister, and made her so swell,
'Tis now almost nine months and she's not yet well.
*Gent* Here, I give you a charm *(He gives her a ring)*
To keep you from harm.
Secured by the ring
Women venture the sting.
*Lass* Oh what shall I give you for such a fine thing?
*Gent* Oh come, come, I'll give you another fine thing.
*Lass* You'll give me another, another fine thing!
*Gent* I'll give you another, another fine thing.

PETER MOTTEUX, *1698*

The scene begins, *Enter a country lass, with a rake, as at haymaking*. She sings, 'O why thus alone must I pass the long day?' Then *Enter a gentleman...*

## The sun was just setting

The sun was just setting, the reaping was done,
And over the common I tripped it alone
When whom should I meet but young Dick of our town,
Who swore e'er I went I should have a green gown.
He pressed me, I stumbled,
He pushed me, I tumbled,
He kissed me, I grumbled
But still he kissed on,
Then rose and went from me as soon as he'd done.

If he be not hampered for serving me so,
May I be worse rumpled,
Worse tumbled and jumbled
Wherever, wherever I go.

Before an old justice I summoned the spark,
And how do you think I was served by his clerk?
He pulled out his inkhorn and asked me his fee.
'You now shall relate the whole businesss,' quoth he.
He pressed me, *&c* –

The justice then came, and though grave was his look,
Seemed to wish I would kiss him instead of the Book.
He whispered his clerk then, and leaving the place
I was had to his chamber to open my case.
He pressed me, *&c* –

I went to our parson to make my complaint.
He looked like a Bacchus but preached like a saint.
He said we should soberly nature refresh,
Then nine times he urged me to humble the flesh.
He pressed me, I stumbled,
He pushed me, I tumbled,
He kissed me, I grumbled
But still he kissed on,
Then rose and went from me as soon as he'd done.

If he be not hampered for serving me so,
May I be worse rumpled,
Worse tumbled and jumbled
Wherever, wherever I go.

## The Young Maid's Portion

Now all my friends are laid in grave
And nothing they have left me
But a mark a year my mother gave — *13 shillings*
By which for to protect me,
Yet I live on the leaguer still *
As brave as any lady

And all is with a mark a year
The which my mother gave me.

I have my pimps at my command,
My coach upon me tending.
If anyone be cut or slashed,
Or anyone offending,
They'll bear me out of all the rout
*As brave, &c —*

My high commode, my damask gown, *high head-dress*
My laced shoes of Spanish leather,
A silver bodkin in my hand,
And a dainty plume of feather,
I'll take tobacco with a grace
*As brave, &c —*

A lord, a knight, a gentleman
Is welcome to my oven;
The finical courtier with his tricks,
Whose beard's but newly shaven:
All's one to me, whos'e'er he be
He's welcome still as may be.
God-a-mercy, mother, for thy gift
Is a portion for a lady.

*1700*

* A 'leaguer-lass' was one attached to an army camp, but the word's meaning was no doubt extended by the fame of a brothel in Southwark kept in the 17th century by a Mrs Holland — fortified with moat, drawbridge, etc, and known as Holland's Leaguer

## The Lusty Young Blacksmith

A lusty young smith at his vice stood a-filing,
*Rub rub rub rub rub rub, in and out hoh,*
When to him a buxom young damsel came smiling
And asked if to work at her forge he would go,
*With a rub rub rub rub rub rub, in and out, in and out hoh.*

'A match,' quoth the smith, so away they went thither,
*Rub rub rub rub rub rub, in and out, in and out hoh.*
They stripped to go to't, 'twas hot work and hot weather.
She kindled fire and soon made him blow,
*With a rub rub rub rub rub rub, in and out, in and out hoh.*

Her husband, she said, could scarce raise up his hammer,
His strength and his tools were worn out long ago.
If she got her journeyman, could any blame her?
'Look here,' quoth our workman, 'my tools are not so,'
*With a rub, &c —*

Red hot grew his iron as both did desire
And he was too wise not to strike while 'twas so.
Quoth she, 'What I get, I get out of the fire,
Then prithee strike home and redouble the blow,'
*With a rub, &c —*

Six times did his iron by vigorous heating
Grow soft in the forge in a minute or so.
As often 'twas hardened, still beating and beating,
But the more it was softened, it hardened more slow,
*With a rub, &c —*

The smith then would go. Quoth the dame full of sorrow,
'Oh what would I give, could my cuckold do so!
Good lad, with your hammer come hither tomorrow,
But pray, can't you use it once more ere you go?'
*With a rub rub rub rub rub rub, in and out, in and out hoh.*

## Early in the dawning of a winter's morn

Early in the dawning of a winter's morn
Brother Dick and I went forth into the barn
To catch ourselves a heat
By threshing of the wheat
From the stack, from the stack, from the stack, the stack.
The straws they flew about
And the flails they kept a rout,
With a thwack, thwack, thwack, thwack, thwack.

Margery came in then with an earthen pot,
Full of a pudding that was piping hot.
I caught her by the neck fast
And thanked her for my breakfast,
With a smack, *etc* –
Up went her tail
And down went the flail
With a thwack, *etc* –

Dick, threshing on, cried out, 'Fie for shame!
Must I beat the bush while you catch the game?
Sow your wild oats
And mind not her wild notes
Of alack,' *etc* –
Faith, I did the job
While the flail bore a bob,
With a thwack, *etc* –

She shook off the straws, and did nothing ail,
Swearing there was no defence against a flail,
But quietly lay still
And bid me fill, fill, fill
Her sack, *etc* —
But 'twas all in vain
For I had spilt my grain
With a thwack, thwack, thwack, thwack, thwack.

## The Country Wake

In our country and in your country
Ruffelers they were a-raking:*
The rarest pastime that ever you see
Was when haycocks they were a-making.

Timmy and Tom, with bottle and bag,
So merrily they were a-quaffing,
If you'd but zeen how Joan's buttocks did wag
You'd bust your heart with laughing.

On another haycock was Vulcan the smith
With Dolly that came from the dairy.
She thought that his back was so full of pith,
Which made her so willing to tarry.

Then rustling Joan came brustling in
And said, 'You are vull of your frolics.
If you will not let black Maggy alone,
Beshrew! she'll take you by the — bald-pate.

Then satchel-arse Ciss, she went to p---
And they went home to conduct her,
And all the way after they did kiss,
And all the way homeward they — plucked her.

Then down in a dale was tumble-down Dick.
The wenches they caught him and held him.
Because he could not give 'em the thing they did lack,
Poor fellow, they threatened to geld him.

Then did you not hear of a country trick?
They say that Tuskin's no dastard, *[allusion lost*
For when country Gillians do play with their Dicks
Then London must father the bastard.

*A broadside version, 'The Merry Haymakers', begins much the same, but after the 'Vulcan the smith' stanza it has the following six, with internal rhymes, survivors perhaps of a lost original:*

Young Bridget came next, and plaguily vexed
In fury she fell upon Robin.
His clatter-de-vengeance, adzuggers! she clawed
'Cause he with young Kate had been bobbing.

With that he made bold with speed to take hold
Of Bridget's young chitter-de-widgeon.
He threw her along, but did her no wrong
Because it was just upon fledging. *she was just old enough*

Her mother came by, and as she came nigh
The sight put her into a laughter.
His butttocks she banged, and bid him be hanged
For playing the fool with her daughter.

The men and the maids, they love their comrades
Above any paltry riches.
Quoth Nancy to Dick, 'Adzuggers! I'm sick
For something thou hast in thy breeches.'

'What, says thou me so? Then to it we'll go.
Thou shalt have thy earnest desire,
For thou art the lass, I swear by the mass,
Which I above all do admire.'

At making of hay they frolic and play,
As you may observe by this ditty.
And when they are cracked, away they are packed —
For virgins away to the city.

* *ruffelers*: usually vagabonds or swaggerers; here just rumbustious villagers

## Pillycock

Pillycock came to my lady's toe
And there the whoreson began to go.
Had he feet?
Ay, marry, had he!
And did he go?
Ay, marry, did he!
*So bolt upright and ready to fight,*
*And Pillycock he lay there all night.*

Pillycock came to my lady's heel
And there the whoreson began to feel.
Had he hands?
Ay, marry, had he!
And did he feel?
Ay, marry, did he!
*So bolt upright , &c —*

Pillycock came to my lady's shin
And there the whoreson began to grin.
    Had he teeth?
    Ay, marry, had he!
    And did he grin?
    Ay, marry, did he!
*So bolt upright, &c –*

Pillycock came to my lady's knee
And there the whoreson began to see.
    Had he eyes?
    Ay, marry, had he!
    And did he see?
    Ay, marry, did he!
*So bolt upright, &c –*

Pillycock came to my lady's thigh
And there the whoreson began to fly.
    Had he wings?
    Ay, marry, had he!
    And did he fly?
    Ay, marry, did he!
*So bolt upright, &c –*

Pillycock came to my lady's ——
And there the whoreson began to hunt.
    Had he hounds?
    Ay, marry, had he!
    And did he hunt?
    Ay, marry, did he!
*So bolt upright and ready to fight,*
*And Pillycock he lay there all night.*

# John and Susan

All in the land of cider
At a place called Brampton Bryan
     Such a prank was played
     'Twixt man and maid
As all the Saints cried fie on. *Puritans*

For gentle John and Susan
Were oft at recreation,
     Which all must grant,
     If not in a Saint,
Was perfect fornication.

Both morning, noon and night, sir,
Brisk John was at her crupper.
     He got in her gears
     Five times before prayers
And six times after supper.

John being well provided
In fine did so solace her
     That Susan's waist,
     So slackly laced,
Showed signs of babe of grace, sir.

But when the knight perceivèd *[knight: see endnote*
That Susan had been sinning
     And that this lass,
     For want of grace,
Loved sporting more than spinning,

To purge his house from scandal
Of filthy fornication,
     And of such crimes
     To show the times
His utter detestation,

He took both bed and bolster,
With blankets, sheets and pillows,
    With Johnny's frock
    And Susan's smock
And burnt 'em in the kiln-house,

With every vile utensil
On which they had been wicked,
    As chairs and stools,
    Old trunks, close-stools
And eke the three-legged cricket. *stool*

But had each thing defilèd
Been burnt at Brampton Bryan
    We all must grant
    The knight would want
Himself a bed to lie on.

## Would you have a young virgin

Would you have a young virgin of fifteen years?
You must tickle her fancy with 'sweets' and 'dears',
Ever toying and playing, and sweetly, sweetly
Sing a love sonnet and charm her ears.
Wittily, prettily talk her down.
Chase her and praise her, if fair or brown.
    Soothe her and smooth her
    And tease her and please her,
And touch but her smicket and all's your own. *smock*

Do ye fancy a widow well known in man?
With a front of assurance come boldly on.
Let her rest not an hour, but briskly, briskly
Put her in mind how her time steals on.
Rattle and prattle, although she frown.
Rouse her and touze her from morn to noon,
Show her some hour y'are able to grapple,
Then get but her writings and all's your own *[her property*

Do ye fancy a punk of a humour free
That's kept by a fumbler of quality?
Ye must rail at her keeper, and tell her, tell her
Pleasure's best charm is variety.
Swear her much fairer than all the town.
Try her and ply her when cully's gone.
        Dog her and jog her
        And meet her and treat her,
And kiss with two guineas and all's your own.

THOMAS D'URFEY, *1709*

## I owed my hostess thirty pound

I owed my hostess thirty pound,
And how d'ye think I paid her?
I met her in my turnip ground
And gently down I laid her.

She oped a purse as black as coal
To hold my coin when counted.
I satisfied her in the whole,
And just by tail she found it.*

Two stones make pounds full twenty-eight, *a stone=14lb*
And stones she had some skill in, *testicles*
And if good flesh bear any rate
A yard's worth forty shilling. *penis; £2*

If this coin pass, no man that lives
Shall dun for past debauches.
Zounds, landlords, send but in your wives!
We'll scour off all their notches.

*From the fifth line to the last, the song is a run of double meanings (in commerce, 'just by tail' = exactly paying off a tally or debt)

## The Willoughby Whim

### A Scotch Song, in a Dialogue between two Sisters

*Molly* Oh Jenny, Jenny, where hast thou been?
  Father and mother are seeking for thee.
You have been ranting, playing the wanton,
  Keeping of Jockey company.

*Jenny* Oh Molly, I've been to hear the mill clack
  And grind grist for the family.
Full as it went I've brought home my sack,*
  For the miller has tooken his toll of me.

*Molly* You hang your smickets abroad to bleach. *smocks*
  When that was done, where could you be?
*Jenny* I slipped down in the quickset hedge
  And Jockey the loon fell after me.

*Molly* My father you told you'd go to kirk.
  When prayers were done, where could you be?
*Jenny* Taking a kiss of the parson and clerk,
  And of other young laddies some two or three.

*Molly* Oh Jenny, Jenny, what wilt thou do?
  If belly should swell where wilt thou be?
*Jenny* Look to yourself! For Jockey is true
  And whilst clapper goes will take care of me.

*The miller did not take a part of the flour as toll in the usual way; Jenny paid him her way (see endnote for other versions of the song)

## The Jolly Fisherman

A fisherman took a fair maid in his boat,
  *Fol de dol lol lol de lol da.*
A fisherman took a fair maid in his boat
And he swore by his oars he would play with her joke.
  *Blood and suet, he swore he would do it,*
  *And she was afraid he would run quite through it.*

'Why sir,' said she, 'if I must dance a jig,
Let me first see if it be not too big.'
  *Blood and suet, etc —*

'Suppose it's too big, it shall do you no hurt
For I'll wrap up one-half in the tail of my shirt.'
*Blood and suet, etc —*

Then he laid this fair maid down on her back,
And he whipped it all in and her daisy went smack.
*Blood and suet, etc —*

As she laid on her back she smiled in his face
And swore that a lady would jump for her place.
*Blood and suet, etc —*

'The pleasure so great, I can hardly laugh.
Take your shirt-tail away and whip t'other half.
*Blood and suet, etc —*

'Come, work it away until you are done,
For I'm poxed if you e'er make both holes into one.'
*Blood and suet, he swore he would do it,*
*And she was afraid he would run quite through it.*

## A young man and a maid, put in all

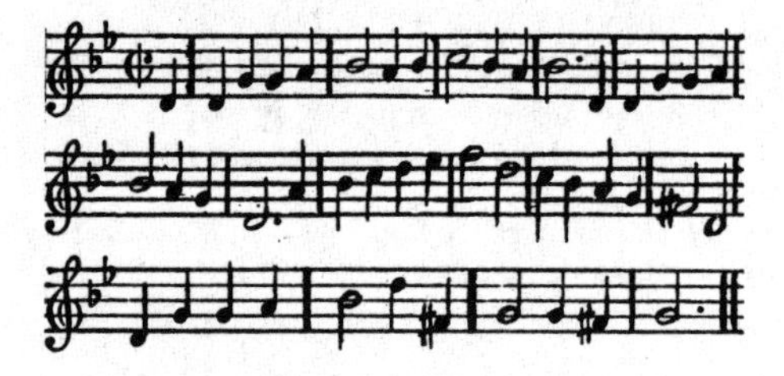

A young man and a maid, *put in all, put in all,*
Together lately played, *put in all.*
The young man was in jest.
O the maid she did protest:
She bid him do his best, *put in all.*

With that, her rowling eyes, *put in all, put in all,*
Turned upward to the skies, *put in all.*
My skin is white, you see,
My smock above my knee.
What would you more of me? *Put in all.*

I hope my neck and breast, *put in all, put in all,*
Lie open to your chest, *put in all.*

The young man was in heat.
The maid did soundly sweat:
A little farther get, *put in all.*

According to her will, *put in all, put in all,*
This young man tried his skill, *put in all.*
But the proverb plain does tell
That use them ne'er so well,
For an inch they'd take an ell, *put in all.*

When they had ended sport, *put in all, put in all,*
She found him all too short, *put in all,*
For when he'd done his best,
The maid she did protest
'Twas nothing but a jest, *put in all, put in all.*

For this song's precursor, 'Jack Hall', and for later versions, see endnote

## The Rakes of Stoney Batter

Come all you roving blades
That ramble through the city
Kissing pretty maids:
Listen to my ditty.
Our time is coming on
When we will be merry.
Kitty, Poll and Nan
Will give us sack and sherry.

*Hey for Bobbin' Joan,*
*Hey for Stoney Batter!*
*Keep your wife at home*
*Or else I will be at her.*

There's Bridget, Peg and Nell
With Nancy, Doll and Susan
To please their sweethearts well
Sometimes will go a-boozing,
But when their cash is gone
They'll hunt for a cully — *a man (client or dupe)*
And bring the splinters home — *money*
To their beloved bully.

*Hey for Bobbin' Joan,*
*Hey for Stoney Batter —*

In summer lasses go
To the fields a-maying,
Through the meadows gay
With their sweethearts playing.
Their smiling winning ways
Show for game they're willing,
Though Jenny she cries, 'Nay,
I won't f—k for a shilling.'

*Hey for Bobbin' Joan,*
*Hey for Stoney Batter —*

'Go, you cunning knave,
No more of coax and wheedle.
By those buttons in my sleeve
I'll prick you with my needle.
What, will you still be bold?
Mammy, call to this man.
For shame, my hands don't hold.
I vow my breath is just gone.'

*Hey for Bobbin' Joan,*
*Hey for Stoney Batter —*

There's Joan, a buxom lass,
Met with lusty Johnny.
They went to take a glass,
He called her dear and honey.
She said, 'You silly clown,
Take me round the middle.
Play me Bobbin' Joan
Or else I'll break your fiddle.'

*Hey for Bobbin' Joan,*
*Hey for Stoney Batter —*

He gently laid her down
And he pulled out his scraper.
He played her such a tune
As made her fart and caper.
She said, 'My dearest John,
You're such a jolly rover
My cloak and gown I'd pawn
That you would ne'er give over.'

*Hey for Bobbin' Joan,*
*Hey for Stoney Batter —*

Come, let us take a roam
Up to Stoney Batter.
Keep your wife at home,
For humpers will be at her.
Hey for cakes and ale,
Hey for pretty misses
That will never fail
For to crown our wishes.

*Hey for Bobbin' Joan,*
*Hey for Stoney Batter.*
*Keep your wife at home*
*Or else I'll stop her water.*

Is your apples ripe?
Are they fit for plucking?
Is your maid within
Ready for the f——g?

*This song is of Irish origin (Stoney Batter is a Dublin district, once noted for raffishness). 'Bobbing Joan' is often mentioned as a fiddle tune for dancing. As the song travelled, singers improvised new verses, perhaps during the dance. Here are more from another broadside —*

Graft your apple trees,
Keep them clean of water.
Keep your wife at home
Or else I will be at her.
Is your apples ripe?
Are they fit for plucking?
Where's your daughter Jane?
Is she fit for humping?

Have you sown your wheat?
Is it ready put in?
Is it almost ripe
Or is it fit for cutting?
Is your corn dry?
Is it fit for thrashing?
You may come and try —
Kissing's all in fashion.

There's Jenny Ling and Diver
Went to town a-walking.
They went to a boozing-ken *alehouse*

To spend their time in courting.
There's Bobbing Joan and Di *
Went to bed together.
All the sport we had
Was kissing one another.

* Evidently an oral error for 'Joan and I'. A Scottish version has this:

Bobbing John and I
Gaed to bed togither.
A' that we could dee
Was kissing ane anither.

## The Surprise

Jolly Tom and Clever-legged Dick
With Blowsy Moll and Maggoty Kate
Into a hop
Happened to pop.
They danced Bobbing Joan till late.
Firking about,
Candles went out,
Tom kissed Moll and Dick kissed Kate.*

Squalling, bawling, pulling and hauling —
Watchman's lantern quick did appear.
Just in the nick
Clever-legged Dick
Nimbly buttoned up his ware. *his penis*
Maggoty Kate,
Somewhat too late,
Struggling lay with all things bare.

Rantum scantum, all in confusion,
Every couple strove to be gone.
Tom upon Moll
Just had a fall,
Game within had just begun.
Fumbling he
Down on his knee
Left poor Blowsy Moll undone.

* One of many instances of 'kissed' meaning much more

## Larry Grogan

You rakes that are jolly and never will marry,
We'll send for sweet Larry, be merry, be merry.
Zounds, boy! Play up a march for us.
Play up, sweet Larry, be nimble, be nimble.
One tune of your chaunter will crown us with honour,
Exceeding harp, hautboy, or fiddle, or fiddle.
Your pipes, Larry Grogan, the Cellians down in, *[reference obscure*
Excelleth the sweetness of singing, of singing.

To hear Lastron Pony, what heart can be stoney, *Irish dance tune*
But dancing and roaring be willing, be willing.
Play up to the humours of those that spend money free.
Turn out the clown and the niggardly, niggardly.
Kick out of doors the whore that is covetous.
Fill up the bowl again, landlady, landlady.

Come play, Larry Grogan, the march of the rovers,
The rakes and the troopers, and drunkards, and drunkards.
Drink about, gentlemen, fill up your bumpers.
Landlady, bring us your pitcher, your pitcher,
And let it flow over — you know Larry Grogan
Will tickle the hole of your twitcher, your twitcher.*

We'll frolic to Wexford, play up to the Hatchets,
And drink off a hogshead at Hammond's, at Hammond's.
From thence to Moll Whealon's, we'll visit the females
And kiss every girl that is handsome, is handsome.
Then sweet young gallants, be airy, be airy,
The glory of the age is sweet Larry, sweet Larry.
If money don't fail us we'll live all like heroes,
But mind, we are never to marry, to marry.

Five thousand per annum, would heaven but grant us
That portion, I'd ramble with Larry, with Larry.
I'd wait on his lady, Susanna or Mary,
But curse me if ever I marry, I marry;
Frolic at taverns, drink and make verses free,
Freely would spend a guinea, a guinea.
What man would I care for? Sweet Larry my master
Would free me in town or in city, in city.

Drink about, Larry, let's laugh and be merry.
The world is only a shadow, a shadow.
We'll frolic and caper. Let's look for the scraper. *fiddler*
Perhaps we may die tomorrow, tomorrow.
If death does approach us we'll play him back home again,
So now let the rogue be civil, be civil.
If not, we'll deny him and live in spite of him.
Good heaven preserve us from evil, from evil.

For leaping or dancing, for tumbling or prancing,
Whoe'er saw a blade like young Larry, young Larry
For wisdom or learning, good parts and behaviour?
But still his opinion is never to marry.
He's wise and ingenious, though young, wild and rakish;
A gentleman really descended, descended.
He's called a young hero, who know him will say so.
Sweet Larry, my verses are ended, are ended.

* *twitcher*: see endnote on this, and for more on Larry Grogan, a noted player of the Irish pipes… whose fame soon travelled to London—

## Larry Grogan, or the London Rakes' Delight

Come boys, let's be jolly and drown melancholy.
    We'll tope off a hogshead of sherry, of sherry.
Let doting old Puritans die in their folly
    While we that are rakes will be merry, be merry.
Each rake with his miss shall tipple and frolic it,
    Peggy and Nancy and Sarah, and Sarah,
And Harry and Jonny and Robin no politic,
    Dicky and Doll of the dairy, the dairy.

We'll dance, sing and caper, rant, rattle and vapour,
    And revel like true sons of thunder, of thunder.

Bawds, panders and bullies, pimps, whores and their cullies,
Amazed and afraid shall knock under, boys, under.
If they resist we'll beat them all back again.
No man our frolic shall hinder, shall hinder.
We'll booze and we'll drink, and when in a merry vein
Turn the house out of the window, the window.

When drunk with good sherry, champagne or canary,
We always are frisky and jolly, and jolly.
Each lass of the town that is free, brisk and airy,
Young Cicely, Bersheba and Polly, and Polly
Shall fly to our arms with am'rous embraces
And meet a return from each gallant, each gallant.
While liquor inspires us we mind no disgraces
But boldly make use of our talent, our talent.

Our bottle's religion, our lasses a region
Of bliss: there our joys we do centre, do centre.
While Bacchus inspires us and Venus she fires us,
We value not Hymen's indenture, indenture.
Those that do marry do often miscarry.
Venùs you know cuckolded Vulcan, old Vulcan.
His horns oft did hinder the sight of his rival,
While Mars in a corner lay skulking, lay skulking.

Since women are fickle and love to be tickled
By those that to them should be strangers, be strangers,
The rake's life is best. Though with pox he is pickled
He need not to fear other dangers, sir, dangers.
For what will come after we have no cause to fret,
Think not at all of tomorrow, tomorrow.
A whole pound of grief will ne'er pay an ounce of debt.
Hang care and cast away sorrow, boys, sorrow.

## The Wagoner

As I was driving my wagon one day,
I met a young damsel, tight, buxom and gay.
I kindly accosted her with a low bow
And I felt my whole body I cannot tell how.
*Gee ho Dobbin! hi ho Dobbin! gee ho Dobbin, gee ho, hi ho.*

I longed to be at her and gave her a kiss.
She thought me but civil, nor took it amiss.
I knew no recalling the minutes were past.

I began to make hay while the sunshine did last.
*Gee ho Dobbin, etc —*

'I've six score of sheep, and each ram has his ewe,
And my cows when they lack to the parson's bull go.
We're made for each other, so prithee comply.'
She blushed, her eyes twinkled, she could not tell why.
*Ah poor Jenny! fearful Jenny! ah poor Jenny! hi ho.*

I kissed her again. She replied with disdain,
'No kisses I want, prithee take them again,'
Then whispered me softly the weather was hot,
And her mind run on something, she could not tell what.
*Ah poor Jenny! coaxing Jenny! ah poor Jenny! hi ho.*

Then down in the wagon this damsel I laid,
But still I kept driving, for driving's my trade.
I rumpled her feathers and tickled her scut
And played the round rubbers at two-handed put. *a card game*
*Well put Roger! well put Jenny! well put Roger, hi ho.*

Her breasts were as soft and as white as new cream
And her motion kept pace with the bells of my team.
When her bubbies went up her plump buttocks went down,
And the wheels seemed to stand, and the wagon go round.
*O brave Roger! drive on Roger! O brave Roger, hi ho.*

Then to it again, to our pastime we went,
And my cards I played fairly to Jenny's content.
I worked at her pump till the sucker grew dry
And then I left pumping—a good reason why.
*Ah poor Roger! broken-backed Roger! gee ho Roger, hi ho.*

I thought ere we parted to've had t'other blow,
When slap went the wagon wheel into a slough,
Which shattered her premises out of repair,
And Roger's pump-handle run the devil knows where.
*Ah poor Roger, flimsy Roger! ah poor Roger, hi ho.*

## On a Famous Toast

Belinda has such wondrous charms
'Tis heaven to lie within her arms,
And she's so charitably given
She wishes all mankind in heaven.

## The Orange Woman

### Sung by Miss Brown at Sadler's Wells*

A hearty, buxom young girl am I,
I come from Dublin city.
I ne'er feared a man, not I,
Though some say, more's the pity,
Well, let them say so once again,
I've got no cause to mind them.
I always fancy pretty men
Wherever I can find them,
*Wherever I can find them.*

I'll never marry, no indeed,
For marriage causes trouble,
And after all the priest has said
'Tis merely hubble-bubble.
The rakes will still be counted rakes:
Not Hymen's chains can bind 'em.
And so preventing all mistakes
I'll kiss where'er I find 'em,
*I'll kiss where'er I find 'em.*

The game of wedlock's all a chance,
Cry Over or cry Under, *heads or tails*
Yet many folks to church will dance,
At which I often wonder.
Some fancy this, some fancy that,
All hope the joy designed 'em.
I'll have my whim, that's tit-for-tat
Wherever I can find 'em,
*Wherever I can find 'em.*

But what a silly jade am I,
Thus idly to be singing!
There's no one here my fruit to buy
Nor any to be flinging. *throwing her coins*
In pretty men all pleasure dwells.
All hope the joy designed 'em,
So now I'll wheel to Sadler's Wells
And there I'm sure to find 'em,
*And there I'm sure to find 'em.*

**Miss Brown*: a popular singer at Sadler's Wells, 1762–7

# The Ruff Toupee

I dressed myself both fine and gay
To take a walk the other day.
A gentleman I chanced to see
Who begged to go along with me.
*And sing, O rare my Ruff Toupee!*
*He paid the reckoning well for me.*

We walked until the moon was up,
Then to a tavern went to sup.
There he a favour asked of me,
If he might see my Ruff Toupee.
*And sing, &c –*

Then straight to him I did reply,
This favour, sir, I must deny.
A guinea down will be the fee
If you do see my Ruff Toupee.
*And sing, &c –*

Soon as the bargain we had struck
He callèd for the waiter up
To pay the reckoning, and so
Then to a bagnio we did go.
*And sing, &c –*

And when we to the bagnio came,
In order to begin the game
He callèd for a bed straightway
That he all night with me might lay.
*And sing, &c –*

When in the morning he arose,
Adorned himself in his fine clothes,
Five guineas more he gave to me,
Well pleasèd with my Ruff Toupee.
*And sing, &c –*

Now all young ladies of renown
That take your walks in London town,
I'd have you all with me agree
And stand up always for your fee,
*And sing, O rare my Ruff Toupee!*
*He paid the reckoning well for me.*

## Chloe's the wonder of her sex

Chloe's the wonder of her sex.
'Tis well her heart is tender.
How might such killing eyes perplex
With virtue to defend her!

But nature, graciously inclined,
Not bent to vex but please us,
Has to her boundless beauty joined
A boundless will to ease us.

## Venus & Bacchus

When Venus and Bacchus by turns did delight
With a bottle all day and a mistress at night,
I thought no condition so happy as mine
When the charms of bright beauty gave a zest to the wine.

But how fleeting's the pleasure, how transient the joy,
When the gods are determined our bliss to destroy!
For alas! I am now grown exceedingly dull:
My casks are all empty, and Celia – and Celia – and Celia is full.

## The Rake's Frolick
### or Stauka an Varaga [The market idler]

Through nations ranging, raking elements,
Spending my days in peace and fellowship,
Oro, and plenty good store.
In each company fill your bumpers high,
With pleasing jollity toast the lasses free,
Oro, and drink your store.

Through Munster I roved with jovial company,
Rowling in sport, resorting pleasantly,
In each barony through the country,
Boozing heartily, cruising gallantly,
Oro, and pleasure galore.

Es Buohileen fast ha saar arr chanosagh,
Da hanigh oan Monister faulhe ee yhallo room,
Oro, gus thouir dhum pog.

Prabig noor see agus leenther knogarea,
Gallim oam chree ga niolodb a tharigid,
Thiogh a saggarth es bemesth cagilthe,
Mo vouhill cabshagh sheen er liobha lume.
    Oro, es na scar lume gidhio.

When first I set sail to range the barony
From sweet Farihy to Kildorrery, *in County Cork*
    Oro, and from that to Red Chair —
It's there the fair maids do treat me heartily,
With full glasses free and impartiality.
    Oro, the truth I'll declare.
On the high road to Castle Oliver
I met a coaxing roving frolicker.
Her mode denoted she was a Palentine, *? palatine, noble*
She wore deep ribbons, her clothes in fashion, sir —
    Oro, her love she received.

. . . *12 more lines in Irish* . . .

There I perceived her state and stature,
Her stately carriage and face most flattering.
    Oro, she wounded me sore.
There I engaged her close in garrison
In the cavern where she followed me.
Who'd refuse such boozing lasses free,
With whom I'd choose to cruise most gallantly?
Win or lose, I'd scourge them heartily.
Their curiosity drowns all poverty.
    Oro, 'tis a time I adore.

. . . *nine more lines in Irish* . . .

It was on a day where play was publicly
With great pleasantry, mirth and jollity,
    Oro, and dancing also.
While we were skipping and kissing heartily,
Staka an varaga, aside she carried me,
Told me her peas was fit for thrashing free.
To tell you in plain, I tasted them certainly.
My flail she fractured, I'm teased with doctor's fee, *he has VD*
    Oro, which makes me condole.

This and the next two songs, printed in Limerick and Monaghan in the 1780s, when English was imposing its domination, show an inventive, erratic delight in adapting English to Irish rhythms and sound-play. I give one of three Irish stanzas. Dublin scholars say the words are in a rough phonetic form, too idiosyncratic for easy translation, but loosely paralleling the English.

## The Answer to Stauka an Vauraga

I am a fair maid that loves good company,
Such as would choose a girl of quality.
Oro, and the boys I adore.

I travelled this nation, submissive and complaisant;
From country to city I rolled in great merriment,
Oro, and am killing galore.

All those who navigate in the seas of tranquillity,
Furl their sails in the midst of extremity,
Steer by their compass unto the lower country —
When the tempest's over, we'll drink in great jollity:
Oro, and have pleasure galore.

One day as I roved by an ancient brave castle, sir,
I met a young lad, and he dressed in the fashion, sir.
Oro, and his eyes they did roll.

He handles me gently, carouses me heartily,
Praises my beauty and hugs me quite lovingly.
Oro, he is the joy of my soul.

He says, My fair maid, if you join me in company,
To Munster we'll go for to see that fair country.
It's the province we'll roll in great jollity.
Oro, and the lip of a bowl!

He is as handsome a lad as any in this country.
He singles, he doubles, he trebles it handsomely. *making love*
Oro, he is valiant and bold.

He lies in my arms without dread or danger.
I lent him some coals to keep fire in his chamber;
Oro, there was snow on the ground.

While we were a-kissing and hugging quite heartily,
Rouling and sporting, under Venus's liberty,
I kindled his coals with a bunch of curiosity. *
Sits at his own fire, and keeps me in memory.
Oro, I'm afraid he'll get cold.

'Tis now I will leave off my raking and rambling.
To Munster I'll go to set up a standing.
Oro, and I'll pass for a maid.

'Tis there the boys out of pleasure will leisure me,
With joy out of measure they'll dingle and jingle me.
With bottle and glasses we'll pass the night merrily,
Saying, Here's a good health to the boy in obscurity.
Oro, my harvest is made.

*curiosity: as in the previous song, a delicate euphemism for the vagina; she confirms she gave him VD, so now he is 'the boy in obscurity'

## Hush Cat from under the Table

You jolly young rakes who loves for to freak,
To sport and play with the girls so pretty,
Attend to my tale while I shall reveal
A humorous sonnet both pleasant and witty.
I happened of late a ramble to take
And met with a maid upon the highway, sir.
I addressed her so sly she soon did comply
In my arms to lie until break of day, sir.

*Hush, she did cry, my mammy's hard by.*
*Come with me tonight, you shall have good quarters,*
*Lie down very snug, like a bug in a rug,*
*And I will lie by you to tie up my garters.*

To Newry I came along with my dame.
She went to a lane and I followed after.
The old woman, sure, she ran to the door
While I on the floor was kissing her daughter.
The cat run about and made such a rout,
While she in a pout with a stick then did storm her.
Cups and saucers were broke. I laughed at the joke
While the old woman groped for puss in the corner.

*Hush cat, come out in a crack,* *hush = whoosh*
*Hush cat, from under the table.*
*Hush cat! I smiled at that.*
*If you had been there you'd laugh while you're able.*

At dawning of day I slipped away.
Without any delay I set to the road, sir.
To Lurgan I came, and met with a dame.
I asked her name and place of abode, sir.
I had excellent room to weave in her loom,

A girl in full bloom, her name it was Nancy.
I pleased her so well that ere long she did swell,
For I was the lad who could tickle her fancy.

*When three quarters were gone she had a young son.*
*Her mother cried hush-a-ba, rocking the cradle!*
*Hush cheep cat, at every whack,*
*That eat the child's pap in under the table.*

*1787*

## Darby O'Golicker

Great boasting of late we have heard of the feat
Of a comical rake called Morgan Rattler,*
But one's come to town will soon cut him down,
And he goes by the name of Darby O'Golicker.

A noted young blade, a blacksmith by trade,
Well known by the lasses to be a great frolicker,
And the ladies all cry when they see him pass by,
There goes the bold hammerman Darby O'Golicker!

His music excels all carillon bells,
His stroke's more sweet than the warbling chorister.
No flute or guitar can ever compare
To the musical hammer of Darby O'Golicker.

At Mullingar Fair, this young Darby was there
With Nancy Adair, that sweet pretty frolicker.
Her gown she did pledge for the triangle wedge*
That was drove by the sledge of Darby O'Golicker.

His excellent music is good for the phthisic.
The fair maids it does physic like a dose of jalap, sir.
No doctor with pills can cure all their ills
Like the essence extracted from Darby O'Golicker.

A maiden so rare with a languishing air,
Whose skin it was fair, her hair it was yellow, sir,
She being distressed, she begged a request
Of one blast of the bellows from Darby O'Golicker.

This ma'am did advance with an amorous glance.
Straightway to a tavern he quickly followed her.
On the table she told ten guineas in gold
Her anvil to pelt with his Darby O'Golicker.

So now to conclude, pray don't think me rude
For singing the praise of this sporting frolicker.
Ah hoo! O Morgan may sleep. Here's the boy that can sweep
Twelve thirteeners off with his Darby O'Golicker.*

*For Morgan Rattler and more on his rivals, see endnote
**triangle wedge*: yet another metaphor for the potent trinity, testicles and penis
**thirteeners*: English shillings (so called because worth 13 Irish pennies). Twelve laid out in a row measured 12 inches, so it is a large phallic boast.

## Moll of the Wood

As I was going along the road
Who should I meet but Moll of the Wood.
I stepped up to her, I did her embrace.
She gave me a terrible smack of the face.

Moll of the Wood and I fell out.
She bat me a thump and I gave her a clout.
I gave her a shilling, she swore it was bad.
'It's a soldier's button,' says Moll of the Wood.

*Moll of the Wood lives alone.*
*She keeps a sporting house of her own,*
*And every man that does pass by,*
*She tips them in with a rolling eye.*

Moll in the Wood got over the stile,
Which made the gentlemen all to smile,
And through the green meadow she tripped it along.
And Moll of the Wood was the pride of my song.

Then I followed her without fear,
Thinking to treat her with wine, ale and beer.
'Get out of my house, you country clown,
Or I'll up with my ladle and crack your crown!'

Moll of the Wood made this reply:
'I've got another young man in my eye.
A country clown I never have had.
I'll have my young drummer,' says Moll of the Wood.

Moll of the Wood went to the fair
To see what pleasure and pastime was there.

She met with the drummer, he being just come.
She learned to beat on his rum-a-dum-dum.

*Moll of the Wood, she lives alone.*
*She keeps a bawdy-house of her own,*
*And every one that does pass by,*
*She tips them in with a gimlet eye!*

## The Lusty Young Coachman

A lusty young coachman his horses was whipping,
With a smack, smack, smack, gee-up and gee-o,
When to him a smiling young damsel came tripping
And asked if to Petticoat Lane he would go,
*With a smack, smack, smack, gee-up and gee-o.*

As he held the coach door her breast swelled with desire.
She liked him much better than any spruce beau
And bid him step in and sit freely down by her,
And what she much wanted she soon let him know,
*With a smack –*

Quite charmed with his fair, on her box he leaped boldly,
For who in his senses would then have said no?
But as he was driving, the damsel cried coldly,
'Pray coachman, whip harder and don't drive so slow,'
*With a smack –*

Ashamed to be foiled when he found her so cunning,
More strength and more skill he resolved then to show.
But though he drove faster, so swift she kept running,
His carriage he feared she would soon overthrow,
*With a smack –*

Then the coachman cried out, 'I can drive you no longer.
My reins you have damaged, my whip broke also,
And you may find one that is knowing and stronger,
For the devil may drive you again, ma'am, for Joe,'
*With a smack –*

Then the coachman got off, left the nymph full of sorrow,
While into his hat a crown piece she did throw.
'Young man, at your stand if I find you tomorrow,
Once more unto Petticoat Lane we will go,'
*With a smack, smack, smack, gee-up and gee-o.*

# My mither built a wee, wee house

My mither built a wee, wee house,
A wee, wee house, a wee, wee house,
My mither built a wee, wee house,
To keep me frae the men O!

The wa's fell in, and I fell out, *walls*
The wa's fell in, and I fell out,
The wa's fell in, and I fell out
Amang the merry men O!

How can I keep my maidenhead,
My maidenhead, my maidenhead?
How can I keep my maidenhead
Amang sae many men O?

Ane auld mouldy maidenhead,
Ane auld mouldy maidenhead,
Ane auld mouldy maidenhead,
Seven years and ten O!

The captain bad a guinea for't. *bid*
A guinea for't, a guinea for't.
The captain bad a guinea for't.
The colonel he bad ten O!

The sergeant he bad naething for't,
Bad naething for't, bad naething for't,
The sergeant he bad naething for't,
And he came farrest ben O! *furthest within*

# Wat ye what my Minny did?

Tune, *How can I keep my maidenhead?*

O wat ye what my minny did, *do you know what*
My minny did, my minny did, *my mother did*
O wat ye what my minny did,
My minny did to me, jo?
She pat me in a dark room, *put*
A dark room, a dark room,
She pat me in a dark room,
A stime I could na see, jo. *a glimmer of light*

An' there cam in a lang man,
A meikle man, a strang man, *mickle: big*
An' there cam in a lang man.
  He might hae worried me, jo,
For he pou'd out a lang thing, *pulled*
A meikle thing, a strang thing,
For he pou'd out a lang thing
  Just like a stannin' tree, jo.

An' I had but a wee thing,
A little thing, a wee thing,
An' I had but a wee thing
  Just like a needle e'e, jo.
But an I had wantet that, *if*
Had wantet that, had wantet that,
But an I had wantet that
  He might hae sticket me, jo.

For he shot in his lang thing,
His meikle thing, his strang thing,
For he shot in his lang thing
  Into my needle e'e, jo.
But had it no come out again,
Come out again, come out again,
But had it no come out again
  It might hae stay't for me, jo.

Collected by Burns, perhaps polished by him, but not published; see endnote

## The Plenipotentiary

The Dey of Algiers, when afraid of his ears,
  A messenger sent to our court, sir.
As he knew in our state that the women had weight,
  He chose one well hung for good sport, sir.
He searched the Divan till he found out a man
  Whose b——ks were heavy and hairy;
And he lately came o'er from the Barbary shore
  As the great Plenipòtentiàry.

When to England he came with his p——k in a flame
  He showed it his hostess at landing,
Who spread its renown through all parts of the town
  As a pintle past all understanding.

So much there was said of its snout and its head
    That they called it the Great Janissary.
Not a lady could sleep till she got a sly peep
    At the great Plenipotentiary.

As he rode in his coach, how the whores did approach
    And stared as if stretched on a tenter.
He drew every eye of the dames that passed by,
    Like the sun to its wonderful centre.
As he passed through the town, not a window was down
    And the maids hurried out in the area.
The children cried, 'Look! there's the man with the cock!
    That's the great Plenipotentiary.'

When he came to the court, oh! what giggle and sport!
    Such squinting and squeezing to view him!
What envy and spleen in the women were seen!
    All happy and pleased to get to him!
They vowed in their hearts, if men of such parts
    Were found on the coast of Barbary
'Twas a shame not to bring a whole guard for the king
    Like the great Plenipotentiary.

The dames of intrigue formed their c—ts in a league
    To take him in turn like good folk, sir;
The young misses' plan was to catch as catch can,
    And all were resolved on a stroke, sir.
The cards to invite flew by thousands each night,
    With bribes to his old secretary,
And the famous Eclipse was not let for more leaps    *a noted stallion*
    Than the great Plenipotentiary.

When his name was announced, how the women all bounced
    And the blood hurried up in their faces.
He made them all itch from the nave to the breech
    And their bubbies burst out all their laces.
There was such damned work to be f—ked by the Turk
    That nothing their passion could vary.
All the nation fell sick for the Tripoli p—k
    Of the great Plenipotentiary.

A duchess whose duke made her ready to puke
    With fumbling and frigging all night, sir,
Being first for the prize, was so pleased with its size
    That she begged to examine its plight, sir.
'Good God!' cried Her Grace. 'Its head's like a mace!

'Tis as big as the Corsican Fairy! *a midget exhibited in London*
I'll make up, please the pigs, for dry-bobs and frigs*
With the great Plenipotentiary.'

And now to be bored by this Ottoman lord
Came a virgin far gone in the wane, sir.
She resolved for to try, though her c—t was so dry
That she knew it must split like a cane, sir.
True it was as she spoke; it gave way at each stroke!
But oh, what a woeful quandary!
With one terrible thrust her whole piss-bladder burst
On the great Plenipotentiary.

The next to be tried was an alderman's bride
With a c—t that would swallow a turtle,
Who had horned the dull brows of her worshipful spouse
Till they sprouted like Venus's myrtle.
Through thick and through thin, bowel-deep he dashed in
Till her c—t frothed like cream in a dairy;
And expressed by loud farts she was strained in all parts
By the great Plenipotentiary.

The next to be kissed on the Plenipo's list
Was a delicate maiden of honour.
She screamed at the sight of his p—k, in a fright,
Though she'd had the whole palace upon her.
'C—t J—s!' she said. 'What a p—k for a maid!
Do pray come and look at it, Cary!
But I'll have one drive, if I'm ripped up alive
By the great Plenipotentiary.'

Two sisters next came, Peg and Molly by name,
Two ladies of very high breeding,
Resolved one should try while the other stood by
To assist in the bloody proceeding.
Peg swore by the gods that the Mussulman's c–ds
Were as big as the buttocks of Mary!
Poll cried with a grunt, 'He has ruined my c—t
With his great Plenipotentiary.'

The next for this plan was an old harridan
Who had swallowed huge p—ks from each nation.
With over-much use she had broke up the sluice
'Twixt her c—t and its lower relation.
He stuck her so full that she roared like a bull,
Crying out she was bursting and weary,

So tight was she stuck by this wonderful f—k
Of the great Plenipotentiary.

All heads were bewitched, and all longed to be stitched;
Even babies would languish and linger,
And the boarding-school miss, as she sat down to p–ss,
Drew a Turk on the floor with her finger.
For fancied delight, how they clubbed for a shite
To f—g in the school necessary, *latrine*
And the teachers from France f—ked *à-la-distance*
With the great Plenipotentiary.

Each sluice-c—ted bawd who was knocked all abroad
Till her premises gaped like a grave, sir,
Hoped luck was so thick she should feel the Turk's p—k,
As all others were lost in her cave, sir.
The nymphs of the stage his fine parts did engage,
Made him free of the grand seminary.
And the gentle signiors opened all their back-doors
To the great Plenipotentiary.

Then of love's sweet reward, measured out by the yard,
The Turk was most blessed of mankind, sir,
For his powerful dart went home to the heart,
Whether stuck in before or behind, sir.
But no pencil can draw this great three-tailed bashaw.
Then each c—t-loving contemporary,
As cocks of the game, let's drink to the name
Of the great Plenipotentiary.

CHARLES MORRIS

* *dry-bobs*: failures to ejaculate; *frigs*: masturbations

## The Rolling Blossom

*Sung at the Beef Steak Club and the Anacreontic Society*

I'm saucy, rolling, leering Bett,
A noted brisk young blowing *loose wench*
I'm up to all your Chick-lane flash
And ev'ry rig that's knowing. *every crafty dodge*
At the New Drop I napped my bub *had a drink*
While Will, my man, was swinging. *was hanged*

At the gin ken I took a swig,
    Reeled home, blind drunk, a-singing.

Then Blackleg George I dearly loved.
    He was my flash-man long, sir.
Could palm an ace or ring the tatts — *cheat with dice*
    Or sing a rolling song, sir:
But caught at marking cards, was kicked
    And bundled from the ken too.
Then being for shoplifting cast,
    He Botany Bay was sent to.

When Phil the flat had stagged my charms — *dupe; discovered*
    He swore none else could please him.
He flew like lightning to my arms
    And begged I would not tease him.
I waited till the fruit was ripe,
    Then thinking to be thrifty,
I left the youth to stretch his pipe: — *to masturbate*
    I had nabbed a bill for fifty. — *stolen a £50 bank-bill*

To Nimming Ned I went to bed, — *thieving*
    Who looked but queer and glumly,
Yet every hit he brought the bit — *he always got some loot*
    And then we spent it rumly. — *[rum=good, splendid*
But happening to kill his man,
    When nabbed, to jail they hauled him.
When cast and scragged, then at their hall — *hanged*
    The slashing surgeons mauled him. — *dissected him*

To Scamping Sam I gave my hand,
Who milled the blunt and tatlers. *money and watches*
He was the man to stop and stand *'Stand and deliver'*
And work among the rattlers. *coaches*
But once the guard let fly his pop *fired his gun*
And Sam became receiver:
The claret ran, it would not stop, *blood*
He died of the leaden fever.

While fat Sal at a tick did tug *a watch*
I helped, as was my duty.
I tipped the cull so close a hug *gave the victim*
She safely nabbed the booty.
The cobweb and the robbing rigs*
I practise every day, sir,
And find a fence for all young prigs
Whene'er they bring their prey, sir.

Now if by chance I should be had
And brought to sad repentance,
And grieve to leave my dear town pad, *her beloved streets*
When Wigsby has passed sentence *the judge*
With curtsy low I'll leave the court.
New-rigged I'll cut a dash, man,
Then sail away to Botany Bay
To Blackleg George, my flash-man.

* *cobweb rig*: some kind of dodge, probably to do with stolen goods

## The Buxom Dairy Maid

I am a young dairy-maid, buxom and tight.
In minding my dairy I take great delight,
In making of butter and cheese that is new,
And a young man to play with my how-do-you-do.

*With my gee-ho Dobbin, drive on your wagon,*
*Drive on your wagon, gee-up and gee-ho.*

The first was young Johnny, a pretty ploughboy.
He called me his honey, delight and his joy.
He kissed me so sweetly, my cheeks gave a pat,
And he's welcome at all times to grind for all that,
*With my gee-ho Dobbin, etc —*

The next a young shepherd, a buxom young lad,
And many's the frolics together we've had.
He used me so kindly and shoved it in tight
And played a sweet tune on the tabor and pipe,
*With my gee-ho Dobbin, etc —*

The wagoners, they are all jolly blades.
They know very well how to please the young maids.
They are hearty and willing, goodnatured and free,
And these are the boys that shall do it for me,
*With my gee-ho Dobbin, etc —*

My mother, she told me of men to beware,
Or else they would draw my poor heart in a snare,
But for all her advice, sure I care not a fig,
For Johnny shall play upon my hairy wig,
*With my gee-ho Dobbin, etc —*

My snatch is my own, the ground is the king's.
It is free for a young man that brings a good thing.
Let him be ever so strong or ever so stout,
I warrant I'll make him quickly give out,

*With my gee-ho Dobbin, drive on your wagon,*
*Drive on your wagon, gee-up and gee-ho.*

## Oh, do it, dear charmer, again

Air — *Meet me by moonlight*

Oh, do it, dear charmer, again
As well as you did it before.
Oh, let me not ask you in vain.
Oh, pray do it nicely once more!
There are girls who are cheaper, I own,
But none who'll so true to you prove,
And where's there a girl on the town
Can match me in point of a move?
So do it, dear charmer, again,
Do it, I prithee, again.

You're just the man for my size,
You know how to please me full well!
Then once more come close to my thighs
Where pleasure and transport doth dwell!

I'll tease you in amorous play
And tickle your beauties all o'er.
To please me you well know the way,
Then why don't you do it once more?
So do it, dear charmer, once more,
Do it, oh, do it once more.

Supposing my belly should swell?
For that you have no cause to care:
There's a kiddy I know in Pall Mall
To whom I the kinchin can swear! *the baby*
Then do not refuse my request.
For rapture again I implore.
Don't you see, my dear boy, I'm undressed?
So prithee come kiss me once more!
Do it, dear charmer, again.
Do it, dear charmer, again.

## Sam Swipes: or, This Way and That Way

A Famous Smutty Stave / Air, *When First I saw Flora*

My name is Sam Swipes, and Sal is my dear.
I labour all day to get her some beer,
And when I come home, if I've had good luck
I lay her down softly and give her a —
This way and that way and which way you will.
I'm sure I've said nothing that you can take ill.

My Sal is a rum one as ever you see, *fine, first-rate*
And chaps at her tail she has had two or three.
There was lanky and short, tall, chubby and fat,
Who all were red-hot for a slap at her —
*This way, &c —*

The first was a butcher, who killing a calf,
All that she wanted, it was the best half.
He took pity, and seeing her in want,
He slapped the calf's tail right bang up her —
*This way, &c —*

. . . *(a fisherman; a parson)* . . .

The next was a soldier who knew how to shoot.
She twigged his long musket and could not stand mute.
He primed it so quickly, and it came to pass
That he banged his musket balls against Sally's —
*This way, &c —*

The next was a builder, so stout and so rare,
Who heard that her kitchen was out of repair.
He brought his strong tools, and at it went smack,
And shoved a wedge ten inches long up her ——
*This way, &c —*

So you see that my Sarah's a rum 'un to go.
The sight of her charms sets each heart in a glow.
She's a precious young pullet, but that I don't mind,
For she always takes care that I have a good ——
This way and that way and which way you will.
I'm sure I've said nothing that you can take ill.

## Mrs Bond: A right-down rummy Ditty

### Air, *Won't you come to the bower?*

Oh, I'm getting still more hot for you, my charming Mrs Bond,
And though you will not smile on me, I never will despond.
The moment when I write to you, indeed quite stiff I stand,
And — and all that I possess is sweating in my hand.
Even randy little duchesses have lured me to their arms
And crumby little countesses have yielded me their charms.
Then only give me leave to go a-fishing in your pond:
I've got a rod so long and strong, and such fine bait, Mrs Bond.
Then won't you let me, won't you let me—tickle you, Mrs Bond?

Every morning I view you at your toilette when you rise,
And watch the towel's motion as you wash your lovely thighs.
I pray for some enchantress to transform me with her wand
To the chamber-pot you hold betwixt your thighs, Mrs Bond.
If the gods would grant my wishes and accomplish my request
I'd seek to be a flea, to skip upon your breast,
Or I'd pray to be a petticoat, of flannel or of blond, *silk lace*
To chafe your panting belly and your bubbies, Mrs Bond.
*Then won't you, &c —*

At eve I seek the privy which your presence may have blessed
And kiss the very timber which your lily duff has pressed.
Even the very paper on which I write this *billet-doux,*
It is gilt-edge, you see, by being s—t upon by you.
Even in my sleep I hourly am attacked.
My laundress and my night-shirt can testify the fact.
My passions are so hot and so exquisitely fond,
My very f—ts have learned to trump the praise of Mrs Bond.
*Then won't you, &c–*

Mrs Bond, you must forgive me, but indeed I cannot wait,
So you'd better ope your pretty mouth and swallow all my bait.
There's one reflection left, to solace me beyond:
I'll never go a-fishing if it is not in your pond.
Then won't you let me, won't you let me—tickle you, Mrs Bond?
Won't you let me, won't you let me—go a-fishing in your pond?

# 3

# *Merriments, mockings, miseries*

## What hap had I to marry a shrew

*A canon for three voices*

What hap had I to marry a shrew,
For she doth give me many a blow
And how to please her, alas, I do not know.

From morn to even her tongue never lies.
Sometimes she brawls, sometimes she cries
And I can scarce keep her talons from my eyes.

When from abroad I do come in,
Sir knave, she says, where have you been?
And please or displease, she lays it on my skin.

Then do I crouch, then do I kneel
And wish my cap were furred with steel
To bear the blows that my poor head doth feel.

But our Sir John — beshrew thy heart! *the parson*
For thou hast joined us, we can't part,
And I, simple fool, must ever bear the smart.

This dates from before 1580; see endnote for an even earlier plaint

## Let Lobcock leave his wife at home

Let Lobcock leave his wife at home
With lusty Jinkin, that clownish groom, *clownish = rustic*
With tee-hee — with two alone;
With ta-ha — farewell, my kind mome. *a gull, a ninny*
Yet we must look kindly when Lobcock comes home.

## When Francus comes to solace

When Francus comes to solace with his whore
He sends for rods and strips himself stark naked,
For his lust sleeps and will not rise before
By whipping of the wench it be awakèd. *of = by*
I envy him not, but wish I had the power
To make myself his wench for one half hour.

SIR JOHN DAVIES, *?1596*

## Faith, wench, I cannot court

Faith, wench, I cannot court thy sprightly eyes
With the bass viol placed between my thighs.
I cannot lisp nor to some fiddle sing
Nor run upon a high-stretched minikin. *treble string*

I cannot whine in puling elegies,
Entombing Cupid with sad obsequies.
I am not fashioned for these amorous times,
To court thy beauty with lascivious rhymes.
I cannot dally, caper, dance and sing,
Oiling my saint with supple sonneting.
I cannot cross my arms or sigh, 'Ay me,
Ay me, forlorn!' Egregious foppery!
I cannot buss thy hand, play with thy hair,
Swearing by Jove thou art most debonair.
Not I, by cock! But shall I tell thee roundly?
Hark in thine ear: zounds! I can —— thee soundly.

## Come drink to me and I will drink to thee

Come drink to me and I will drink to thee,
And then we shall full well agree.
I have loved the jolly tankard full seven winters and more.
I lovèd it so long, till that I went upon the score. *owing the alehouse*

He that loves not the tankard is no honest man
And he is no right soldier that loves not the can:
Tap the canikin,
Toss the canikin,
Troll the canikin,
Turn the canikin.
Hold, good son, and fill us a fresh can
That we may quaff it round about, from man to man.

## Of all reckonings I love good cheer

Of all reckonings I love good cheer
  With honest folks in company,
And when drink comes, my part for to bear,
  For still methinks one tooth is dry.

*Trudge away quickly to fill the black bowl*
  *Devoutly as long as we bide.*
*Now welcome, good fellows, both strangers and all.*
  *Let madness and mirth set sadness aside.*

Love is a pastime for a king,
  If one be seen in phys'nomy, *be good-looking*
But I love well this pot to wring,
  For still methinks one tooth is dry.
*Trudge away quickly, etc —*

Masters, this is all my desire:
  I would no drink should pass us by.
Let us now sing and mend the fire
  For still methinks one tooth is dry.
*Trudge away quickly, etc —*

Master butler, give us a taste
  Of your best drink, so gent—ly,
A jug or twain, and make no waste
  For still methinks one tooth is dry.
*Trudge away quickly, etc —*

Master butler, of this take part.
  Ye love good drink as well as I.
And drink to me with all your heart,
  For still methinks one tooth is dry.
*Trudge away quickly to fill the black bowl, &c —*

## A Letter from a Lover to his Beloved

O love whose power and might
  None ever yet withstood,
Thou forcest me to write—
  Come, turn about, Robin Hood.

Sole mistress of my rest,
  Let me thus far presume

To make this bold request:
  A black patch for the rheum.*

Your tresses finely wrought
  Like to a golden snare
My loving heart have caught
  As Moss did catch his mare. *[proverbial: caught napping*

Your eyes, two stars divine,
  Methinks renew this errand
In silent speech to mine:
  A buttock for a warrant. *[a play on kissing the Bible*

O woman, wilt thou never
  But think I still do flatter?
I vow I love you ever
  But it is no great matter.

What is't I would not do
  To purchase one sweet smile?
Bid me to China go
  And I'll sit still the while.

Grant favour, else I die.
  Love so my heart bewitches
It makes me howl and cry.
  Oh how my elbow itches!

Tears overflow my sight
  With waves of daily weeping,
And in the restless night
  I take no ease for sleeping.

Cupid is blind, men say,
  But yet methinks he seeth.
He hit mine heart today.
  A turd in Cupid's teeth!

My mistress she is fair
  But yet her late disgraces
Have made me to despair.
  A pox of all good faces!

But since my simple merits
  Her loving looks must lack,
Come, stop my vital spirits
  With claret, white and sack.

Regard my great mishap,
Jove, father of the thunder.
Send down thy thunder-clap
And rend her smock asunder.

But since that all relief
And comfort do forsake me
I'll hang myself for grief.
Nay then, the devil take me!

## Her Answer

Your letter I received,
Bedecked with flourishing quarters.
So women are deceived.
Go hang you in your garters.

I cannot choose but pity
Your restless mourning tears.
Because your plaints are witty
You may go shake your ears.

To purchase your delight
No labour shall you leese. *lose*
Your pains I will requite:
Maid, cut him bread and cheese.

'Tis you I fain would see,
'Tis you I only think on.
My looks as kind shall be
As the devil's over Lincoln.*

If ever I do turn,
Great queen of lightning-flashes,
Send down thy fire and burn
His codpiece into ashes.

I can by no means miss thee,
But I must have thee one day.
O sweetheart, come and kiss me
Where I did sit on Sunday.

******patch*: of black taffeta, stuck on the face to hide pimples or sores; soon a fashion accessory, cut into pretty shapes

**devil over Lincoln*: old catchphrase inspired by an image of the devil on the south side of Lincoln Cathedral

## Beware, fair maids, of musky courtiers' oaths

Beware, fair maids, of musky courtiers' oaths.
Take heed what gifts and favours you receive.
Let not the fading gloss of silken clothes
Dazzle your virtues or your fame bereave,
For lose but once the hold you have of grace,
Who will regard your fortune or your face?

Each greedy hand will strive to catch the flower
When none regards the stalk it grows upon.
Each nature seeks the fruit still to devour
And leave the tree to fall or stand alone,
Yet this advice, fair creatures, take of me:
Let none take fruit unless he take the tree.

Believe no oaths nor much-protesting men.
Credit no vows, nor their bewailing songs.
Let courtiers swear, forswear and swear again,
Their hearts do live ten regions from their tongues,
For when with oaths they make thy heart to tremble,
Believe them least, for then they most dissemble.

Beware lest Caesar do corrupt thy mind
And fond ambition sell thy modesty.
Say though a king thou ever virtuous find,
He cannot pardon thine impurity.
Begin with king, to subject thou wilt fall,
From lord to lackey, and at last to all.

JOSUAH SYLVESTER

Some versions have a different ending:

For if with one, with thousands thou'lt turn whore.
Break ice in one place and it cracks in more.

## Away with sickly wenches, whitely faced

Away with sickly wenches, whitely faced,
And those whose heads with amber locks are graced.
Those puling creatures are unfit for men.
They cry 'they're sick' when we have need of them.
Wouldst choose out one unto a man most true?
Choose then out one of clear deep-sanguined hue

With black-brown hair, in whose sweet face is set
Two sparkling lamps, yet black as blackest jet;
With dimpled chin, with lips pure ruby-red.
This wench with action shalt thou find in bed:
Aye, active, nimble, hah! her stirring spright
Hates sluggish sleep, loves motion all the night.
Choose such a one. I'll choose so for my part.
Such, men should love. Such love men with their heart.

WILLIAM GODDARD, *1615*

## Cedendum necessitati

*yielding to necessity*

Franciscus swears he'll be no more forsworn,
No more will swagger, surfeit or be drunk,
No more his locks will wear at length, but shorn,
No more converse or solace with his punk, *whore*
No more chaste widows, maids or wives abuse,
No more lewd songs or bawdy terms repeat,
No more tobacco midst of dinners use,
No more detract, lie, flatter, cog or cheat.
For true it is, time now hath better taught him,
Since late that scurvy Wood-street Counter caught him. *debtors' prison*

HENRY PARROT, *1615*

## On Mr Pricke, a Master of Arts in Christ's College in Cambridge*

In a Jùly moister than December
Christ's College lost a privy member.
Love and death their arrows did pick:
Love hit the clout but death hit the prick. *the target; the bulls-eye*
And lecherous earth did ope her womb
Deceasèd Pricke for to entomb.
Widows lament and maidens make their moans,
For now the Pricke is laid beneath the stones. *[as it is not in life*

*Cambridge had various Prickes; this one must have been Edmund Pricke of Christ's, who died July 1618. Some secondhand versions of this popular jest make Pricke a Christ Church man, but Oxford had no Prickes.

## Here six foot deep

Here six foot deep
In his last sleep
The Lord of Lampas lies,*
Who his end made
With his own blade
Between his mistress' thighs.

If through that hole
To heaven he stole,
I dare be bold to say
He was the last
Who that way passed
And first that found the way.

**Lampas*: probably derived from Lampsacus, seat of the worship of Priapus

## The Young Man's Careless Wooing All Done out of Old English Proverbs

I prethee, sweetheart, grant me my desire
For I am thrown, as the old proverb goes,
Out of the frying-pan into the fire
And there is none that will pity my woes.
Then hang or drown thyself, my muse,
For there is not a T—— to choose. *turd*

Most maids are false; though some seem holier,
Yet I believe they are all of a kind.
Like will to like, quoth the devil to the collier.
They will prove true when the devil is blind.
Let no man yield to their desire
For the burnt child doth dread the fire.

What though my love as white as a dove is?
Yet you would say, if you knew all within,
That shitten-cum-shites the beginning of love is,*
And for her favour I care not a pin.
    No love of mine she e'er shall be,
    Sir-reverence of your company.*

Though her disdainfulness my heart hath cloven,
Yet am I of so stately a mind
I'll ne'er creep in her arse to bake in her oven.
'Tis an old proverb that cat will to kind.
    No, I will say until I die,
    Farewell and be hanged, that's twice goodbye.

Alas, what rejoicing or comfort can I take
From her that regards not the worth of a lover?
A T— is as good for a sow as a pancake.
Swallow that gudgeon, I'll fish for another.
    She nought regards my aching heart.
    Tell a mare a tale, she'll let a fart.

But this is my counsel to all men that do woo:
Look well before you handle your gear,
For if you wink and shite you shall ne'er see what you do.
Thus one may take a wrong sow by the ear,
    And nothing gained by this assault
    But what the cat left in the malt.

I am as sure as my shoes are made of leather
Without good advice or fortunate helps
We two shall ne'er set our horses together,
She'll so rage like a bear that is robbed of her whelps.
    Therefore of me it shall ne'er be said
    I have brought an old house upon my head.

Fall back or fall edge, I never will bound be
To make a match with tag, rag or longtail.
He that's born to be hanged shall never drowned be.
Best is best cheap, if I miss not the nail.
    Shall I toil gratis in their dirt?
    First they shall do as doth my shirt. *kiss my arse*

* Proverbial piece of psychology, perhaps inspired by the sharing of privies

* *sir-reverence*: from 'saving your reverence', a phrase to excuse bluntness, coarseness, etc; and thence a euphemism for excrement

## A Riddle

It is a kind of pleasing thing,
A pricking and a piercing sting.
It is Venus' wanton wand.
It hath no legs and yet can stand.
A bachelor's button thoroughly ripe,
The kindest new tobacco-pipe.
It is the pen that Helen took
To write in her two-leavèd book.
It's a prick-shaft of Cupid's cut,
Yet some do shoot it at a butt.
And every wench by her good will
Would keep it in her quiver still.
The fairest yet that e'er had life
For love of this became a wife.

## Will Bagnall's Ballad

A ballad, a ballad, let every poet
　　A ballad make with speed,
And he that hath wit, now let him show it
　　For never was greater need.
And I that never made ballad before
Will make one now, though I never make more.
　　*O women, monstrous women!*
　　*What do you mean to do?*

. . . . . .

Where is the decency become
　　That your fore-mothers had?
In gowns of cloth and caps of thrum
　　They went full meanly clad.
But you must jet it in silks and gold.
Your pride, though in winter, is never a-cold.
　　*O women, etc —*

Your faces tricked and painted be,
　　Your breasts all open bare
So far that a man may almost see
　　Unto your lady-ware.
And in the church, to tell you true,
Men cannot serve God for looking at you,
　　*O women, etc —*

And many there are of those that go
    Attired from head to heel
That them from men you cannot know,
    Unless you do them feel.
But oh, for shame! (though they have none)
'Tis better to believe, and let them alone.
    *O women, etc —*

Both round and short they cut their hair,
    Whose length should women grace.
Loose like themselves their hats they wear,
    And when they come in place
Where courtship and compliments must be
They do it like men, with cap and knee. *instead of curtseying*
    *O women, etc —*

They at their sides, against our laws,
    With little poignards go,
Which surely is, I think, because
    They love men's weapons so.
Or else it is, they'll stab all men
That do refuse to stab them again.
    *O women, etc —*

Doublets like to men they wear
    As if they meant to flout us,
Trussed round with points and ribbons fair.
    But I pray, let's look about us,
For since the doublet so well doth fit 'um
They'll have the breeches if they can get 'um.
    *O women, etc —*

. . . . . . .

And women all, whom this concerns,
    Though you offended be
And now in foul and railing terms
    Do swagger and scold at me:
I'll tell you, if you mend not your ways
The devil will fetch you all one of these days.
    *O women, monstrous women!*
    *What do you mean to do?*

See also page 212; and endnote for more on these assertive women of 1620

## 'Tis late and cold, stir up the fire

'Tis late and cold, stir up the fire;
Sit close and draw the table nigher.
Be merry and drink wine that's old,
A hearty medicine 'gainst a cold.
Your beds of wanton down the best,
Where you may tumble to your rest.
I could wish you wenches too
But I am old and cannot do.

Call for the best, the house may ring.
Sack, white and claret let them bring.
Drink apace while breath you have.
You'll find but cold drink in the grave.
Plover, partridge for your dinner,
And a capon for the sinner
You shall find ready when you are up,
And your horse shall have his sup.
    Welcome, welcome shall fly round,
    And I shall smile, though under ground.

JOHN FLETCHER, *1623*

Sung by an innkeeper's ghost — the most genial ghost of Jacobean drama

## The Way to woo a Zealous Lady

I came unto a Puritan to woo
And roughly did salute her with a kiss.
She shoved me from her when I came unto:
'Brother, by yea and nay, I like not this.'
And as I her with amorous talk saluted,
My articles with Scripture she confuted.

She told me that I was too much profane
And not devout neither in speech nor gesture,
And I could not one word answer again
Nor had not so much grace to call her Sister,
For ever something did offend her there:
Either my broad beard, hat, or my long hair.

My band was broad, my 'parel was not plain, *lacy collar*
My points and girdle made the greatest show; *ribbons*

My sword was odious, and my belt was vain,
My Spanish shoes were cut too broad at toe;
My stockings light, my garters tied too long,
My gloves perfumed and had a scent too strong.

I left my pure mistress for a space
And to a snip-snap barber straight went I.
I cut my hair, and did my corps uncase
Of 'parel's pride that did offend the eye.
My high-crowned hat, my little beard also,*
My pecked band, my shoes were sharp at toe.

Gone was my sword, my belt was laid aside,
And I transformèd both in looks and speech.
My 'parel plain, my cloak was void of pride.
My little skirts, my metamorphosed breech!
My stockings black! My garters were tied shorter.
My gloves, no scent. Thus marched I to her porter.

The porter spied me and did lead me in,
Where his sweet mistress reading was a chapter.
'Peace to this house, and all that are herein,'
Which holy words with admiration rapt her,
And ever, as I came her something nigh,
She, being divine, turned up the white o' th'eye.*

Quoth I, 'Dear Sister,' and that liked her well.
I kissed her and did pass to some delight.
She, blushing, said that long-tailed men would tell.
Quoth I, 'I'll be as silent as the night,
And lest the wicked now should have a sight
Of what we do, faith, I'll put out the light.'

'O do not swear,' quoth she, 'but put it out,
Because that I would have you save your oath.
In troth, you shall but kiss me, without doubt.'
'In troth,' quoth I, 'here will we rest us both.'
'Swear you,' quoth she, 'in troth? Had you not sworn,
I'd not have done't, but took it in foul scorn.'

A fine commentary on the potency of 'correct' language, clothes and hair

* His new, Puritan look begins at 'My high-crowned hat'

* *white o' th'eye*: as in religious or in sexual ecstasy

## A Bacchanal Song in a Masque before Their Majesties, 1636

*Bacchus, Iacchus, fill our brains* *
*As well as bowls with sprightly strains.*

Let soldiers fight for pay or praise
And money be the miser's wish;
Poor scholars study all their days
And gluttons glory in the dish.
'Tis wine, pure wine revives sad souls.
Therefore give us the cheer in bowls.

Let minions marshal every hair
Or in a lover's lock delight,
And artificial colours wear:
We have the native red and white.
*'Tis wine, etc —*

Take pheasant poules or calvered salmon,*
Or how to please your palates think.
Give us a salt Westphalia gammon —
Not meat to eat, but meat to drink. *to make one drink*
*'Tis wine, etc —*

Some have the tisick, some the rheum, *phthisic (tuberculosis)*
Some have the palsy, some the gout;
Some swell with fat and some consume,
But they are sound that drink all out.
*'Tis wine, etc —*

The backward spirit it makes brave;
That lively which before was dull.
Those grow good fellows that were grave
And kindness flows from cups brimfull.
*'Tis wine, etc—*

Some men want youth and some want health,
Some want a wife and some a punk. *a whore*
Some men want wit and some want wealth,
But he wants nothing that is drunk.
'Tis wine, pure wine revives sad souls.
Therefore give us the cheer in bowls.

*Bacchus, Iacchus, fill our brains*
*As well as bowls with sprightly strains.*

AURELIAN TOWNSHEND

* *Iacchus:* solemn name for Bacchus

* *pheasant poules:* young pheasants; *calvered salmon:* one old recipe says to cook it in vinegar with oil and spices

## Hang sorrow and cast away care

Hang sorrow and cast away care
And let us drink up our sack.
They say 'tis good to cherish the blood
And for to strengthen the back. *for making love*

'Tis wine that makes the thoughts aspire
And fills the body with heat.
Besides 'tis good if well understood
To fit a man for the feat.

Then call and drink up all.
The drawer is ready to fill.
A pox of care! What need we to spare?
My father hath made his will.

## The pot, the pipe, the quart, the can

The pot, the pipe, the quart, the can
Hath spoilèd many an honest man.
The hare and horn, the hawk and whore
Hath quite undone as many more.

# If any so wise is

If any so wise is
That sack he despises
Let him drink his small-beer and be sober.
Whilst we drink and sing
As if it were spring,
He shall drop like the trees in October.

But be sure overnight
If this dog do you bite
You take it henceforth for a warning:
Soon as out of your bed,
To settle your head
Take a hair of his tail in the morning.*

And be not so silly
As to follow old Lilly,*
For there's nothing but sack that can tune us.
Let his *ne assuescas*
Be put in his cap-case, *portmanteau*
And sing *bi-bi-to vi-num jejunus.* *'Drink wine if you're hungry'*

*The 'hair of the dog' notion goes back a long way. John Heywood in his versified proverbs, 1546, has this:

I pray thee, let me and my fellow have
A hair of the dog that bit us last night.
And bitten were we both to the brain aright.
We saw each other drunk in the good ale-glass.

*William Lilly, author of the then prevailing Latin grammar, which evidently contained a moral sentence with *ne assuescas* (Don't make a habit of it)

# A pox on the jailer

A pox on the jailer and on his fat jowls.
There's liberty lies in the bottom of bowls.
A fig for the rascal whate'er he can do.
His dungeons are deep: so are our cups too.
Then drink we a health in despite of our foes
And make our cold irons cry clink in the close.

Originally a song in William Cartwright's *The Royal Slave*, 1636; published in this smoother form in 1652 (and no doubt sung by imprisoned Cavaliers)

## Have you observed the wench in the street?

Have you observed the wench in the street?
She's scarce any hose or shoes to her feet,
Yet she is very merry, and when she cries she sings,
I ha' hot codlings, hot codlings! *baked apples*

Or have you ever seen or heard
The mortal with the lion-tawny beard?
He lives as merrily as any heart can wish
And still he cries, Buy a brish, buy a brish! *brush*

Since these are merry, why should we take care?
Musicians, like chameleons, must live by the air.
Then let's be blithe and bonny, and no good meeting baulk,
For when we have no money we shall find chalk. *for tavern credit*

## Wilt thou be fat? I'll tell thee how

Wilt thou be fat? I'll tell thee how
　　Thou shalt quickly do the feat,
And that so plump a thing as thou
　　Was never yet made up of meat.
Drink off thy sack! 'Twas only that
Made Bacchus and Jack Falstaff fat.

## She lay all naked in her bed

She lay all naked in her bed
　　And I myself lay by;
No veil but curtains round her spread,
　　No covering but I.

Her head upon one shoulder seeks
  To lean in careless wise.
All full of blushes were her cheeks,
  Of wishes were her eyes.

The blood still flushing in her face *still = constantly*
  As on a message came
To show that in another place
  It meant another game.

Her cherry lips, soft, sweet and fair
  Millions of kisses crown,
Which ripe and uncropped dangle there
  And weigh the branches down.

Her breast that swelled so plump and high
  Bred pleasant pain in me,
That all the world I would defy
  For that felicity.

Her thighs and belly soft and neat
  To me were only shown.
To have seen such meat and not have eat
  Would have angered any stone.

Her knees lay up and gently bent
  And all was hollow under,
As if on easy terms they meant
  To fall unforced asunder.

Just so the Cyprian dame did lie *Venus*
  Expecting in her bower
When too long sport had kept the boy *Adonis*
  Beyond his promised hour.

'Dull clown,' said she, 'that dost delay
  This proffered bliss to take!
Canst thou not find a sweeter way
  Similitudes to make?'

Mad with delight I thundered in
  And threw my arms about her.
But pox upon't! I waked agin
  And there I lay without her.

## Yes, I could love, could I but find

Yes, I could love, could I but find
A mistress fitting to my mind:
Whom neither pride nor gold could move
To buy her beauty, sell her love;
Were neat, yet cared not to be fine
And loved me for myself, not mine;
Not lady proud nor city coy
But full of freedom, full of joy;
Not wise enough to rule a state
Nor fool enough to be laughed at;
Not childish young nor beldam old;
Not fiery hot nor icy cold;
Not richly proud nor basely poor;
Not chaste, yet no reputed whore.
    If such a one I chance to find
    I have a mistress to my mind.

## On a Justice

A justice walking o'er the frozen Thames,
The ice about him round began to crack.
He said to's man, 'Here is some danger, James.
I pray thee, help me over on thy back.'

## A Lady to a Young Courtier

Love thee! Good faith, not I.
I've something else to do.
Alas, you must go learn to talk
Before you learn to woo.
Nay fie, stand off, go to, go to!

Because y'are in the fashion
And newly come to court
D'ye think your clothes are orators
T'invite us to the sport?
Ha ha, who will not jeer thee for't!

Ne'er look so sweetly, youth,
Nor fiddle with your band. *large lacy collar*
We know you trim your borrowed locks *wig*

To show your pretty hand,
But 'tis too young for to command.

And why so confident
Because that lately we
Have bought another lofty word
Into our pedigree? *[he has paid Charles I for a title*
Your inside seems the worse to me.

Go practise how to jeer
And think each word a jest.
That's the court wit. Alas, y'are out
To think when finely dressed
You please me or the ladies best.

Mark how Sir Whacham fools:
Ay, marry! there's a wit
That cares not what he says or swears
So ladies laugh at it.
Who can deny such blades a bit?

DR HENRY HUGHES

## Anger Soon Appeased

When John Cornutus doth his wife reprove
For being false and faithless in her love,
His wife to smooth those wrinkles on his brow
Doth stop his mouth with 'John come kiss me now.' *[old song*

## Merry Doll

I blame not lusty Doll that strives so much
To keep her light heart free from sorrow's touch.
She'll dance and sing, 'Ahem, boys, hey all six!' *
She's steel to the back, all mirth, all meretrix.

*Perhaps an enticing call in a dance; meretrix seems a harsh word for her

## On Isabella, a Courtesan

He who would write an epitaph
Whereby to make fair Is'bell laugh
Must get upon her and write well,
Here underneath lies Isabell.

## On an Arrant Whore

She was so exquisite a whore
That in the belly of her mother
She turned her —— so right before
Her father ——— them both together,
And lest her sire should not thrust home
She frigged her father in her mother's womb.

## The Oxford Scholar

As I was riding on a day
One chanced to ask me by the way
How Oxford scholars passed their time,
And thus I answered all in rhyme:

When first from our beloved home
We to the town of Oxford come
The first thing is to buy a gown;
The next, the best sack in the town.

And then a tutor we must have,
And ten to one he'll be a knave
Who ne'er looks after's all the day,
So that at night we come to pray.

This fellow sends unto our friends
For money for his private ends
And locks it up all in his trunk
While we must upon tick be drunk.

We never ask him for a groat
But wish 'twere all stuck in his throat;
Till at the quarter-day there comes
The dunners with their bouncing sums.

Imprimis, for an Aristotle —
Which we perhaps pawned for a pottle;
And Euclid — which away did pack
For the better element of sack.

Item, for Vasquez' Rhetoric
And Borgias for the selfsame trick —
Which, wanting coin, for ale we gave 'em,
When all their rhetoric could not save 'em.

Item, for Homer — poor blind poet
(O that our tutors did but know it!)
For old tobacco we make flee,
Till smoke makes us as blind as he.

And then sometimes we kiss a lass,
But th' honest proctors let that pass
Till after twelve o'clock at night.
'Tis ten to one too they are right.

But then our tutor gravely speaks:
I wonder you will do these freaks,
But unless you do your lives amend
You never will come to good end.

And thus we pass our time away;
Evening and morning duly pray,
While the costive chaplain for his sense
Strains as for a sir-reverence.*

Then hang all studying to no end.
At length the spirit will pretend.
Then let us sit and drink our fill.
We can be preachers when we will.*

* As if straining to move his bowels

* Anglican church livings were only for Oxford or Cambridge graduates

# An Encomium

I sing the praises of a fart.
That I may do't by rules of art
I will invoke no deity,
But buttered peas and furmity, *frumenty*
And think their help sufficient
To fit and furnish my intent.
For sure I must not use high strains
For fear it bluster out in grains.
When Virgil's gnat and Ovid's flea
And Homer's frogs strive for the day*
There is no reason in my mind
That a brave fart should come behind,
Since that you may it parallel
With any thing that doth excel.
    Music is but a fart that's sent
From the guts of an instrument.
The scholar but farts when he gains
Learning with cracking of his brains,
And when he has spent much pain and oil
Thomas and Dun to reconcile *Aquinas; Duns Scotus*
And to learn the abstracting art,
What does he get by't? Not a fart.
The soldier makes his foes to run
With but the farting of a gun;
That's if he make the bullet whistle,
Else it's no better than a fizzle.
And if withal the winds do stir up
Rain, 'tis but a fart in syrup.
They are but farts, the words we say:
Words are but wind, and so are they.
Applause is but a fart, the crude
Blast of the fickle multitude.
Fine boats that ply the Thames about
Be but the farts several docks let out.
Some of our projects were, I think,
But politic farts: foh, how they stink!
As soon as born, they by-and-by
Fart-like but only breathe and die.
Farts are as good as land, for both
We hold in tail, and let them both;
Only the difference here is that

Farts are let at a lower rate.
I'll say no more, for this is right:
That for my guts I cannot write
(Though I should study all my days)
Rimes that are worth the thing I praise.
What I have said, take in good part.
If not, I do not care a fart.

*Virgil wrote a poem on a gnat, *Culex;* Homer is credited with the battle of the frogs and mice, *Batrachomyomachia*; where is Ovid's flea?

## A Song on a Tenement

If any man doth want a house,
Be he prince, baronet or squire
Or peasant (hardly worth a louse)
I can fit his desire.
I have a tenement, the which
I know will fit them all.
'Tis seated near a stinking ditch.
They call it Cunny-hall.

It doth lie beyond bonny ground
At the foot of Belly-hill.
This house is easy to be found
By whosoever will.
For term of life, or years, or days
I'll let this pleasant bower.
Nay, rather than a tenant want
I'll let it for an hour.

About it grows a lofty wood
To shade you from the sun.
Well watered 'tis, for through it
A pleasant stream doth run.
If hot, you there may cool yourself;
If cold, you'll there find heat.

For greatest, 'tis not too little;
For least, 'tis not too great.

My house, I must confess 'tis dark
Be it by night or day,
But if you once be got therein
You cannot miss your way.
And when you're in, make boldly on
As fast as e'er you can,
But if you come to the end thereof
You come where ne'er did man.

But I must covenant with him
That takes this house of mine,
Either for years or else for months
Or for some shorter time,
That once a day he wash it
And sweep it round about,
And if that he do fail of this
I'll seek a new tenant out.

## On One that Laughed at Him in Church

What though I were not pewed, but stood in yoke*
Below there with the three-pound-and-a-cloak
Squire of your person and the quick-tongued crew
Of those that cry 'What do you lack?' — must you
Needs laugh at me? Was't not enough that I,
Bathed in the fair sweat of humility,
Would so have washed away my sin? But you,
Scorning my meeker station, must pursue
My publican-like sorrows with disdain,
Proud Pharisee! as if you hoped t'attain
Heaven by your laughter. Yet my votes will pay *prayers*
Your evil back with good, and thus I pray:
May she some face within this temple see
Which she beside her own may think to be
Stuck full of beauties (though not so, but like
To hers indeed); which, once seen, may it strike
Hot love into her, and when she courts it, pass
Like her own kissed shadow from her glass.
May that bright virgin which doth now sit nigh her,
When she comes near choose ever to sit by her

That we may see her highlight colour tends
To dimness when this sparkling light ascends.
May every spring of virtue in her fade.
That ambling piece of diligence, her maid,
May she betray her secrets. And may I,
Because I thought her once fair, ere I die
Dictate false English in a verse. And dead,
May she without a text be burièd,
To keep me company; or an epitaph*
If Wither make it not. But stay, she'll laugh
If I myself so dread a sentence give.*
May she a longing widow ever live;
But if she'll marry, be't one that no more
Can than the last could that she had before.

*The gentry sit in the privacy of pews, for which they pay. The poet stood at the back, with such low people as pedlars and the lady's (ill-paid) footman, to atone for his 'sin'. Was it that he dared to woo her or even tried to seduce her?

*'May she die so poor that there is no money for a funeral sermon or a gravestone epitaph – as I shall die'

*This might be taken to mean that he is the poet George Wither; but at that date Wither had been made a byword for inept verse, so the sense seems to be, 'Or if she does have an epitaph, let Wither make it'

## To be a whore, despite of grace

To be a whore, despite of grace,
Good counsel and an ugly face,
And to distribute still the pox
To men of wit
Will seem a kind of paradox;
And yet
Thou art a whore, despite of grace,
Good counsel and an ugly face.

CHARLES COTTON

## An Epitaph on a Whore

In this cold monument lies one
Which I know who has lain upon
(The happier he); whose sight might charm
And touch might keep King David warm.

Lovely as is the dawning east
Was this marble's frozen guest;
As glorious and as bright as day,
As odoriferous as May,
As straight and slender as the crest
Or antler of the one-beamed beast; *unicorn*
Whom I admired as soon as knew,
And now her memory pursue
With such a superstitious lust
That I could fumble with her dust.
She all perfections had, and more;
Tempting, as if designed a whore,
For so she was, and some there are
Whores, I could wish them all as fair.
Courteous she was, and young, and wise,
And in her calling so precise
That industry had made her prove
The sucking schoolmistress of love.
But death, ambitious to become
Her pupil, left his ghastly home
And seeing how we used her here,
The rawbone rascal ravished her;
Who, pretty soul, resigned her breath
To practise lechery with death.

CHARLES COTTON

## Dr Smith's Ballad

Will women's vanities never have end?
Alack, what is the matter?
Shall poets all their spirits spend
And women yet never the better?
Will Bagnall's ballad hath done no good *[see page 195*
To the head that is hid in the taffety hood,
Which makes the virtuous chew the cud
And I till now their debtor.

I once resolvèd to be blind
And ne'er put pen to sheet.
Though all the race of womankind
Were mad, I would not see't.
But now my heart's so big it struts

And hold I cannot for my guts.
With as much ease as men crack nuts
My rhymes and numbers meet.

And first I will begin to touch
Upon their daubing paint.
Their pride that way it is so much
It makes my muse grow faint.,
And when they are got into a new suit
They look as though they would straight go to't. *make love*
The devil's in't and's dam to boot.
'Twould anger any saint.

Their soaring thoughts to books advance.
'Tis odds it may undo 'um,
For ever since Dame Eve's mischance
That villainous itch sticks to 'um, *desire for knowledge*
And when they have got a little smack
They talk as if nothing they did lack
Of Wither, Drayton or Balzac —*
'Twould weary a man to woo 'um.

Their faces are besmeared and pieced
With several sorts of patches,
As if some cats their skins had fleeced
With stars, half-moons and notches. *fashionable face patches*
Prodigious signs there keep their stations
And meteors of most dreadful fashions.
Booker hath no such prognostications. *John Booker, astrologer*
Now out upon those wretches!

With these they are disfigured so
They look as untoward as elves.
Their husbands scarce their wives can know
Nor they sometimes themselves.
And every morning they feed their chops
With caudles, broths and honey-sops
And lap it up as thick as hops —
Ne'er think of him that delves.

. . . . .

Sometimes they in the water lurk
Like fish with silver fins,
And then I wish I were the Turk
And these my concubines.

But to tell you the truth without any erring,
They are neither fish, flesh nor good red herring,
And whensoe'er you find them stirring
They will put you in mind of your sins...

DR JAMES SMITH

* George Wither, Michael Drayton and the French writer Guez de Balzac

## When I see the young men play

When I see the young men play,
Young methinks I am as they,
And my aged thoughts laid by,
To the dance with joy I fly.
Come, a flowery chaplet lend me.
Youth and mirthful thoughts attend me.

Age begone! We'll dance among
Those that young are, and be young.
Bring some wine, boy! Fill about!
You shall see the old man's stout
Who can laugh and tipple too
And be mad as well as you.

## A Catch

A boat, a boat, bring to the ferry,
For we come over to be merry,
To laugh and sing and drink old sherry,
For this is life as soldiers lead,
To laugh, to drink and to roar,
For every wench maintains her blade
And every blade his whore.

## On the Praise of Fat Men

*[Extracts from a panegyric of nearly 500 lines]*

But now for rules before we eat
And how to choose right battening meat.
For spoon-meat, barley-broth and jelly
Very good is for the belly.
For morning's draught, your Northdown ale

Will make you oily as a whale.
But he that will not out-flesh wit
Must at the good canary sit,
For 'tis a saying very fine,
Give me the fat man's wit in wine,
For he's as merry as weanling pig
That to the hog's-trough dances jig.
  Your beef, your pork, your veal, your mutton
(So it be good as knife e'er cut on),
Your pigs, your capons, turkeys, coneys
Your feeding wight thinks worth his moneys.
But he whose longing's to grow thicker
Must mingle with good meat, good liquor.
Your brawn washed down with muscadine
Will make your cheeks look plump and fine.
If you would have a double chin
Drink no small beer, for that's too thin;
For he that means to feed his chops high
Apt is to fall into a dropsy.
Therefore your high, rich wines are fit
T'augment the flesh and help the wit.
'Twill make the buttocks firm as brawn
And skin as pure white as lawn.
Turn haunches up with lady fine
And thy fat arse shall hers outshine.

. . . . .

Fat man and wife together went
To cleanse each other's fundament,
For so well-grown was either belly
They could not do't themselves, I tell ye.
This I dare boldly say, sans sinning,
Shitten-cum-shites is love beginning. *[proverbial: see p194*
This further know: fat folks do scummer
As much as cows do give in summer,
And that must be a fruitful tail
That at one dunging fills a pail.
  Nor is't amiss that I recite
The parley that they did use at shite
(Kind words are worth a world of money):
*Qu.* Dost thou piss, love?
                *Ans.* No, I shite, honey.
Such questions would the good man ask
When wife was troubled with the lask, *diarrhoea*

For she when laskish shit so thin
It might have served to shave a chin.
Something is needful to be said
Of love they used to show in bed.
Large paunches did so shorten arm,
Own privy members could not warm,
But commonly like loving friends
Their sausage-plumpèd fingers' ends
In winter morning you might catch —
Her hand on cod, he fingering notch.
Thus they do keep their fingers warm,
Doing to neither any harm...

## A Relation of a Quaker that to the Shame of his Profession Attempted to Bugger a Mare near Colchester

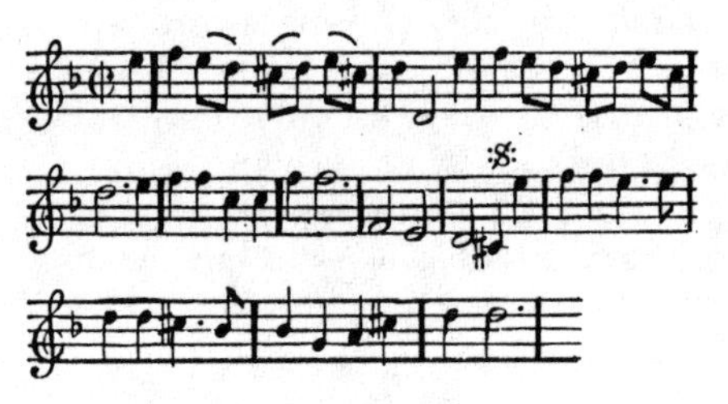

All in the land of Essex
Near Colchester the zealous,
On the side of a bank
Was played such a prank
As would make a stone-horse jealous. *stallion*

*Help, Woodcock, Fox and Naylor,**
*For Brother Green's a stallion.* [he was one Ralph Green
*Now alas! what hope*
*Of converting the Pope*
*When a Quaker turns Italian?* *

Unto our whole profession
A scandal 'twill be counted
When 'tis talked with disdain
Amongst the profane
How Brother Green was mounted.

And in the good time of Christmas,
Which though our Saints have damned all,*
  Yet when did they hear
  That a damned Cavalier
E'er played such a Christmas gambol?

Had thy flesh, O Green, been pampered
With any cates unhallowed? *fancy food (delicates)*
  Hadst thou sweetened thy gums
  With pottage of plums?
Or profane minced-pie hadst swallowed?

Rolled up in wanton swine's flesh
The fiend might have crept unto thee.
  Then fullness of gut
  Might have caused thee to rut,
And the devil have so rid through thee.

But alas! he had been feasted
With a spiritual collation
  By our frugal mayor,
  Who can dine with a prayer
And sup with an exhortation.

'Twas mere impulse of spirit,
Though he used the weapon carnal.
  'Filly foal,' quoth he,
  'My bride thou shalt be:
Now how this is lawful, learn all.

'For if no respect of persons
Be due 'mongst the sons of Adam,
  In a large extent
  Then may it be meant
That a mare's as good as a madam.'

Then without more ceremony
Nor bonnet veiled, he kissed her.
  He took her by force
  For better, for worse,
And used her like a Sister. *a Puritan woman*

Now when in such a saddle
A Saint will needs be riding,
  Though I dare not say
  'Tis a falling away,
May there not be some backsliding?

'No, surely,' quoth James Naylor,
' 'Twas but an insurrection
Of the carnal part,
For a Quaker in heart
Can never lose perfection.

'For so our masters teach us:*
The intent being well directed,
Though the devil trapan
The adamical man
The Saint stands uninfected.'

But alas! a pagan jury
Ne'er judges what's intended.
Then say what we can,
Brother Green's outward man
I fear will be suspended. *hanged*

And our Adopted Sister
Will find no better quarter;
But when him we enrol
For a Saint, filly foal
Shall pass at least for a martyr.

Now Rome, that spiritual Sodom,
No longer is thy debtor:
O Colchester, now
Who's Sodom but thou?
Even according to the letter.

*Help, Woodcock, Fox and Naylor,*
*For Brother Green's a stallion.*
*Now alas! what hope*
*Of converting the Pope*
*When a Quaker turns Italian?*

SIR JOHN DENHAM, *1653*

*Francis Woodcock of the Assembly of Divines; George Fox, founder of the Quakers; James Naylor, Quaker activist

**Italian*: a nation often vilified by the English as being fond of unnatural acts

**Christmas*: in 1644 parliament decreed that 'monthly fasts should be continued, especially on Christmas... instead of a sensual feast'

**masters*: Denham supplies a sidenote, 'the Jesuits' (some Puritan reasoning was indeed jesuitical)

## On a Little Dog Presented to a Lady

This dog may kiss your hand, your lip,
Lie in your lap and with you sleep,
On the same pillow rest his head,
Be your companion in your bed.

Now he that gave it doth not crave
Any reward of what he gave;
But he would think himself more blest
If you'd but use him as a beast.

## A Pastoral Song

A silly poor shepherd
    Was folding his sheep.
He walkèd so long
    He got cold in his feet.
He laid on his coals
    By two and by three
But the more he laid on
    The cuc-colder was he.

Alas, good wife,
    What shall we do now?
To buy us more fuel
    We'll sell the brown cow,
To buy us more coal
    To warm thee and me.
But the more he laid on
    The cuc-colder was he.

Some shepherds, quoth she,
    Themselves warm can keep
By feeding their flocks
    And folding their sheep,
But when you come home
    With your tar-box and crook
Oh it grieves me to see
    How cuc-cold you do look!

Alas, wife, I walk
    Through dew, dirt and mire

While you perhaps warm
    Yourself without fire
With a friend in a corner
    In such sort as whereby
The warmer you are
    The cuc-colder am I.

## Sensual Delight

Are you grown so melancholy
That you think of naught but folly?
  Are you sad, are you mad, are you worse?
  Do you think want of chink is your curse? *cash*
    Do you love for to have
    Longer life, or a grave?
    Then this will cure you.

First I would have a bag of gold
That should ten thousand pieces hold,
  And all that in your lap would I pour
  For to spend on your friend or your whore,
    For to play away at dice
    Or to shift you from your lice,
    And this will cure you.

Next I would have a soft bed made
Wherein a virgin should be laid
  That will play any way you devise,
  That will stick like an itch to your thighs,
    That will bill like a dove,
    Lie beneath or above,
    And this will cure you.

Next the bowl that Jove divine
Drunk nectar in, filled up with wine,
    And all that, like a Greek, you should quaff
    Till your cheeks they look red, and you laugh
        Unto Ceres and to Venus,
        Unto Bacchus and Silenus,
        And this will cure you.

Next seven eunuchs should appear
Singing in sphere-like manner here *like 'music of the spheres'*
    In the praise of the ways of delight
    Venus can use with man in the night
        When she seemeth to adorn
        Vulcan's head with a horn, *cuckolding him*
        And this will cure you.

But if no gold nor women can,
Nor wine nor song make merry, man,
    Let the bat be your mate and the owl, *[bat/mate rhyme*
    Let the pain in the brain make you howl,
        Let the pox be your friend
        And the plague be your end,
        And this will cure you.

## The Cleanly Slut

It was my chance to pass by
    Where a sackful of puddings hung to sell. *[black puddings*
In truth it was at the sign of the Pie
    And where a cleanly slut doth dwell.

I entered in to spend an old groat.
    The house was clean —you know what I mean?
The cat was locked in the cupboard fast,
    The dogs were licking the dishes clean.

The cow was tied in the chimney's end
    And she was fed as fat as a rake.
The sheep was folded up in a pen
    And for want of meat began to quake. *meat = food*

The hens got into the garden at noon,
    The bees got up and was ready to swarm.
The thrashers they fell fast asleep
    And then the geese got into the barn. *[to eat the grain*

This put me into a mighty fright.
    Then I looked in at the parlour door.
The sow had pigged in the bed at night.
    I never saw such a sight before.

The good wife she lay fast asleep,
    Snorting and farting like a great sow.
Her daughter she full sadly did weep:
    She was got with child and she knew not how.

The good man he lay under the table,
And for to stand he was not able.
The brewer's dog had bit him so sore*
He could do nothing else but shite and roar.

All things in the house were basely broke
    And nothing in the right place was set,
And still for drink I was like to choke
    But the devil a drop that I could get,

Which when I perceived away came I,
    Both weary and wet, and wondrous dry.
But if I live a hundred years longer
    I'll never come at the sign of the Pie.

* *dog*: as in 'a hair of the dog that bit me last night'

## A Contest Between the Court and Country

You courtiers scorn us country clowns, *bumpkins*
    We country clowns do scorn the court.
We can be as merry upon the downs
    As you are at midnight, with all your sport,
        *With a fadding.**

You hawk, you hunt, you lie upon pallets,
    You eat and drink the Lord knows how.
We sit upon hillocks and pick up our sallets
    And sup upon sillabubs under a cow,*
        *With a fadding.*

Your masques are made of knights and lords
    And ladies that are fresh and gay.
We dance with such music as bagpipes affords
    And trick up our lasses as well as we may,
        *With a fadding.*

Your suits are made of silk and satin
And ours are made of good sheep's gray.
You mix your discourses with pieces of Latin,
We speak our old English as well as we may,
*With a fadding.*

Your rooms are hung with cloth of Arras,
Our meadows are decked as well as may be;
And from this pastime you never shall bar us,
Since Joan in the dark is as good as my lady,
*With a fadding.*

**fadding*: as in Autolycus's sardonic/suggestive phrase in *The Winter's Tale*, 'delicate burdens of dildos and fadings' (pronounced faddings)

*Milk straight from the cow, instead of cream whipped with sugar and wine

## I Went to the Tavern

I went to the tavern, and then,
I went to the tavern, and then,
I had good store of wine
And my cap full of coin,
*And the world went well with me then, then,*
*And the world went well with me then.*

I went to the tavern again,
Where I ran on the score
And was turned out o' th' door,
*And the world went ill with me then, then, &c –*

When I was a bachelor then
I'd a saddle and horse
And I took my own course,
*And the world went well with me then, then, &c –*

But when I was married, O then
My horse and my saddle
Were turned to a cradle
*And the world went ill with me then, then, &c –*

When I brought her home money, then
She never would pout
But clip me about, *hug me*
*And the world went well with me then, then, &c –*

But when I was drunk, O then
She'd kick, she'd fling

Till she made the house ring,
*And the world went ill with me then, then, &c –*

So I turned her away, and then
I got me a miss
To clip and to kiss
*And the world went well with me then, then, &c –*

But the 'paritor came, and then *apparitor: church officer*
I was called to the court,
Where I paid for my sport,
*And the world went ill with me then, then, &c –*

I took my wife home again,
But I changed her note,
For I cut her throat
*And the world went well with me then, then, &c –*

But when it was known, O then
In a two-wheeled charet *cart*
To Tyburn I was carried,
*And the world went ill with me then, then, &c –*

But when I came there, O then
They forced me to swing
To heaven in a string,
*And the world went well with me then, then,*
*And the world went well with me then.*

## The Beneficial Wedding

And I have a mind to be married,
And so has you know who.
We both too long have tarried,
And therefore I mean to woo.
Then I did give her a buss
And she gave me a ring,
And so we bussed and kissed and bussed
And kissed like anything.

Her grandsire gave her a cow
And her grannam a ewe and lamb.
She said she'd suckle it too
Until it had left the dam.
Her uncle gave her a hog,
Her aunt a teeming sow

For bacon and souse to keep the house *pickled meat*
And make 'em puddings enow.

Her father gave her a gown,
Her mother a petticoat
Which was of a mingled brown,
The best that could be bought.
Her brother gave her a cock
And her sister a breeding hen
To tread and breed, and breed and tread,
And tread and breed again.

Her cousin took a care
To give her a rug was new;
His wife did give her a pair
Of sheets and blankets too.
But she had a special friend
That was a young upholster
(You must not know the reason now),
Did give her a bed and bolster.

A friend did give her a waistcoat
And hose and shoes and hat.
Another did give her a laced coat,
But 'tis no matter for that.
So long as 'tis our own,
No matter how it come.
They keep her fine, and give her wine,
But no more of that but 'mum'.

Another did take her a house
And paid a twelvemonth rent,
And furnished me and my spouse
With what at the wedding was spent.
Then we desired to know
What trade we both should drive.
They said good ale would never fail
If ever we meant to thrive.

We both are fitted now, I think,
With store of household stuff
And likewise clothes, meat and drink
As much as is enough.
But if we chance to want
My wife has store of friends,
Which I connive at, because they're private,
And so our wedding ends.

*1672*

# The Town Gallant

Let us drink and be merry, dance, joke and rejoice
With claret and sherry, theorbo and voice. *a large lute*
The changeable world to our joy is unjust.
All treasure's uncertain, then down with your dust: *money*
In frolics dispose your pounds, shillings and pence
For we shall be nothing a hundred years hence.

We'll kiss and be free with Moll, Betty and Nelly;
Have oysters and lobsters and maids by the belly.*
Fish dinners will make a lass spring like a flea:
Dame Venus (love's goddess) was born of the sea.
With Bacchùs and with her we'll tickle the sense
For we shall be past it a hundred years hence.

Your most beautiful bit, that hath all eyes upon her,
That her honesty sells for a hogo of honour,*
Whose lightness and brightness doth shine in such splendour
That none but the stars are thought fit to attend her,
Though now she be pleasant and sweet to the sense,
Will be damnably mouldy a hundred years hence.

The usurer that in the hundred takes twenty,
Who wants in his wealth and pines in his plenty,
Lays up for a season which he shall ne'er see,

The year of one thousand eight hundred and three.
His wit and his wealth, his law, learning and sense
Shall be turned to nothing a hundred years hence.

Your chancery lawyer who by subtlety thrives
In spinning out suits to the length of three lives,
Such suits which the clients do wear out in slavery
Whilst the pleader makes conscience a cloak for his knavery,
May boast of his subtlety in th' present tense
But *non est inventus* a hundred years hence. *he'll devise nothing*

Then why should we turmoil in cares and in fears,
Turn all our tranquillity to sighs and to tears?
Let's eat, drink and play till the worms do corrupt us.
'Tis certain that *post mortem nulla voluptas.* *no pleasure after death*
Let's deal with our damsels that we may from thence
Have broods to succeed us a hundred years hence.

THOMAS JORDAN, *1675*

* *maids*: young skates; but with double meaning
* *hogo*: a high-flavoured dish, and also a stink

## On a Lady and her Chambermaid

A chambermaid was got with child,
For which her lady did call her whore
And said that she had her house defiled
And vowed she would turn her out a-door.
'Who got the child,' says she, 'you jade?'
'Your husband, and please you, madam.'
'Why, where, you whore?' 'Forsooth,' she said,
'In the truckle-bed at Hadham.' *

'Why, where was I? I'll know the truth.
Come, tell me or else I'll make ye.'
'In the high-bed fast asleep, forsooth,
And I was afraid to wake ye.'
'Why did you not cry out, you drab,
When first you saw he begun it?'
'Truly forsooth, I was never a blab
Of my tongue. Would you 'a' done it?

'And besides, forsooth, you know
That I your humour know too well,
That when y'are suddenly waked you'll throw

And tear, like to a fiend of hell.
Nay, you'll cry out with loud alarms
And fling what your fingers touches,
That I had rather be in my master's arms
Than ever to come in your clutches.'

'Why did you not then sooner go,
You arrant quean, before 'twas known?' *whore*
'Truly, madam, 'tis even so,
Because that you had none o' your own,
And truly, madam, the truth to tell,
I did think I well did plot it,
Thinking you would use it well
For his dear sake that got it.'

* *truckle-bed*: low bed for servant, in the same room as the curtained fourposter

## In Praise of Eating

What'a devil ails our poets all,
For drink, for drink thus always to call
And nothing goes down but drink?
Friends, whither are your stomachs flown,
That you the noble food disown,
Which better deserves your ink?

Food! Aye, there's a substantial word,
And it begets a substantial t---
That breeds grass for cows and sheep.
The country bumpkin he comes for it
And at night it rideth in a charet*
When all men are asleep.

Alas for drink! 'Tis not worth your metre.
Drink makes piss, and piss makes saltpetre
That murders and blows up the people.
You may drink claret and have the gout.
I'll eat, and drink little, and go without
And laugh at the drunken cripple.

Let ladies the exchanges range, *[the shopping malls of their day*
The shambles shall be my exchange, *the meat market*
Which I count a nobler place.
What do I care for pins or points?

Let me behold the solid joints
    That keep up the human race.

The noble sirloins there do lie,
A joint well known to satisfy,
    Though you feed ne'er so fiercely.
And there you may see glorious buttocks
Of many a cow and many a fat ox.
    Oh, how they taste with parsley!

The brisket must not be forgot.
'Tis meat for a prince while it is hot
    If cabbage do attend it;
Though if the turnips be of Hackney *
I will not covet any sack nigh
    To inspire me to commend it.

. . . . . .

Who will not commend the high-soaring larks?
Or a pigeon pie worth three or four marks
    With rabbits life-guarded about?
The woodcock, partridge and the teal,
The pheasant and turkey, which the commonweal
    Can never be without?

. . . . . .

The man that drinketh all his life,
What can he do unto his wife?
    Poor soul, she rests in quiet,
But such a restless quiet 'tis
That never ends till she doth kiss
    The man that eats good diet.

. . . . . .

Peace, therefore, Brome, for liquor so fierce.*
The cooks are angry at thy verse
    And ha' sworn the fiddlers to cripple
If against next term they ha' ne'er a new song
Which may to the praise of food belong
    As well as to that of tipple.

* *charet*: cart (of the men who did their nightly rounds collecting the contents of household latrine buckets)

* *Hackney*: then noted, like Islington, for market gardens and farms – whose fertility was enhanced by the nightly charets

* *Brome*: Alex Brome (1620-66), writer of bacchanalian songs

## Since the pox or the plague

Since the pox or the plague of inconstancy reigns
    In most of the women o' th' town,
What ridiculous fop would trouble his brains
    To make the lewd devils lie down?

No more in dull rhyme or some heavier strain
Will I of the jades or their jilting complain.
My court I will make to things more divine,
The pleasures of friendship, freedom and wine.

We'll Venus adore
For a goddess no more,
That old lady whore;
But Bacchus we'll court,
Who doth drinking support.
Let the world sink or swim.
Sirrah, fill to the brim!

*set by* HENRY PURCELL

## The Deist

*To the tune of 'Old Simon the King'*

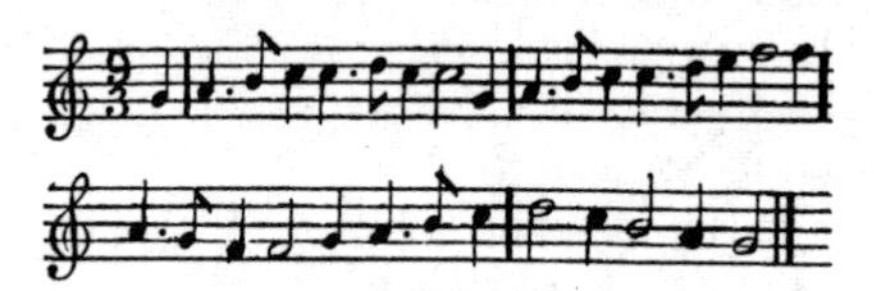

Religion's a politic law
    Devised by the prigs of the schools    *thieves; universities*
To keep the rabble in awe
    And amuse poor bigoted fools.

And they for good victuals and bub    *drink*
    Will bellow their nonsense aloud
And cant out a tale of a tub
    To fright the poor ignorant crowd.

And therefore in every town
    There's a pimp that we call a parson,
Equipped with a band and a gown    *clerical collar*
    And a cushion to set his fat arse on.

And after the text is taken
  To unriddle mystical writings,
He proves pease and beans to be bacon
  And slippery eels to be whitings.

Though the apple was but a fib,
  Yet he vouches it to be true;
And that Eve was made of a rib —
  Pray, gentlemen, what think you?

And that Cain in the land of Nod,
  Where the blockhead was all alone
Like an owl in an ivy tod,
  Built a city as big as Rome;

That a quarrelsome son of a whore
  Slew ten thousand with a jawbone,
And after, to vex them the more,
  Ran away with the gates of the town;

That foxes were tied by the tails,
  And castles were built in the air;
That windmills went without sails,
  And Samson's strength lay in his hair.

Come, these are but idle frolics,
  For his strength lay no more in that
Than it did in his pintle and bollocks
  Or a hair of Dalilah's twat.

And thus for reward he will cant
  And poach up the whites of his eyes,
For rather than Roger should want
  He will tell you a thousand lies.

But if niggardly humour controls
  And you cram not his cellar and shelves
Old Nick may take care of your souls
  And your kids may go christen themselves.

. . . . . . .

I laugh at the Pope's devices,
  Bulls, pardons and militant fights,
His incense and nonsense and spices
  Are nothing but shitten-cum-shites.

I pity the flogging old shaver,
  Who pretends he does miracles show,

And makes flesh and blood of a wafer
    A baker has just made of dough.

Let Huddleston fumble his beads*
    And ogle a buttock at mass;
And Stillingfleet prove what he reads*
    Or else he may kiss my arse.

I'm not to be frighted at all
    Or out of my reason driven.
As well as St Peter and Paul,
    Poor fucksters will go to heaven.

Give me health, vigour and victuals,
    And a cunt to mortify lust.
The rest are but tattle-cum-tittles
    And flutter about like the dust.

To marry or keep a plump whore,
    All's one as to matter of sin.
Use arsehole, or tarse-hole before,
    It signifies just not a pin.

*tarse = penis*

Nuncle Solomon, nicknamed the wise,
    Built a temple, none like it before him,
Yet found 'twixt his concubines' thighs
    The best way to his sanctum sanctorum.

And his dad, after God's own heart,
    Who did atheist Goliah o'ercome,
Made Uriah be slain with a dart,
    Having seen pretty Bathsheba's bum.

Nay, one whom we once did obey,
    And after his copy should write,
Has fucked five hundred, they say,
    Though one did his bollocks beshite.

*Charles II*

. . . . .

Though Adam ne'er married his Eve,
    He soon found out what was what,
And fucked her, we all do believe.
    Pray, what says the parson to that?

If a friar can crupper a nun,
    Though half-starved, lousy and lean,
Your bishop as sure as a gun
    Will thrum the hard arse of a dean.

Come, the pulpit pad's but a cheat. *robber*
'Tis a twang through the nostrils bewitches,
And none believe what they repeat
But blockheads and ignorant bitches.

Let's lead a life honest and moral,
One God and one Caesar adore,
And ne'er be so foolish to quarrel
For Luther's or Babylon's whore.

And therefore, sirs, 'tis not amiss
To take my advice, though in jest.
Let's know what religion first is
And then let us fight for the best.

*Deist*: one manuscript, Firth c.16, Bodleian, makes the title The Atheist; and deists, rejectors of revealed religion, were indeed often seen as crypto-atheists

* *Huddleston*: John Huddleston (1608–98), Benedictine monk, heard Charles II's deathbed confession and administered the Roman Catholic sacraments

* *Stillingfleet:* Edward Stillingfleet (1635–99), chaplain to Charles II, denounced the 'atheistic drollery' of the poet Rochester and other 'scoffers'

## I'll tell my mother, Jenny cries

I'll tell my mother, Jenny cries,
And then a poor languishing lover dies,
But i'faith I believe the gipsy lies.
For all she looks so grave and wise,
She longs to be tickled, to be tickled, to be tickled,
She longs to be tickled, O she longs to be tickled.

*set by* DR JOHN BLOW

This catch and the next eight came into print between 1678 and 1701 but were all in circulation well before the latter date. Blow, organist of the Chapel Royal and Westminster Abbey, was one of Purcell's teachers. No doubt each of them devised some of the words. Purcell was certainly credited with words as well as music. 'A Rebus on Mr Henry Purcell's Name' declares:

His skill and performance each auditor wins,
But the poet deserves a good kick on the shins.

## Fie, nay, prithee John

Fie, nay, prithee John,
Do not quarrel, man!
Let's be merry and drink about.

—Kiss my arse, I caren't a turd
For any man that wears a sword.
Lay down your money on the board.
Sir, I'll play it out.

—You be damned, you brazen face.

—You sneaking dog, I'll whip your arse.

—Here, take my band and hold my hat. *band = collar*

—Hey, boys, for that!

## To thee, to thee and to a maid

To thee, to thee and to a maid
That kindly will upon her back be laid
And laugh, and sing, and kiss, and play,
And wanton out a summer's day:
Such a lass, kind friend, and drinking
Give me, great Jove, and damn the thinking.

*set by* PURCELL

## Sir Walter enjoying his damsel one night

Sir Walter enjoying his damsel one night,
He tickled and pleased her to so great a height
That she could not contain t'wards the end of the matter
But in rapture cried out, O sweet Sir Walter! *[pronounced Watter*
O sweet Sir Walter, O sweet Sir Walter,
O sweet Sir sweet Sir Walter!
O switter swatter switter swatter switter swatter
switter swatter switter swatter sir!

*set by* PURCELL

## 'Tis woman makes us love

'Tis woman makes us love,
'Tis love that makes us sad,
'Tis sadness makes us drink,
And drinking makes us mad. *set by* PURCELL

## Full bags, a brisk bottle

Full bags, a brisk bottle and a beautiful face
Are the three greatest blessings poor mortals embrace,
But alas! we grow muckworms if bags do but fill
And a bonny gay dame often ends in a pill.
Then hey for brisk claret, whose pleasures ne'er waste.
By a bumper we're rich, and by two we are chaste.

*set by* PURCELL

## Once, twice, thrice I Julia tried

Once, twice, thrice I Julia tried.
The scornful puss as oft denied.
And since I can no better thrive
I'll cringe to ne'er a bitch alive.
So kiss my ar—,
So kiss my ar—, disdainful sow.
Good claret,
Good claret is my mistress now. *set by* PURCELL

## A Catch set by Doctor Blow

In a cellar at Sodom at the sign of the T—— *twat*
Two buxom young harlots were drinking with L—. *Lot*
Some say they were his daughters — no matter for that.
They resolved they would souse their old dad with a pot.
All flustered and boozy, the frolicsome sot
As great as a monarch between them was got,
Till the oldest and wisest thus opened the plot:
'Pray show us, dear daddy, how we were begot.'
'Gadzooks! ye young jades, 'twas the first oath, I wot.
The devil of a serpent this humour has taught.'
'No matter!' they cried, 'you shall pawn for the shot*
Unless you will show us how we were begot.'

THOMAS D'URFEY, *1690*

**pawn for the shot*: be left to pay for the drinks

## Say, good Master Bacchus

Say, good Master Bacchus, astride on your butt,
Since our champagne's all gone and our claret's run out,
Which of all the brisk wines in your empire that grow
Will serve to delight your poor drunkards below?
Resolve us, grave sir, and soon send it over
Lest we die, lest we die of the sin of being sober.

## Phillis, the fairest of love's foes

Phillis, the fairest of love's foes
    But cruel as a dragon,
The terror of the powdered beaus —
    But what, what has she, what, what, what has she,
    What, what has she to brag on?
For while she keeps her legs so close
    Her arse has scarce a rag on.

Compelled through want, this wretched maid
    Did sad complaints begin,
Which surly Strephon hearing, said
    It were both shame and sin
To pity, to pity, to pity, to pity such an idle jade
    Who'd neither kiss nor spin;
To pity such an idle jade
    Who'd neither kiss nor spin.

In a British Library manuscript, Harl.6914, the last line is 'Who'd neither fuck nor spin', a reminder that in print 'kiss' is often a euphemism

## Love is now become a trade

Love is now become a trade.
All its joys are bought and sold.
Money is a feature made
And beauty is confined to gold.

Courtship is but terms of art:
Portion, settlement and dower
Softens the most obdurate heart.
The lawyer is the only wooer.

My stock can never reach a wife;
It may a small retaining whore.
Let men of fortune buy for life:
A night a purchase for the poor.

*set by* PURCELL

## Corinna, I excuse thy face

Corinna, I excuse thy face,
Those erring lines which nature drew,
When I reflect that every grace
Thy mind adorns is just and true.

But oh, thy wit what god has sent,
Surprising, airy, unconfined!
Some wonder sure Apollo meant
And shot himself into thy mind.

THOMAS CHEEK

Henry Purcell set this and other songs in Thomas Southerne's play *The Wives' Excuse*, 1691 (revived by the Royal Shakespeare Company, 1994)

## The London Lady's Vindication of Topknots

Young women and damsels that love to go fine,
Come listen a while to this ditty of mine.
In spite of all poets, brave girls, we will wear
*Our towers and topknots, with powdered hair.*

I am a young woman, 'tis very well known,
And I am resolved to make use of my own.
In spite of all poets, brave girls, we will wear
*A tower and topknot with powdered hair.*

They talk of a calf which was seen in our dress,*
Yet let us take courage, girls, nevertheless.
In spite of these rumours, we'll constantly wear
*Our towers and topknots and powdered hair.*

. . . . . .

Were we to be ruled by some sort of men
We should go like women of fourscore and ten.
In spite of those coxcombs, brave girls, we will wear
*Rich towers and topknots, with powdered hair.*

Like beautiful angels we strive to appear,
The hearts of our husbands in order to cheer.
Then what is the reason that we may not wear
*Rich towers and topknots, with powdered hair?*

If we are the pleasure and joy of their life,
Pray, when can they take more delight in a wife
Than at the same time when rich garments they wear
*With towers and topknots, and powdered hair?*

We see the young misses and jilts of the town
Have six storeys high as they walk up and down.
Then pray tell me why should not honest wives wear
*Rich towers and topknots, &c — ?*

If we a'n't as fine and as gaudy as they
Who knows but our husbands might soon run astray.
Consider this, women, and still let us wear
*Our towers and topknots, &c.*

It is but a folly to tell us of pride
While we have these arguments still on our side.
As long as we live we will flourishing wear
*Rich towers and topknots, &c.*

Nay, further I'll tell ye: the case it is thus,
That all is not saved that is put in the purse.
A shopkeeper's lady, she utters much ware *does a good trade*
*When dressed in her topknot, &c.*

What man would not have his wife richly arrayed
Whenas he well knows it enlarges his trade?
Come, come, I must tell ye, 'tis fit we should wear
*Rich towers and topknots, &c.*

Sometimes when our husbands are out of the way,
Pray tell me, what huffing young gallants will stay
If that a fine delicate wife was not there?
*Then hey for the topknots with powdered hair!*

Some young men may flout us, yet mark what I say:
There's no woman living now prouder than they.

Observe but the many knick-knacks which they wear
*More costly than topknots or powdered hair.*

Their wig, watch and rapiers we daily behold,
And embroidered waistcoats of silver and gold.
Likewise turn-up stockings they constantly wear,
*More costly than topknots or powdered hair.*

If pride be a sin and a folly, why then,
Ha'n't we a far better example from men?
If gaudy apparel those gallants do wear
*We will have our topknots with powdered hair.*

*A direct reference to a comical broadside song, 'The Farmer's Wife's Complaint Against the Ladies' Commodes and Topknots' (see endnote)

## The Coy Lass Dressed up in her Best Commode and Topknot

Do not rumple my topknot,
I'll not be kissed today.
I'll not be hauled and pulled about
Thus on a holiday.
Then if your rudeness you don't leave,
No more is to be said.
See, this long pin upon my sleeve
I'll run up to the head,
And if you rumple my headgear
I"ll give you a good flout on th'ear.

Come upon a working day
When I have my old clothes on.
I shall not be so nice nor coy
Nor stand so much upon.
Then haul and pull, and do your best,

Yet I shall gentle be.
Kiss hand and mouth, and feel my breast
And tickle to my knee,
I won't be put out of my road:
You shall not rumple my commode. *wire-framed head-dress*

## A Drunken Dialogue

*He (drinking in a tavern)*

Should I not lead a happy life (*hick*),
Were but my bottle like my wife?
Were but my bottle like my wife (*hick*).
My bottle empties when I swill,
My bottle empties when I swill (*hick*),
But my wife swells up, but my wife swells up,
But my wife, my wife swells up when we bill (*hick*).

Would, when I drink — would, when I drink, my bottle fill,
And when I kiss, and when I kiss, my wife not swell,
All would be well.
I would so (*hick*) so swill,
I would so (*hick*) so fill,
I would so (*hick*) so bill,
That daily, daily I would spend my life
Drinking, filling,
Hugging, billing
My merry merry merry merry merry merry merry merry
bottle and my wife.

*Enter his wife*

Still at your pot,
You drunken sot,
You drunken, drunken, drunken sot!
You, till I come,
Will never come home,
And when you're there you curse and swear,
You curse, you ban, you damn and swear,
Then prove abed
A lump of lead.
Will you never leave your beastly pot,
You odious, filthy, drunken sot?

*He* Do you think, you scold,
I'll be controlled (*hick*)?

Do you think, you scold, I'll be controlled?
No more be said, no more be said,
Or at your head,
As I'm a sot, souse flies the pot.
But first I think I'll save the drink,
But first I think I'll save the drink.

*She* Hold, leave a sup.
Don't, don't drink all, all up.
*He* Here, taste, taste and know *[Gives her the pot*
Why, why, why I'll not go.

*She drinks*
How sweet, how sweet! Oh, how it cheers and warms my heart!
Oh dear! methinks, methinks I suck my mother.
Here's to you, my love, have t'other quart.
And then, what then? And then another. *[She drinks again*

CHORUS *(both)*
Come, now we're friends; come, now we're friends,
And all, all, all is right,
And all, all, all is right.
Drink, drink, drink, drink all day
But love, love, love at night. *(Repeat)*

From Pierre Motteux's play *Love's a Jest*, 1696, set by John Eccles

## Dialogue Between two Chairmen waiting at a Tavern Door

Hey ho! hey ho! hey ho! hey ho! *(Yawning)*
The clock has just struck four.
Hey ho! hey ho! hey ho! hey ho!
The chimes too tell the hour,
And morning cocks that crow.
Hey ho, hey ho, hey ho!

My lord, my lo— *(Yawning)*
My mad Lord Rantepoll,
Sure now his guts are full
Will think, will think 'tis time to go.

No no no no, 'tis too soon, 'tis too soon, 'tis too soon,
He's yet not crammed to the top.

Faith, Tom, let's home. Pox on him, pox on him, pox on him,
He ne'er budges till the sun be up.
Hey ho, hey ho!
Ods bud! As poor as I am grown,
I'd rather lose his nasty crown *five shillings for the night's work*
Than wait, than wait, wait on such a fop.

And so had I,
Confound me if I lie,
I'd rather lose his nasty crown
Than wait, than wait, than wait on such a fop.

What pranks has he been playing all this day
Before and since we brought him to the play!
He pulled a parson by the ears
As he was going to say prayers
And rabbit-like from cassock stripped. *as if skinning a rabbit*
Next minute met a senator *a member of parliament*
And him through midriff whipped. *[superficially, one hopes*
'*(Hick)* You rogue,' says he, '(*hick*) you rogue,' says he,
'I'll maul you, I'll maul you
For the want, for the want, for the want, the want
Of money in the nation (*hick*),
Land taxes (*hick*) and the damning capitation (*hick*).'

Then windows breaking, children scaring,
Women ruffling, cuckolds daring,
Bullies frighting, slow of fighting,
Nor old nor young, degree nor sexes sparing.
He twice raised the mob
And we twice relieved him:
From Counter and Newgate and gallows reprieved him, *two jails*
By handling of poles and stout words of defial, *sedan-chair poles*
From Counter and Newgate and gallows reprieved him.
We brought him off safe to the Theatre Royal.

No sooner got there and secure from the rout,
But the troublesome bear put the actors all out
By squabbling in the pit
With a rake they call a wit
About two confounded whores,
Who conveyed him out of doors,
And for supper at last saved the fool and his feather,
And here in the tavern they're drunk drunk drunk drunk drunk
drunk drunk all together

And here in the tavern they're drunk drunk drunk drunk drunk
drunk drunk all together
They're drunk drunk drunk drunk drunk,
They're drunk all together.
They're drunk drunk drunk drunk drunk drunk drunk all together.
They're drunk drunk drunk drunk drunk,
They're drunk all together.

Then Tom, to the army let's away,
Then Jack, to the army let's away.
No longer wait at tavern door,
But take King William's royal pay. *William III*
No longer wait at tavern door,
But take King William's royal pay.
Sit up all night and pimp no more,
Pimp no more,
Sit up all night and pimp no more.

THOMAS D'URFEY, *1697, set by* JOHN ECCLES

## Hark, the cock crowed

Hark, the cock crowed, 'tis day all abroad.
It looks like a jolly fair morning.
Up, Roger and James, and drive out your teams,
Up quickly to carry the corn in.

Davy the drowsy and Barnaby bowzy *boozy*
At breakfast we'll flout and we'll jeer, boys.

Sluggards shall chatter with small-drink and water
While you shall tope off the March beer, boys. *strong beer*

Lasses that snore, for shame give it o'er:
Mouth open, the flies will be blowing.
To get us stout hum when Christmas is come, *extra strong beer*
Away where the barley is mowing.

In your smock-sleeves too, go bind the sheaves too
With nimble young Rowland and Harry.
Then when work's over, at night give each lover
A hug and a buss in the dairy.

Two for the mow and two for the plough
Is then the next labour comes after. *lovemaking*
I'm sure I hired four, but if you want more
I'll send you my wife and my daughter.

Roger the trusty, tell Rachel the lusty
The barn's a rare place to steal garters.
'Twixt her and you then, contrive up the mow then,
And take it all night for your quarters.

## Joan to her Lady

Lady, sweet now, do not frown
Nor in anger call me clown, *country bumpkin*
For your servant Joan may prove
Like yourself, as deep in love,
And as absolute a bit

Man's sweet liquorish tooth to fit.
*The smock alone the difference makes,*
*'Cause yours is spun of finer flax.*

What avails the name of Madam?
Came not all from Father Adam?
Where does one exceed the other?
Was not Eve our common mother?
Then what odds 'twixt you and Joan?
Truly, in my judgment none.
*The smock, &c —*

Ladies are but blood and bone,
Skin and sinews: so is Joan.
Joan's a piece for man to bore
With his wimble; you're no more.
*Then what odds, &c —*

It is not your flaunting 'tires — *fine clothes*
Are the cause of men's desires.
They're other darts which lusts pursue: — *?parts*
Those Joan has as well as you.
*Then, &c —*

What care we for glorious lights?
Women are usèd in the nights,
And in night, in women-kind
Kings and clowns like sport do find.
*Then, &c —*

Were there two in bed together,
There's not a pin to choose 'twixt either.
Both have eyes and both have lips,
Both have thighs and both have hips.
*Then, &c —*

When your hand puts out the candle
And you at last begin to handle,
Then you go about to do
What you should be done unto.
*Then, &c —*

Who can but in conscience say,
'Fie, fie, for shame, away, away!'
Putting finger in the eye,
Till you have a fresh supply.
*Then what odds 'twixt you and Joan?*
*Truly, in my judgment none.*

## A New and Old Medley

Doff with your clogs and ceckers*
And don with your hose and shoon
And away to John at the Cock at Pegham,
And we shall have a new tune, *tol lol.*

Says old Sir Simon the King
To young Sir Simon the Squire,
Old father Jenkinson kissed mother Wilkinson
Round about our coal fire.

As I went over the water
For want of company
I met with a lass a-scratching her arse—
'Will you buy milk for furmity?' *frumenty*

There were threescore women run naked
And fourscore of them were blind.
He run and she run and I run
And so we run all of a mind.

If a man should lie with my wife
I'll kill him if I can.
I'll stick my nose in his arse.
Zounds! A man's but a man.

Somebody come light me a candle.
My wife she will die in my arms.
I dare not look at her for laughing:
Come, somebody knock out her brains.

My father's a lady of honour,
My mother's a justice of peace,
My arse is an apple-pie maker
And you may come to the feast.

There was an old woman of Wigan,
She shit in a bottle of hay, *a bundle*
She run threescore miles to a meeting
And shit and pissed all the way.

When I have got money I'm merry,
When I have got none I am sad.
When I am sober I'm civil
And when I am drunk I am mad.

And hey for a pipe of tobacco
And hey for a bottle of wine
And hey for a pretty girl
That will turn her bare belly to mine.

Marjoram grows by thyme,
Thyme it grows by sage.
Clap your belly to mine
And put the bird into the cage.

The beginning of Sellenger's Round *old dance tune*
The cow leapt over the moon,
The maid she shit in the creampot
And we'll have a dumpling soon.

Take an old whore and roast her,
Baste her well with cheese,*
Lay her out in a frosty night,
It's ten to one but she'll freeze.

Take her in the next morning,
Lay her in a bed of straw,
Then set fire to her arse,
Ten to one but she'll thaw.

Coverly's cow's in the corn.
Nobody helps her out.
Coverly's wife's beshit,
And nobody lends her a clout.

Joan, shall I feel your coney?
Joan, shall I feel it now?
How the devil, said she, will you feel my coney,
And my petticoats hang so low?

There was an old woman, and she
And me crept into a tree,
And when she came there her arse it was bare
And her conjuring cap you might see.

Did not you know Tom Dod?
And did not you know Tom Dod?
His breeches was tore behind and before
And his twopence went niddity-nod.

There was an old woman, cock-ram her,
She lived at the sign of the Hammer.
She died of the colic. I laughed at the frolic,
To see how the sexton did jam her.*

Will you buy any beer of me?
Will you buy any beer of me?
For I have a barrel to broach
A little above my knee.

'Tis eighteenpence a quart,
And half-a-crown to trust,
Sixteen shillings a gallon,
And that makes twenty just.*

* *ceckers*: also cockers or caukers – heavy studded boots (the singer and friends are changing out of working clothes for a night of merriment)

*Allan Ramsay, the early 18th-century Edinburgh song-collector, noted similar lines in a margin of his manuscript collection (Egerton 2023, British Library):
We'll take an auld wife and roast her
And baste her with butter and cheese.

*This stanza and the two preceding ones are early limericks

*Eighteenpence + half a crown = 4 shillings; a nonsense reckoning

## Gossip Joan

Good-morrow, Gossip Joan,
Where have you been a-walking?
I have for you at h–o—me
A budget full of talking,
Gossip Joan.

My sparrow's flown away
And will no more come to me.
I've broke a glass to–da—y,
The price it will undo me,
Gossip Joan.

I've lost a Harry groat — *coin of Henry VIII*
Was left me by my granny.
I cannot find it o–u—t
Though I've searched every cranny,
Gossip Joan.

My goose has laid away,
I know not what's the reason.
My hen has hatched to–da—y,
A week before the season,
Gossip Joan.

I've lost my wedding ring,
Was made of silver gilded;
And drink would please a k–i—ng,
The whorish cat has spilled it,
Gossip Joan.

My duck has eat a snail
And is not that a wonder?
The horns bud out at ta–i—l
And split her rump asunder,
Gossip Joan.

My husband he was drunk
And all the night lay snoring.
I told him in the m–o—rn
That he had been a-whoring,
Gossip Joan.

My pocket is cut off,
'Twas full of sugar-candy.
I cannot stop my co–u—gh
Without a gill of brandy,
Gossip Joan.

Oh, I am sick at heart!
I pray give me some ginger.
I cannot sneeze nor fa–r—t,
Therefore put up your finger,
Gossip Joan.

O pity, pity me!
Or I shall go distracted.
I've cried till I can't s–e—e
To think how things are acted,
Gossip Joan.

Let's to the gin-shop go
And wash down all my sorrow.
My griefs in part you kn–o—w,
The rest I'll tell tomorrow,
Gossip Joan.

## The Curtain Lecture

Being drunk last night, I found
My wife was in a pet.
Do what I could for my heart's blood,
She still would scold and fret.
And thus her chat she did begin:
'Is this your coming-in?
The clock strikes one, you'll be undone.
Is this a life to lead?'

'My dear,' said I, 'I don't deny
But what you say is true.
I do intend my life to mend.
*Lend me the pot to spew.'*

'You filthy beast, you have increased
My sorrow, grief and care
By drunkenness. I do confess
I'm almost in despair.
For you drink, and sure I think
You will destroy a woman's joy
Which I should have, you drunken knave.
My very heart will rue.'

'No, no,' I cried, 'my charming bride,
Believe me, this is true:
I do intend my life to mend.
*Lend me the pot to spew.'*

'Take it yourself, you wicked elf.
I am not bound to wait
Upon you here. Alas! I fear
You'll ruin my estate
Which I brought. I little thought
That in wine the land of mine
You would have spent. I do lament.
My very heart doth rue.'

I groaning cried, 'My charming bride,
A love I have for you,
And I intend my life to mend.
*Lend me the pot to spew.'*

'How you look! I never took
You for a drunken man,

But now I find you prove unkind,
Consuming all you can
In taverns still. There do you swill,
Destroy your health, consume your wealth.
O this is more than can be bore.
Alas! what shall I do?'

'Love, do not weep, but let me sleep
Another hour or two,
For by degrees I shall have ease
*If you'll lend's the pot to spew.'*

*1715*

## A Dialogue between Miss Molly and her Mother about a Hoop

What a fine thing have I seen today !
*O mother, a hoop!*
I pray let me have one and don't say nay .
*O mother, a hoop!*
You must not have one, dear Moll, to be sure,
For hoops men's eyes and men's hearts do allure.
*No Molly, no hoop, no Molly, no hoop!*

Dear mother, let women wear what they will
*O mother, a hoop!*
Men's eyes and men's hearts will be roving still
*O mother, a hoop!*
Whether decently clothed or sluttishly dressed—
Some men prefer these, and others the rest.
*O mother, a hoop!*

Men wear laced hats, and ladies laced shoes
*O mother, a hoop!*

Men with canvas and whalebone stiffen their clothes.
*O mother, a hoop!*
Then why should the men the ladies abuse
For applying the same things to the same use?
*O mother, a hoop!*

Pray hear me, dear mother, what I have been taught.
*O mother, a hoop!*
Nine men and three women o'erset in a boat.
*O mother, a hoop!*
The men were all drowned, but the women did float,
And by the help of their hoops they got all safely out.
*O mother, a hoop!*

Dear Molly Joan, thou talk'st very well.
*O Molly, no hoop!*
Thou always in wit and good sense did excel.
*O Molly, no hoop!*
For I have one scruple remaining behind,
Which if thou canst solve, a hoop shall be thine.
*O Molly, no hoop!*

I'm told as two ladies were running a race
*O Molly, no hoop!*
One fell on her back, the other on her face
*O Molly, no hoop!*
And when they were fallen, their hoops did unveil
What nature intended that they should conceal.
*O Molly, no hoop!*

Dear mother, you know that nature ordains
*O mother, a hoop!*
Quite different habits to women and men.
*O mother, a hoop!*
Through all ages and nations it ever was so,
And why, dear mother, should it not be so now?
*O mother, a hoop!*

Besides, dear mother, if a fall's to be blamed
*O mother, a hoop!*
What man or what woman can there be named
*O mother, a hoop!*
Who never did fall? Had yourself never fallen
You'd ne'er had a son—nor a daughter, now calling
For a hoop, dear mother, a hoop, a hoop, O mother, a hoop!

Dear daughter, I own your reasoning's strong.
*O Molly, a hoop!*
I wonder I could withstand it so long.
*O Molly, a hoop!*
I grant your request, and you shall have a hoop,
And with it through land and through water may swoop.
O Molly, a hoop, a hoop! O Molly, I grant you a hoop.

Dear mother, I thank you for this mighty favour
*O mother, a hoop!*
For now I can laugh in the face of any creature
*O mother, a hoop!*
Who void of good breeding, good manners, good nature,
Dares attack the hoop-wearers with his fulsome satire.*
O mother, a hoop, a hoop! O mother, I thank you, a hoop!

*Rhyming as natt'r / satt'r

## On the Ladies' Hoops and Hats Now Worn

Our grannums of old were so piously nice
That to show us their shoe-tie was reckoned a vice,
But lord! could they now but peep out of the ground
And see the fine fashions their daughters have found.
How their steps they reveal, and oblige the lewd eye
With the leg's pretty turn, and delicate thigh,
When the modern free hoops, so ample and wide,
Uplift the fair smocks with an impudent pride
And betray the sweet graces they chastely should hide.

But how wanton is beauty! How capricious the fair!
Their hats are all flapped with so modest an air,
Each maiden you meet a veiled vestal you'd swear.
Impropriety strange! How wild the extremes!
How the hats suit the hoops just like water and flames!
What whimsies are these, what comical farces!
They hide all their faces and show us their ar—s.
But from hence an excuse for the ladies may rise,
For when conscious their nethermost charms treat our eyes
Perhaps they may blush. 'Tis a sign of some grace
When their breech is exposed, to cover their face.

*1719*

## The Lass with the Velvet A–se

There was a buxom lass and she had a velvet a—,
Which made her for to bounce and to vapour.
Whene'er she went to sh—
If 'twas ne'er such a little bit,
O she always wiped it with brown paper,
With brown paper,
With brown paper,
She always wiped it with brown paper.

This lass, whose name was Jane, O she kept her a—se so clean
That she won the heart of one Mr Draper.
He married her outright,
So she got a husband by't,
And all because she wiped her a—se with brown paper,
With brown paper,
With brown paper,
And all because she wiped her a—se with brown paper.

Ye lasses short and tall, pray take example all,
And learn for the future to use brown paper.
So here's a health to every lass
That mundifies her a— *cleanses*
Not forgetting good Mrs Draper.
Good Mrs Draper,
Good Mrs Draper,
Not forgetting good Mrs Draper.

## The Hubble Bubbles

### A Ballad to the tune of O'er the Hills and far away

Ye circum- and uncircumcised,
Come hear my song and be advised.
Sell all your lands, sell all your flocks
And put your money in the stocks.

*Hubble bubble, bubble hubble now's in play.*
*Come buy our hubble bubbles whilst you may,*
*For there's hubble bubble, bubble hubble night and day*
*At Jonathan's and Garraway.**

Ye Scotchmen who love laws so well,
Ye Irish who have bulls to sell,

Ye Hollanders, come here and buy,
For there's gelt got by this ally. *money*

*Hubble bubble, bubble hubble low and high,*
*Come all away to Change Alley.*
*Come ye hubble bubbles o'er the hills and far away*
*To Jonathan's and Garraway.*

Now purchase in if you be wise
For stocks will either fall or rise,
And how can stocks be at a stay,
Since time and riches fly away?

*Hubble bubble, bubble hubble come away:*
*Let every hubble bubble have his day,*
*For there's spick and span new hubble bubbles for your pay*
*At Jonathan's and Garraway.*

Come all who would by fishing gain,*
Venture like gamesters on the main.
Whate'er you lose projectors get,
For you're the gudgeons in their net. *dupes*
*Hubble bubble &c.*

Come all who would large gain secure,
Our ships upon the sea insure,
And those the surest gain must find
Who trust to faithless sea and wind.
*Hubble bubble &c.*

Ye privy counsellors draw nigh,*
Come ease yourselves of your money.
Here cent for cent is money told,
For all goldfinders must find gold.
*Hubble bubble &c.*

Come all ye nymphs of gay desire,*
Insure your house and selves from fire.
A house insured brings better rent.
Come then, insure your tenement.
*Hubble bubble &c.*

Italian songsters, come away,
Our gentry will the piper pay.
Come hasten here, for before 'tis long
Op'ra stock will be sold for a song.
*Hubble bubble &c.*

A bubble is blown up with air,
In which fine prospects do appear.
The bubble breaks, the prospect's lost,
Yet must some bubble pay the cost.

*Hubble bubble, bubble hubble, all is smoke.*
*Bubble bubble, hubble bubble, all is broke.*

Farewell your woods, your houses, lands,
Your pastures and your flocks,
For now you have nought but yourselves in the stocks.

THOMAS D'URFEY

* Coffee-houses in Change-alley, precursors of the London Stock Exchange
* Here the song-sheet has a sidenote, 'The Fishery hubble bubble'
*A sidenote says, 'Project for Emptying Necessary Houses' (privies), and there is word-play in 'privy counsellors', 'ease yourselves', 'cent [scent] for cent' and 'goldfinders' – slang for men who emptied privies
* A sidenote says 'Insurance from Fire'; the nymphs are prostitutes ('gay' until the late 20th century was a slang term for anyone, female or male, on the game); 'fire' signifies venereal disease, 'tenement' the body for hire
One copy of this is dated 1720, so it must have been written just before the bursting, that year, of the biggest bubble of all, the South Sea Bubble

## A Coquet's Fate

Cloe, a coquet in her prime,
The vainest, ficklest thing alive—
Behold the strange effects of time—
Marries and dotes at forty-five.

So weathercocks that for a while
Have veered about with every blast,
Grown old and destitute of oil
Rust to a point and fix at last.

RICHARD LEVERIDGE

## The Old Bachelor's Advice
### to all young Bachelors

You find from the beginning
That women did perplex.
Their whole delight's in teasing,
For to torment and vex.

They all are sly and wheedle,
Will noose you if they can.
They ogle, prick with needle—
All women are trapan. *cheat, snare*

Like crocodiles cry o'er you,
Then catch you in the snare.
They fondly seem to adore you.
They're all a bite: take care.
All women are alluring
And have bewitching charms.
In them there's no confiding
Though folded in their arms.

## What though I am a London dame

What though I am a London dame *[dame: young woman*
And lofty looks I bear–a?
I carry sure as good a name
As those who russet wear–a.
What though my clothes are rich brocades,
My skin it is more white–a
Than any of the country maids
That in the fields delight–a.

What though I to assemblies go
And at the opera shine–a?
It is a thing all girls must do
That will be ladies fine–a.
And while I hear Faustina sing*
Before the king and queen–a

My eyes they are upon the wing
To see if I am seen–a.

My pekoe and imperial tea
Are brought me in the morn–a;
At noon, champagne and rich tokay
My tables do adorn–a.
The ev'ning then does me invite
To play at dear quadrille–a, *fashionable card game*
And sure in this there's more delight
Than in a purling rill–a.

Then since my fortune does allow,
I'll live just as I please–a.
I'll never milk my father's cow
Nor press his coming cheese–a,
But take my swing both night and day —
I'm sure it is no sin–a.
And as for what the grave-ones say,
I value not a pin–a.

**Faustina*: dating the song to 1726–8, when the mezzo-soprano Faustina Bordoni was lured to London for enormous fees to sing for Handel

The song is a mock (but a double-edged one) to a long-popular ballad by Martin Parker (died 1656) lauding country virtues, which begins:

What though I am a country lass?
A lofty mind I bear–a.
I think myself as good as those
That gay apparel wear–a.
My coat is made of homely grey,
Yet is my skin as soft–a
As those that with the chiefest wines
Do bathe their bodies oft–a.

## Stand by! Clear the Way!

What though they call me country lass,
I read it plainly in my glass
That for a duchess I might pass —
Oh could I see the day!
Would fortune but attend my call,
At park, at play, at ring, at ball
I'd brave the proudest of 'em all
With a 'Stand by! Clear the way!'

Surrounded by a crowd of beaux
With smart toupets and powdered clothes, *fancy wigs*
At rivals I'll turn up my nose,
    Oh could I see the day!
I'll dart such glances from these eyes
Shall make some nobleman my prize,
And then, oh how I'll tyrannize
    With a 'Stand by! Clear the way!'

Oh then for grandeur and delight,
For equipage, for diamonds bright
And flambeaux that outshine the night —
    Oh could I see the day!
Thus ever easy, ever gay,
Quadrille shall wear the night away
And pleasure crown the growing day
    With a 'Stand by! Clear the way!'

HENRY CAREY

Carey (author of 'Sally in Our Alley') also set the song. It was sung by Mrs Theophilus Cibber in *The Provok'd Husband* (John Vanbrugh and Colley Cibber), which was the best thing Drury Lane could offer in 1728 after Cibber had turned down what became the hit of that year, *The Beggar's Opera*. Cibber imposed an extra stanza on Carey, closing lamely with:

Of love and joy I'd take my fill,
The tedious hours of life to kill.
In everything I'd have my will
    With a 'Stand by! Clear the way!'

## Newcastle Ale

### Tune, *Lillibullero*

Fair Venus, the goddess of beauty and love,
    Arose from the froth that swam on the sea.
Minerva leaped out of the cranium of Jove,
    A coy, sullen slut, as most authors agree.
Bold Bacchus, they tell us, the prince of good fellows,
    Was his natural son, but attend to my tale!
For they that thus chatter mistake quite the matter:
    He sprung from a barrel of Newcastle ale.
        *Newcastle ale, boys, Newcastle ale,*
        *No liquor on earth is like Newcastle ale.*

Then having surveyed well the cask whence he sprung
And finding it empty, disconsolate grew;
He mounted astride, set his a—e on the bung,
And away to the gods and the goddesses flew.
But when he looked down and saw the fair town
To pay him due honours not likely to fail,
He swore on all earth the place of his birth
Was the best, and no liquor like Newcastle ale.
*Newcastle ale, boys, Newcastle ale,*
*No liquor on earth is like Newcastle ale.*

Ye doctors who more execution have done
With bolus and potion and powder and pill
Than hangman with halter and soldier with gun
Or miser with famine or lawyer with quill,
To dispatch us the quicker you forbid us malt liquor
Till our bodies grow thin and our faces look pale.
Observe them who pleases, what cures all diseases
Is a comforting dose of good Newcastle ale.
*Newcastle ale, boys, Newcastle ale,*
*No liquor on earth is like Newcastle ale.*

Ye bishops and deacons, priests, curates and vicars,
Come taste, and you'll certainly find it is true
That Newcastle ale is the best of all liquors,
And who understand the good creature like you?
It dispels every vapour, saves pen, ink and paper,
For when you're disposed from the pulpit to rail
It will open your throats: you may preach without notes
When inspired with full bumpers of Newcastle ale.
*Newcastle ale, boys, Newcastle ale,*
*No liquor on earth is like Newcastle ale.*

Let each lover that talks of flames, darts and daggers
With Newcastle ale ply his mistress but hard.
The lass that once tastes it will drink till she staggers,
And all his past service and sufferings reward.
He may turn her, and twist her, and do what he list, sir.
Engage her but briskly, he soon must prevail.
Fill, fill the glass often, for nothing can soften
The heart of a woman like Newcastle ale.
*Newcastle ale, boys, Newcastle ale,*
*No liquor on earth is like Newcastle ale.*

Later printings claimed the glory for other towns, notably Nottingham

# *Augustan Graffiti: An Interlude*

## The Merry-Thought
### or, The Glass-Window and Bog-House Miscellany

Taken from The Original Manuscripts written in *Diamond* by Persons of the First Rank and Figure in Great Britain; relating to Love, Matrimony, Drunkenness, Sobriety, Ranting, Scandal, Politicks, Gaming, and many other Subjects *Serious* and *Comical*. Faithfully Transcribed from the Drinking-Glasses and Windows in the several noted *Taverns, Inns* and other *Publick Places in this Nation.* – Amongst which are intermixed the Lucubrations of the polite Part of the World, written upon Walls in Bog-Houses, &c.

*[1730–1732*

### *Red Lion at Southwell, in a window*

Clarinda lay here
With a young cavalier
With her heart full of fear
For her husband was near. *February 2, 1728*

### *The Temple Boghouse* *[in one of the Inns of Court]*

No hero looks so fierce in fight
As does the man who strains to sh–te.

### *The Middle Temple Boghouse*

Because they cannot eat, some authors write;
And some, it seems, because they cannot sh-te.

## *The Star at Coventry, in a window*

Drunk at Comb-alley, horrid drunk,
Hither I came and met my favourite punk,
But she as well might have embraced a log.
All night I snored and grunted like a hog.
Then was not I a sad confounded dog!
    I'll never get drunk again
    For my head's full of pain
    And it grieves me to think
    That by dint of good drink
I should lie with my Phillis in vain.

*R.H., 1712*

## *The Boghouse at Pancras-Wells*

Hither I came in haste to sh–t
But found such excrements of wit
That I to show my skill in verse
Had scarcely time to wipe my a–se.

*Underwritten*

D—n your writing,
Mind your sh–ting.

## *On a wainscot at the Crown at Harlow*

Whilst Lady Mary slept at ease,
Secure from jealousy and fleas,
Her lord, with vig'rous love inclined
To kiss her maid and ease his mind.
The maiden did not long resist
But gently yielded to be kissed
And in the dance of lovers move
With sprightly bounds to show her love.
When in the height of am'rous fire
She cried, 'My lord, I've one desire.
Tell me, my peer, tell me, my lord,
Tell me, my life, upon your word,
Who does it best, my dame or me?'
And then she fell in ecstasy.
My lord, in fire of his love,
Called her his minion, turtle dove.
'You have the only art to please,'

All this he swore upon his knees:
'Your dame is like a log of wood.
Her love is never half so good.'
'My lord,' says she, 'all that I know
For all the world has told me so.' *April 1717*

## *On a Person of Quality's Boghouse*

Good Lord! Who could think
That such fine folks should stink?

## *In a Boghouse at the Bush at Carlisle*

Within this place two ways I've been delighted,
For here I've f—, and likewise here have sh—d.
They both are healthful; nature's ease requires 'em.
And though you grin, I fancy you desire 'em.

*Underwritten*

What beast alive could bear to f—
In such a filthy hole as this is?
The nauseous stink might, one would think,
Disturb his taste for amorous kisses.

*Underwritten*

This was wrote by some beau — the fop you may know —
His squeamish exception would make one believe it.
Though the smell where we sh–t is not grateful a bit,
Yet I ne'er knew a c—y that savoured of civet. *1718*

## *Woodstock, in a window*

Have you not in a chimney seen
A sullen faggot, wet and green,
How coyly it receives the heat
And at both ends doth fume and sweat?
So fares it with the harmless maid
When first upon her back she's laid.
But the kind experienc'd dame
Cracks and rejoices in the flame.

## *In a window at an inn on the West Country road*

The cook, confound her, boiled no roots,
The hostler never cleaned my boots,
The tapster too would hardly stir,
The drawer was a lazy cur,
The chamberlain had made no bed,
The host had maggots in his head,
But Millicent, who kept the bar,
Was worse than all the rest by far.
She was as many others are.
I kissed her till she had her fill.
I thought it love, and with her will,
But then ——————
She made a da–n'd confounded bill.

*See the bill, gentlemen:*

Thrice was I reckon'd for my meat,
Thrice was I reckon'd for Miss Milly's treat,
Thrice was I reckon'd for my dirty boots,
Thrice was I reckon'd for not having roots,
Thrice was I reckon'd by the lazy fellows,
And thrice I swore I wish'd them at the gallows.
And if I come here any more,
Then call me a son of a whore.

*Captain R.T., 1718*

## *In a boghouse at the Nag's Head in Bradmore*

Such places as these
Were made for the ease
Of every fellow in common,
But a person who writes
On the wall as he sh–tes
Has a pleasure far greater than woman
For he's eas'd in his body and pleas'd in his mind
When he leaves both a turd and some verses behind.

*Underwritten*

You are eas'd in your body and pleas'd in your mind
That you leave both a turd and some verses behind,
But to me which is worse I can't tell, on my word:
The reading your verses or smelling your turd.

### *In a boghouse over the water, at the Spread Eagle in Bunny in Nottinghamshire*

The nicest maid, with the whitest rump,
May sit and sh–te, and hear it plump.*

### *From a Boghouse at the George Inn, Whitchurch*

From costive stools, and hidebound wit;
From bawdy rhymes, and hole besh–t;
From walls besmear'd with stinking ordure
By swine who ne'er provide bumfodder —
*Libera nos* *

This is a small selection from this innovative publication. It came out in six-penny instalments as gentlemen responded to an appeal from its printer, one James Roberts (he specially mentions offerings 'from both the universities'). When he uses dashes, no doubt the boghouse walls were not so coy.

*This goes back to a song in *Choyce Drollery*, 1656, 'Upon a House of Office over a River', stanza 18:

There nicest maid with naked rump,
When straining hard had made her mump,
Did sit at ease and hear it plump.

*Waste paper was scarce in those days of few newspapers. Here is one of several hits at people who, lacking even the humble alternative, grass or leaves, wiped fingers on boghouse walls. 'Bumfodder' is the origin of 'bumf'.

---

## The Cullies' Invitation

O you merry, merry souls,
  Christmas is a-coming.
We shall have flowing bowls,
  Dancing, piping, drumming;
Delicate minced-pies
  To feast every virgin;
Capon and goose likewise,
  Brawn and a dish of sturgeon.
Then for your Christmas-box
  Sweet plum-cakes and money;
Delicate holland smocks,
  Kisses sweet as honey.

. . . . .

There is your dainty does
    With their rising bubbies,
Eyes as black as sloes,
    Lips as red as rubies.
Robin chooses Kate,
    Simon buxom Mary,
Every one his mate,
    Dancing of Hey-down-derry.
With the cushion dance
    There is kissing, billing.
Every youthful glance
    Shows the damsels willing.

Roger tickles Sue
    Both with a pipe and tabor.
Robin bobtails Prue,
    Verily his neighbour.
When the hop breaks up,
    Betty, Bridget, Robin
Through the streets they troop,
    All together mobbing,
Both with sparks and clowns,
    Hot as if they fainted;
Some in ragged gowns,
    Others patched and painted.

O the merry, merry mob
    Minds not worldly treasure.
Bridget, Joan and Bob
    Hug their dancing pleasure,
Mirth and music sweet,
    Seeming as we hear them
Lords in their conceit;
    Ladies can't come near them.
From all parts they come,
    Jovial lads and lasses,
To the fee fau fum
    While they jig their arses.

. . . . .

O you pretty, pretty rogues,
    Sweet as sugar-candy,
There are cakes and cogues,     *drinks*
    Bottle-ale and brandy
For to cheer your hearts
    At the men's expenses.

They will show their parts
    To refresh your senses.
Nancy, Kate and Nell
    Dressed up brisk and topping,
Come to Clerkenwell.
    There's the finest hopping
As was ever known.
    Sue and Isabella
Dances Bobbin' Joan,
    Buffcoat Has No Fellow.

. . . . . .

O this love's decoy
    Sets the girls a-longing,
Some for puddings white, *white pudding = penis*
    Better worth than money,
But the chief delight
    Is sweet matrimony.

. . . . . .

O you pretty, pretty girls,
    If you would have blisses
Better worth than pearls
    Or ten thousand kisses,
Then the hop frequent,
    Lay aside your needle.
Here is sweet content —
    Tant-tant-tant turn-tweedle.

Girls, come to the hop,
    Do but make a trial.
'Tis a lover's shop.
    Here's bass and bass-viol.
There's both whiff and dub *[significance unknown*
    Dancing by the dozen.
Girls, the meanest shrub
    Has her kissing cousin.

Since the mob of late,
    Harry, Joan and Dolly,
Having no estate,
    Live so brisk and jolly
In their youthful airs,
    And all joy commences
Free from worldly cares,
    Who would be a princess?

# The Harlot's Progress
## Being the Life of the noted Moll Hackabout

**[Extracts from verses inspired in 1732 by William Hogarth's 'Harlot's Progress' prints: Moll, dying, is disposing of her worldly wealth]**

My bunch of rods, for flogging-cull *man who likes to be flogged*
When he is jaded, dry or dull,
To modest Edm--d Cu–l I give *Edmund Curll, notorious publisher*
That he in lechery may revive,
With ballads and some bawdy books
(I thought to leave to pastry-cooks)
As a reward for what he's done,
I leave betwixt him and his son.

. . . . .

To Mother Tho<ma>s, now the oldest
Of all the bawds of fame, and boldest,
I leave my cu–d–ms, fifty gross, *condoms [see endnote*
And all my pills, a dozen dose,
With this advice: get all you can
From that vile perjured creature man,
Or fair or foul, or right or wrong,
With hands and heart, with tail and tongue.
And when you've purchased an estate,
And bawdy tricks are out of date
With you through riches, age and poxes,
Then build a hospital for doxies. *loose women*
Endow it with a handsome bounty
And then a saint the world will count ye.

. . . . .

Leave other legacies to the poor:
'Twill lay you blessings great in store.
Your wicked life will not be named
So much as by a lecher maimed;
Your virtue, sanctity and so forth
All round the town and country go forth;
And you by this, with Guy may trick*
That cunning friend of yours, Old Nick.

*Thomas Guy (died 1724) made a big profit on South Sea stock by selling just before its crash, and built the hospital that still bears his name

## The Harlot Unmasked

How happy a state doth the damsel possess
Who would be no greater, nor can be no less:
On her quim and herself she depends for support,
And is better than all the prime ladies at court.
What though she in grogram and linsey does go,
Nor boasts of gay clothing to make a fine show,
A girl in this dress may be sweeter by far
Than she that is stitched by a Garter and Star,
*Than she that is stitched by a Garter and Star.*

Though her hands they are red and her bubbies are coarse,
Her quim, for all that, may be never the worse.
A girl more polite with less vigour may play,
And her passion in accents less charming convey.
What though a brisk fellow she sometimes may lack
When warm with desire, and stretched on her back:
In this too, great ladies examples afford,
Who oft put a footman in room of a lord,
*Who oft put a footman in room of a lord.*

Or should she endeavour new conquests to make,
In this too she mimics the pinks of the state,
Whose aim is all one, for to get a good stroke,
As all her concern's to supply her *black joke.*
Each night when sport's over and love's fountain's dry,
She, weary with stitching, contented does lie,
Then wakes in the morning so brisk and so keen.
If so happy a harlot, then who'd be a queen?
*If so happy a harlot, then who'd be a queen?*

## The Malt-man

The malt-man comes on Monday,
He craves wonder sair, — *very pressingly*
Cries, *Dame, come gi' me my siller*
*Or malt ye sall ne'er get mair.**
I took him into the pantry
And gave him some good cock-broo; — *chicken broth*
Syne paid him upon a gantree, — *then; a stand for ale barrels*
As hostler wives should do. — *inn-keepers' wives*

When malt-men come for siller,
    And gaugers with wands o'er soon,*
Wives, tak them a-down to the cellar
    And clear them as I have done.
This bewith, when cunzie is scanty,*
    Will keep them frae making din.
The knack I learned frae an auld aunty,
    The snackest of a' my kin. *most artful*

The malt-man is right cunning
    But I can be as slee, *sly*
And he may crack of his winning *brag*
    When he clears scores with me:
For come when he likes, I'm ready,
    But if frae hame I be
Let him wait on our kind lady,
    She'll answer a bill for me.

* Pay me what you owe or you'll get no more malt (for brewing)
* *gaugers*: excise-men, with wands to measure the contents of barrels
* *bewith*: something taken in lieu; *cunzie*: money

## The Golden Cuckold

Now husband, the day is a-coming,
    Horn-fair is now drawing near.
Therefore you must go and do duty.
    You're summoned indeed to appear
With the rest of the hornified cuckolds.
    I'd have you lead heavenly lives
And flock to Horn-fair now by couples
    Along with your beautiful wives.

I have tipped your horns with great splendour.
    As fine as a lord you'll appear
With pick-axe and shovel in order.
    Horn-fair comes but once in a year.
'O wife, you have been ungrateful
    Thus to put horns on my crown.
I thought I had been as sufficient
    As ever a man in the town.'

Dear husband, was marriage designèd
    For to confine us to one man?

We are in the right to get money,
    Dear husband, you know, if we can.

. . . . .

You fumbling dog, now I swear
    If you offer to chatter or prate
I'll break all my ladles to shatters
    Across your hornified pate.

Look under the candlestick, cuckold.
    A single groat you'll find there
I hid for to put in your pocket,
    Your charges to bear at Horn-fair.
'Then wife, prithee put up your ladle,
    My implements ready prepare.
I'll summons all the rest of my neighbours
    To go with me unto Horn-fair.'

You buttocking whores of St Giles's
    That play for a penny a time,
Before get your cuckolds in order
    With everything decent and fine.
You Billingsgate lasses so pretty — *fish-market girls*

Who loves to play with your bum,
Before get your husbands all ready,
My girls, at the beat of a drum.

Old whores that do carry the basket,
That loves for to tope royal gin,
Although that you are old and past it
Your husbands are all summoned in.
The next to the pretty milk-woman
Who does the trick under a tree,
We know that in horns you are dealing
So we summons your husbands to be.

You pretty young girls in the market
That dresses so neat and so trim,
That horns on your husbands have grafted,
We likewise do summons them in.
Since most of our sex they are guilty,
Dear husband, why should you despair?
Your horns shall be charmingly gilded,
My dear, for to go to Horn-fair.

For more about Horn-fair, see endnote

## Of honest malt liquor let English boys sing

Of honest malt liquor let English boys sing.
A pox take French claret — we'll drink no such thing.
But London-brewed staple, stout Burton and Lincoln,
They'll find us good matter to talk or to think on.
To king, lords and commons toast a health ere we rise:
Though we lower our pockets, yet we raise his excise.

## The St Giles's Frolick
## or a Smith's Ramble for New Adventures

I the other night was drunk
And somewhat merry.
Went in search of a punk; *whore*
Not finding any,
To St Giles's I did stroll. *notorious low-life London district*
Whores there is plenty:

At every corner of the street
    Not less than twenty.

Sweep-foot O, mop-spinning Nan,
    Hugging and billing.
'Nan, you whore, let's have a dram.'
    'Yes, Tom, I am willing.'
To a gin-ken straight they went. — *house selling gin*
    I laughed till my sides ached
To hear them bawl, 'Bring half a pint
    Of old strip-me-naked!'

Next down a cellar I did peep,
    Hearing a growling:
A hanged man covered with a sheet,
    The Pats o'er him howling. — *Irishmen holding a wake*
'O harrah, dear, why would you die
    And leave your dear honey?
I wish the t'ief you'd ne'er come nigh
    Nor never touched his money.'

Next in Church-lane one I know well
    At Black Rachel snatches.
In summer-time nosegays she sells,
    In winter-time matches.
He hugged and kissed and called her dear.
    The black bitch did finny — *[? – a misprint?*
Whilst he was bobbing at her ware
    She nailed all his money.

Then I rolled to Maynard-street.
    Some whores I heard scolding.
Through a keyhole I did peep —
    Such a scene beholding.
Says Bess to Kate, 'I think of late
    We have got our hire' —
Of pox and itch much moan did make,
    Anointing by the fire. — *applying ointment*

In Monmouth-street a drunken buck
    Met with a madam.
Soon as the bargain they had struck
    She to a watchman had him:
'Let me your watchbox occupy,
    I'll bug to you a shilling. — *pay you*

Here, damn you, don't the bit deny.' *money*
The scout cried, 'I am willing.' *watchman*

Short's Gardens I next did see:
Two whores a-fighting.
'You bitch,' says one, 'you slanged me *cheated me*
In the bit dividing.'
The patrol, upon my soul,
Did to the roundhouse take them.
Half-naked they were dragged away,
With cold shivering and shaking.

Down Holborn Hill homeward I steered.
I saw a rig funny. *a trick, a diversion*
A blackamoor there met a whore
And swore he'd feel her c—y.
'Twas on a butcher's block, O look,
He gave poor bun the colic.
It growing day, I came away
Well pleased with my frolic.

## The Flying Highwayman

Young Morgan was a lusty blade,
No youth had better courage.
Much gold he got on the highway
That made him daily flourish.

Grand bagnios were his lodging then
Among the flashy lasses.
Soon he became a gentleman
And left off driving asses.

'I scorned poor people for to rob:
I thought it so my duty.
But when I met the rich and gay,
On them I made my booty.

'Stand and deliver! was the word.
I must have no denial.
But alas! poor Morgan has changed his note
Now he is brought to trial.

'I robbed for gold and silver bright
For to maintain my misses,

And we saluted when we met
With most melodious kisses.

'After sweet meat comes sour sauce,
Which brought me to repentance,
For now at last I'm tried and cast
And going to receive my sentence.

'Upon Hounslow Heath and Putney too
I oft made my approaches.
Like lightning I and my horse did fly
When I heard the sound of coaches.

'When first of all I was called up
In order for my trial,
With my beaver hat and surtout coat
I stood a bold denial.

'I stood as bold as John of Gaunt
All in my rich attire.
I ne'er seemed daunted in the least,*
Which made the court admire.

'From Newgate through St Giles's Pound
Me and my Moll were carted, *to Tyburn*
But when we came to the gallows tree
Me and my Moll were parted.

'So I take my leave of all my friends,
Likewise my flashy blowing, *blowen: mistress*
For now at last I am tried and cast,
Out of the world I'm going.

'I thought I heard the people say
As I rode though the city
That such a clever youth as I,
To die it was a pity.*

'I thought I heard such cries as those,
Which set my tears a-flowing,
But now, alas! I'm tried and cast
And out of the world am going.

'I am the captain of the gang
All in my low condition,
But now I'm going to be hanged
I'll throw up my commission.

'So why should I refuse to die,
  Now here or ever after?
The captain he leads on the van,
  His men must follow after.'

No doubt the lost original of this much-reprinted song was more coherent; but cinematic quick-cutting, taking the hero right to the gallows-tree, is part of the form. Young Morgan was so popular that a sequel was concocted: reprieved, he goes to France, buys a black pudding, uses it as a mock hold-up pistol, and is soon prosperous again — robbing the despised French

* 'John of Gaunt' suggests that this line may originally have been 'I seemed a blade they could not daunt' (with an abab rhyme-scheme throughout)

* As John Gay has it in *The Beggar's Opera*: 'The youth in his cart hath the air of a lord, / And we cry, There dies an Adonis!'

## The Modern Lass in High Dress

Come all ye bucks and lads of fire,
Come see a modern nymph's attire.
Here's everything to please your eyes,
And every joyous passion raise.

See how my sable locks bedeck
In wanton curls my ivory neck.
Behold my brawny shoulders bare,
Behold my bubbies round and fair.

Look down my back e'en to my waist,
With thousand joys your fancy feast.
Through plackets see my hips, how plump, *slit in her skirt*
And ev'ry motion of my rump.

See how my hoop's contrived to show
The beauties of my limbs below,
My well-shaped leg and taper thigh,
And more perhaps if winds blow high.

So little skill our grandams knew,
They would not set a foot to view
And straight would make a wondrous rout
If bubby peeped from tucker out.

But we their offspring, far more sage
Than that prepost'rous prudish age,
All naked like our mother Eve
Will show the charms kind nature gave.

## Ye brimstones of Drury

Ye brimstones of Drury and Exeter-street, *whores*
Ye frows of the Strand and ye molls of the Fleet,
Whose soft tender hearts have by man been betrayed,
And from virtue, though 'gainst inclination, have strayed,
Obey the glad summons and quickly repair
To Fielding's new warehouse for cracked earthenware.*

Here Nancy no more shall be napped for a gown *napped=get VD*
Nor be tempted to do naughty tricks for a crown,
No more by a fulsome old bawd be oppressed,
But here (if she can) forever live chaste.
*Obey the glad summons—*

From the luscious titbit to the bouncing jack-whore,
From the bunter in rags to the gay pompadour,
Chaste Fielding invites you. Oh, give him applause,
Who lost both his daylights in Venus's cause.*
*Obey the glad summons—*

. . . . . .

No longer by night shall each draggle-tail trull
Through hail, rain and snow tramp to pick up a cull;
No longer in cursing and blasting delight,
But here on her knees pray devoutly each night.
Oh Fielding, when this can be done, I declare
You deserve a reward for your pastoral care;
You deserve a reward, sir, at Pa-d--g--n Fair.*

*Sir John Fielding (the novelists's half-brother), a notable Bow Street magistrate, in 1758 established an asylum for reclaiming prostitutes and sheltering poor girls. Many girls in bawdy-houses were 'not more than 12', he said (the age of consent until 1885)

*Sir John became blind at 19 — owing to an accident, he said

*'Paddington Fair Day' was a hanging day at Tyburn; a puzzlingly bitter jibe

## The Kennel-Raker

*kennel=gutter*

Though I sweep to and fro, old iron to find,
Brass pins, rusty nails, they are all to my mind,
Yet I wear a sound heart true to great George our king,
And though ragged and poor, with clear conscience can sing —
*Though I sweep to and fro, yet I'd have you to know*
*There are sweepers in high life as well as in low.*

The statesman he sweeps in his coffers the blunt *money*
That should pay the poor soldiers that honour do hunt.
The action though dirty, he cares not a straw:
So he gets but the ready, the rabble may jaw.
*Though I sweep to and fro, &c —*

I'm told that the parson — for I never go
To hear a man preach what he'll never stick to —
'Tis all for the sweepings he tips you the cant.
You may pray by yourselves else, depend, sirs, upon't.
*Though I sweep to and fro, &c —*

One sweeps you from this life, you cannot tell where,
And what place you go to the doctor don't care
So he brings in his bill your long purses to broach,
Then he laughs in his sleeve as he rides in his coach.
*Though I sweep to and fro, &c —*

Your counsel may plead, but pray what is it for?
His eye's on your fob whilst he chatters the law.
Tongue-padding, he rakes ye and sweeps you quite clear
Of what's better than iron, you need not to fear. *[of gold*
*Though I sweep to and fro, &c —*

But honesty's best in what station we are:
For the grand sweeper Death we can sooner prepare.
Your statesman, your parson, your physic and law
When death takes a sweep are no more than a chaw.
*Though I sweep to and fro, yet I'd have you to know*
*There are sweepers in high life as well as in low.*

## Bob and his Landlady

Upon the march it was my lot
A billet for to share
Into an inn, which made me grin
To see my dame so fair.
My landlord he proved kind to me
And I got quarters there;
And it's true I kissed my landlady,
Let that stand there.

*Let that stand there, my dear,*
*Let that stand there.*
*'Tis true I kissed my landlady,*
*Let that stand there.*

Our lousy landlord blamèd me
For doing of this deed,
Because I did relieve his wife
When in the time of need.
Being a petty constable,
For him I did not care.
It's true I kissed his pretty wife,
Let that stand there.

*Let that stand there, my dear, &c —*

Our orders were for Ireland
Fresh quarters to prepare,
Which made my handsome landlady
Begin to curse and swear,
Saying, 'I'll go along with Bob,
Let Bob go e'er so far.
My Bob's the lad that kissed me well,
Let that stand there.'

*Let that stand there, my dear, &c —*

'Farewell, my loving landlady,
I must pursue the rout.'
'Dear Bob,' says she, 'pray stay with me.
Let's take the other bout.
I'll rob the cuckold of his gold
And thou the same shalt share,
For thou'rt the lad that kissed me well,
Let that stand there.'

*Let that stand there, my dear, &c —*

Then twenty guineas in my hand
She lovingly did squeeze.
'Dear Bob,' says she, 'pray think on me
When you are on the seas.
Pray think on me: I will agree
With all your fate to share,
For thou'rt the man that kissed me well,
Let that stand there.'

*Let that stand there, my dear,*
*Let that stand there.*
*'Tis true I kissed my landlady,*
*Let that stand there.*

## The Whores' Downfall

Near to Temple Bar lived two trading women,
Jane and Madam Carr, dressed in silver trimming.
These that used to serve roaring sons o' thunder,
Now before they'll starve are glad to knock under.

Madam she was head, Jenny journeywoman,
Ere trading it was dead, when they valued no man,
Having store of sparks of all sorts and sizes,
Chubs and lawyers' clerks, men that paid good prices.

Sailors gave a crown, lawyers half a guinea,
Ready money down. Likewise they had many
Loving yea-and-nays with their linèd breeches. *rich Quakers*
Those were golden days, when they rolled in riches.

Gallants of the best came to them in coaches,
Much like squires dressed, and as sound as roaches,
Treating them with wine for a little billing.*
Now they trudge the street, glad of half a shilling.

'As your dearest friend, now I tell you, Jenny,
If trading does not mend, five pounds to a penny
We must feed on sprats the ensuing winter,
Though the finest girls that e'er abroad did venture.*

'Besides, that is not all' (so she fell a-weeping).
'We may chance to fall into limbo's keeping. *Bridewell jail*
Oh! the hemping block causes lamentation, *for beating hemp*
Many a bitter knock, tears of tribulation.'

'Madam, let's go home and not rove no longer.
Here we trudge the streets both with cold and hunger.
Here we starve and pine — see, my joints are shaking.
Not one cross of coin this night have we taken.

'Not one single souse, though I dearly lack it. *not a sou*
Madam, I'll quit your house and no longer track it.'
'Hold you!' madam cried, and with anger turning,
'That shall soon be tried — pay me for your learning.'

'Had you not my work for a little keeping?
Was ever Jew or Turk so much over-reaching?
Take the other cup and leave off your biting.'*
Madam's back was up so they fell to fighting.

'For your bully Ralph's breakfast, supper, dinner,*
Did not you pawn my smock, cap, topknot and pinner?
This you know is true, madam, with no gammon. *no pretence*
Pay your doctor too, quit your old physician.'

As these words did pass, grabbling Tom stood listening.*
He fairly checked them both as he would two chickens.
To the workhouse quod, there he led them grunting.
On the hempen block, here he left them thumping.

* A few internal rhymes are lost; here 'Wine it was their treat' would work
* For 'girls' try mots (wenches)
* *bully*: pimp/protector; for a rhyme he should be Jock
* To grabble is to seize (this seems a cobbled-up ending to a longer original)

## The Boman Prig's Farewell*

Tune, *Old Simon the King*

To the hundreds of Drury I write
And the rest of my filching companions;
To the buttocks that pad it all night, *streetwalkers*
Along with a crew of raskallions.
I now who am rubbed to the Whit *Newgate jail*
Can rattle my darbies with pleasure *shackles*
And laugh at the culls I have bit *victims*
For I have still store of their treasure.

This time I expect to be nubbed. *hanged*
My duds they grow wondrous seedy.
I prithee now send me some grub,
A slat or a bore for the needy.*
But pray don't you bring it yourself:
Harmans are at the Old Bailey. *constables*
I'd rather you would send it behalf, *by someone on your behalf*
For if they tout you they'll nail you. *if they spot you*

Behold, in my paper I leave
How my indictment was raised.
This time I expect no reprieve
That my poor corpse may be saved.
My smish and my joseph I leave *shirt (chemise) and coat*
And the rest of my duds all behind me.
If the nubbing cull I don't deceive *hangman*
Then the devil knows where for to find me.

Moll Spriggins was drunk th'other night
And tipped us a jorum of diddle, *a jug of gin*
And said she was stitched very tight *treated outrageously*
By Pitchford that plays on the fiddle.
He snaffled her clout, poll and tail,*
For which he was hiked to the Whit, sir,
But now the bitch pads it in jail
And laughs at the culls she has bit, sir.

Then adieu to all kins and knots, *thieves; gangs*
To kid-layers, files and trapanners,*
To the buttocks and other fine flats *low whores, and others*
And all fellow men that have manners.
Here's a health to all beauman prigs,
From the rum pad down to the prancer. *bold robber; horse-thief*

We will mill all the culls with our fibs *mill=fight; fibs=b lows*
And teach them a new morris-dance, sir.

This time I expect no reprieve.
The sheriff's come down with his warrants.
An account I behind me must leave
Of birth, education and parents.
Our bolts are knocked off in the Whit, *leg-irons*
Our friends to die penitent pray us.
The nubbing cove pops from the pit *the hangman arrives*
And into the tumbril conveys us.

Then from the Whit to the tree
As ordered by my sad sentence.
The gownsman he there does meet me
And talks a long time of repentance.
But when I am tied up to the gib
I look like a fool in the forest.*
My eyes from the light they are hid.
The tumbler draws off, then I'm morrised.*

* *boman prig*: clever thief; in stanza 5 it is 'beauman', showing the derivation
* *slat or a bore*: a puzzle; a later version has 'flat'; another tries 'a bottle or two'
* He stole her handkerchief, headgear and gown
* *kid-layers*: who rob messenger-boys; *files*: pickpockets; *trapanners*: swindlers
* This fragment of Shakespeare ('I met a fool i' the forest', *As You Like It*, II, 7) must somehow have became a catch-phrase
* *tumbler*: tumbril; the man kicks as if dancing (see endnote on hangings)

## De Night before Larry was stretched

### An Irish Slang Song, to be pronounced as spelled

De night before Larry was stretched
De boys all dey ped him a visit,
And bait in der sacks too dey fetched. *food in their pockets*
Dey sweated der duds till dey ris it, *pawned their clothes*
For Larry was ever de lad,
When a boy was condemned to de squeezer, *noose*
Would pop all de duds dat he had *pawn*
To help his comrade to a sneezer *a dram*
*And warm his gab 'fore he died.*

De boys dey came crowding in fast,
Dey drew all their stools round about him.
Nine glims round his trapcase were placed. *candles*
Oh, he could not be well waked widout dem.
When one of us axed, could he die
Widout having truly repented,
Says Larry, 'Dat's all in my eye
And first by de clergy invented
*To fatten dir gobs wid a bit.'*

'I'm sorry, dear Larry,' says I,
'To see you in dis situation
And blister my limbs if I lie,
But I'd 's liff it had been my own station.' *as lief*
'Oghone! it's all over,' said he,
'For de neckcloth I'll be forced to put on,
And by dis time tomorrow you'll see
Your poor Larry as dead as a mutton.
*Bekaise why? My cause it was good.'*

De cards being called for, dey pled,
Den Larry found one of dem cheated.
A dart at his napper he med *head*
(De boy being easily heated)
And sed, 'Be de holy, you teeffe, *thief*
I'll splinter your skull wid my daddle. *fist*
You cheat me bekaise I'm in grief,
But soon I'd demolish your noddle
*And tip you your claret to drink.'* *your blood*

De clargy stepped up wid his book *priest*
And spoke him so neat and so civil.

Larry tipped him a Kilmainham look — *Kilmainham jail*
And pitched his big wig to de devil.
Den gently raising his head
He took a sup out of de bottle
And sighing most bitterly said,
'Oh! de hemp will be soon round my t'rottle
*And squeeze my poor windpipe to death.'*

So melting these last words he spoke,
Our griff it found vent in a shower. — *grief*
As for my part, I t'ought my heart broke
For to see him cut down like a flower.
On his travels I saw him next day.
O de t'rottle! By the hoky, I could kill him, — *hangman*
But Larry not one word did say,
Nor change till he came to King William,*
*And den, why his colour grew white.*

When he came to de nubbing chit — *the gallows*
He was tucked up so neat and so pretty.
De rumbler shoved off from his feet — *the cart*
And he died wid his face to de city.
He kicked too but dat was all pride,
For soon you might see 'twas all over,
And when dat de noose was untied,
At home, why, we waked him in clover
*And sent him to take a ground sweat.*

* *King William:* statue of William III then in front of Trinity College, Dublin

## Female Ware

Come all ye country yea-and-noes,
Ye Temple rakes and City beaux
And ancient flogging cullies.
Walk in and see my female ware,
The black, the brown, the red, the fair,
All free from c—ps and bullies, — *claps*
*All free from c—ps and bullies.*

I've widows, wives and pretty maids,
Fine dapper dames and lusty jades
Of every age and stature:
High-flyers, Quakers, Meeters, Saints

Who scorn your washes and your paints,
All beautiful by nature.

My wine is good, both white and red.
Its fumes ne'er get into the head,
The heart it cheers and lightens.
My nectar too is quite complete:
If you walk in I will you treat,
The eye it always brightens,

The wieldy cit may ease his cares
Upon my beds or strong-backed chairs
With nymphs that's most complying.
They'll wriggle well, they'll ride St George — *perform on top*
Or a frigid dotard smartly scourge
Till you cry, 'My dear! I'm dying!'

If you don't find all this is true
When of my house you take a view
And see my regulation,
Say I'm a jilting fat-a—e b—d — *fat-arse bawd*
As e'er hired p—ps or took reward — *pimps*
Or dwells within the nation,
*Or dwells within the nation.*

## Sandman Joe

*As sung at the Anacreontic Society**

Oh the other day as Sandman Joe
Up Holborn Hill was jogging,
His rawboned steed it scarce could go,
But still the dog kept flogging.

*His rawboned steed, scarce fit for the crows,*
*Just starved to death could scarce go,*
*While gallus Joe his rump he rubbed* — *strong, handsome; whipped*
*And roaring cried, White sand O!**
*Why here's your lily lily lily lily white sand O!*

To sell his sand ere far he'd got,
'Twas near a neighbouring alley,
When turning of his head about
He saw his flash girl Sally.

*His rawboned steed, scarce fit for the crows,*
*Could scarce stand when he cried Whoa!*
*But to keep him up his rump he rubbed,*
*And roaring cried, White sand O!*
*Why here's your lily lily lily lily white sand O!*

He stared a while, then turned his quid.
Why, blast you, Sall, I loves you!
And for to prove what I have said,
This night I'll soundly fuck you.
Why then, says Sall, my heart's at rest
If what you say you'll stand to.
His brawny hands her bubbies pressed
And he roaring cried, *White sand O!*
*Why here's your lily lily lily lily white sand O!*

Said Sall to Joe, Where shall we go
To get some gin to warm us?
Up at St Giles's Pound, said Joe,*
For there the gin won't harm us.
*His rawboned steed, scarce fit for the crows, etc* —

When to St Giles's they had got
They made themselves quite merry.
They five times drained the quartern pot — *quarter of a pint*
With glorious gin so cheery.
*His rawboned steed, etc* —

Oh then they kissed, and then shook fist.
My dearest Joe, I know ye:
As sound a dog as ever pissed.
This night I'll doss with Joey.
Then away they went with hearts content
To play the game you all know,
While gallus Joe he wagged his arse
And roaring cried, *White sand O!*
*Why here's your lily lily lily — lil-ly — li–l–ly white — sand — O!*

* *Anacreontic Society* : a club of gentlemen who met at a superior tavern, the Crown and Anchor in the Strand. And a short walk away, this song was enjoyed by a lower class of reveller. Francis Place, who preserved it as an example of 18th-century coarseness, says it was sung on Saturday nights 'in an open space at the back of St Clement's in the Strand, at the front of an alehouse called the Crooked Billet, by two women who used to sham dying away as they concluded the song — amidst roars of laughter'.

* *white sand*: for household use, scouring pots, etc

* *St Giles's Pound*: now the part of Oxford Street north of Soho Square

# Christening Little Joey, or the Devil to Pay

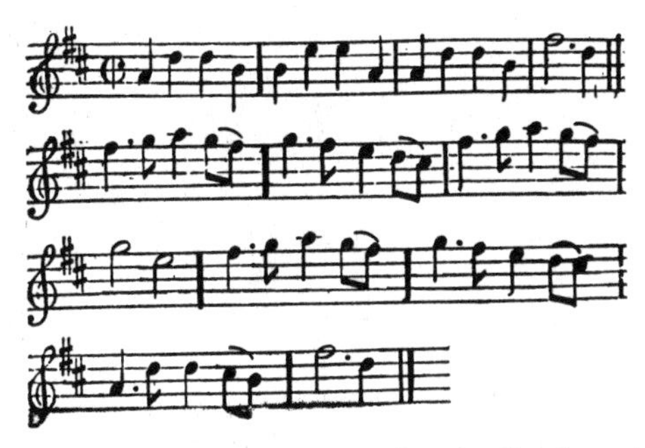

Come list a while, I'll tell you how, to Joe the Sandman's joy, sir,
The moll with whom he used to snooze brought forth a chopping
boy, sir;
And by the statute of Hedge-lane, as Joey must pass for dad, sir,
When that they did christen him, a roaring booze they had, sir.
*Sing rumpty roudy &c*

When three weeks old, then Blear-eyed Bob, Sam Sweep and
Dustcart Chloe
To give the little kid a name invited were by Joey.
And Filching Fan was likewise there, a brim with bird-lime fingers,*
And Mumping Moll brought Chanting Dick, the prince of ballad-
singers. *Sing rumpty roudy &c*

Sir Jeffery Dunstan, Garratt's mayor, a Whig of high renown, sir,*
Brought Buntinelle, a brimstone who cried matches through the
town, sir.
With Irish Pat Miss Blarney came, O bless the wriggling cratur!
When Langolee came in her head, her tail would wag by nature.*
*Sing rumpty roudy &c*

When all were met, to church they went, but such a queer procession
Of seedy culls and bunting brims, 'tis almost past expression.
When dominie had named the kid, why back again they piked it.
A flash of lightning was prepared for every one that liked it.
*Sing rumpty roudy &c*

The lads they swigged their barley swipes, as short-cut they were
smoking.
The girls drank tea and pattered flash, with gallows fun and joking.
And when that they had sluiced their gobs, wit striving to excel wit,
The lads began to gnaw their nobs and tip the frows the velvet.*
*Sing rumpty roudy &c*

Sam Sweep he sucked Miss Blarney's jowl, which Irish Paddy
smoking, *noticing*
Soon lent his lantern jaws a lick — 'Oh, I believe I spoiled your
joking!
You gallows whore, last night I caught your cull and you i' the privy.
The pains of hell shall be delight to the kick of the arse I'll give ye.'
*Sing rumpty roudy &c*

He would have done it then and there, but Mumping Moll she held
him.
'You bitch! Why meddle you?' says Dick. Upon the ground she felled
him.
Sir Jeffery interfered and got a blow from Bob the Blinker
When Bunting Nell bounced in between and tipped the cull a clinker.
*Sing rumpty roudy &c*

Now Sandman Joey getting up to quell the general riot,
Swore 'Damn his eyes', he'd mill 'em all unless they'd all be quiet:
'I'd scorn to use a gemman so that to his treat had ax'd me.
Within my ken to breed a row, why 'tis not genteel, blast me!'
*Sing rumpty roudy &c*

So peace took place, and supper came to treat their curious cronies:
A bullock's melt, a nice hog's maw, sheep's head and stale polonies.*
Till twelve o'clock they swigged gin hot, when all as blind as Chloe
Reeled home (save those the watchmen got) from christening little
Joey.
*Sing rumpty roudy &c*

This too was sung at the Anacreontic Society (to the tune of 'Daniel Cooper'). A brief glossary: *brim, brimstone,* whore; *mumping,* begging; *piked it,* hurried; *flash of lightning,* glass of gin; *swipes,* beer; *gallows (gallus),* great; *sucked,* kissed; *mill,* punch, beat; *ken,* house

**Sir Jeffery Dunstan*: at the time of each parliamentary election, the humble voteless people of the village of Garratt (a name surviving in Garratt Lane, Wandsworth) held a tumultuous burlesque election; from the early 1780s until 1796 their 'mayor' was 'Sir' Jeffery, a radical-minded dealer in old wigs

**Langolee*: in a popular Irish song, yet another word for the male organ

**gnaw their nobs*: unexplained; *tip the frows the velvet*: use their tongues when kissing the women

**bullock's melt*: one meaning of melt (or milt) is spleen, but as another is semen, perhaps it is slang for the animal's penis or testicles

# Ye scamps, ye pads, ye divers

Ye scamps, ye pads, ye divers and all upon the lay,*
In Tothill Fields gay sheep-walk like lambs ye sport and play.
Rattling up your darbies, come hither at my call: *fetters*
I'm jigger-dubber here, and you're welcome to mill doll,*
*With my tow de row, &c.*

At your insurance-office the flats you've taken in. *dupes*
The game you've played, my kiddy, you're always sure to win.
First you touch the shiners — the number up, you break.*
With your insuring policy I'd not insure your neck,
*With my tow de row, &c.*

. . . . . . .

My peepers, who've we here now? Why, this is sure Black Moll.
Why ma'am, you're of the fair sex, and welcome to mill doll.
The cull with you who'd venture into a snoozing-ken *brothel*
Like blackamoor Othello should — 'put out the light — and then —'
*With my tow de row, &c.*

I say, my flashy coachman, that you'll take better care,
Nor for a little bub come the slang upon your fare. *
Your jazy pays the garnish, unless the fees you tip.*
Though you're a flashy coachman, here the gagger holds the whip,
*With my tow de row, &c.*

*We're scamps, we're pads, we're divers, we're all upon the lay,*
*In Tothill Fields gay sheep-walk like lambs we sport and play.*
*Rattling up our darbies, we're hither at your call.*
*You are jigger-dubber here, and we're forced for to mill doll,*
*With my tow de row, &c.*

This was sung in a pantomime, *The Choice of Harlequin* — a great success as an afterpiece at Covent Garden Theatre in 1781-2. The rogues are addressed by the turnkey (jigger-dubber = door-locker) of a prison in Tothill Fields, then a marshy waste beyond Westminster Abbey (sheep-walk = exercise-yard)

*'You highway robbers, footpads, pickpockets and others living by crime'

**mill doll*: beat hemp (for ropemaking), a prison punishment

**insurance-office:* a dubious agency that sold lottery tickets, plus insurance against their being losers; *the number up, you break*: at the time of the draw the rogues vanish

* *bub*: drink; *come the slang*: practise a cheat (very early such use of 'come')

**jazy*: jasey, wig, which he must hand over if he has no cash for the garnish that every new prisoner must pay to the jailer and to old prisoners

## Toast All

Dinner o'er, and grace said, we'll for bus'ness prepare,
Arranged right and left in support of the chair.
We'll chorus our song as the circling toast passes,
And manage our bumpers as musical glasses.
*Sing Tantararara, Toast all.*

To your lips, my convivials, the burgundy lift:
May we never want courage when put to the *shift*! *smock*
Here's what tars dislike, and what ladies like best.
What's that? You may whisper, why, 'tis *to be pressed.*
*Sing Tantararara, &c.*

Ye fowlers who eager at partridges aim,
Don't mark the maimed covey, but mind better game:
'Tis beauty's the sport to repay sportsmen's trouble,
And there *May our pointers stand stiff in the stubble.*
*Sing Tantararara, &c.*

. . . . . .

Asthmatical gluttons exist but to eat.
They purchase repletions at each turtle treat.
Our feast boasts a flavour unknown to made dishes.
Here's *Life's dainty, dressed with the sweet sauce of kisses.*
*Sing Tantararara, &c.*

Fair befall every lass, fair may fine ladies fall.
No colour I'll fix on, but drink to them all,
The black, the brunette and the golden-locked dame —
*The lock of all locks, and unlocking the same.*
*Sing Tantararara, &c.*

. . . . . .

Here's *Bathsheba's cockpit, where David stood sentry;*
*Eve's custom-house, where Adam made the first entry;*
Here's *The pleasant placed waterfall 'midst Bushey Park;*
*The nick makes the tail stand; The farrier's wife's mark.*
*Sing Tantararara, &c.*

*That the hungry be filled with rich things,* let us say,
*And well pleased the rich be sent empty away.*
Here's *The miller's wife's music; The lass that's lamb-like;**
And *The fence of the farmer on top of love's dyke.*
*Sing Tantararara, &c.*

But why from this round-about phrase must be guessed
What in one single syllable's better expressed?
That syllable then I my sentiment call,*
So here's to that word which is, *One word for all.*
*Sing Tantararara, Toast all.*

* *lamb-like*: as another song of the time has it, 'I love the lass that's plump and free, / That like the lamb will wag her tail'
* 'The syllable' was long a euphemism for cunt

## The Milkmaid

### A parody on The Ploughboy *

A flaxen-headed milkmaid
As simple as may be,
And next a pretty dairy-maid,
I chanted o'er the lea.
But now a saucy chambermaid,
I've got a better place.
I'll dress my head with ribbons fine,
Set off my handsome face.

When housekeeper promoted
I'll snip a butcher's bill,
My lady's pockets empty —
My own I mean to fill.
And lolling in my chariot,
A lady great I'll be.
You'll forget the little milkmaid
That chanted o'er the lea.

I'll try to get a husband.
No matter for the pelf:
So I can have a title,
Why then, I please myself.
Her Ladyship I long to be,
A lord or knight I crave.
If he is rich in honours,
No matter if a knave.

I hope to be a peeress
And see a birthday ball,
With footmen dressed so gaily
My carriage for to call.
When lolling in my chariot

A lady great I'll be.
You'll forget the little milkmaid
That chanted o'er the lea.

I'll send my lord to India
His pockets for to fill.
So he does get their treasure,
The nabobs he may kill.*
With gold and diamonds loaded
When he returns again,
For honours and for riches
I'll be foremost in the train.

A Knight of Bath or Garter
I'll purchase him, I vow,
And then forget those merry days
When milking of my cow.
So lolling in my chariot
A lady great I'll be.
You'll forget the little milkmaid
That chanted o'er the lea.

* *The Ploughboy*: popular song in John O'Keeffe's *The Farmer*, 1787, with similar dreams of great things but less social comment

*Written soon after the impeachment of Warren Hastings for his ruthless pillaging conquests in India

## Jenny Sutton

Come, charge your glasses! Let us raise
From dull oblivion's slumber
A gallant nymph well worth your praise,
Whose feats no man can number.
Her hand, like Caesar's, grasped at all,
Till envy marked her station,
Then like great Caesar did she fall
By foul assassination.

*For every letch alike prepared,*
*She valued not a button,*
*And culls of every humour shared*
*The charms of Jenny Sutton!*

A by-blow on the world she burst,
By furious love engendered,
Replete with every spark of lust

That youth and vigour rendered.
The parish reared her, till she knew
For what her parts were able.
Away from workhouse then she flew
And quartered in a stable.
*For every letch alike prepared, &c—*

An empty stall supplied a bed.
A dung-heap was her bolster.
The gin and cheese on which she fed
She kept within a holster.
A single pin at night let loose
The robes that veiled her beauty;
Then down she lay for public use
To every man on duty,
*For every letch alike prepared, &c—*

A brat she bore so mixed of hues
That every corps denied it,
And whether Greys, or Buffs, or Blues
Was never yet decided.
Though troops of all sorts did surround
Her couchée and her levée,
The piebald imp was never owned
By light horse or by heavy.
*For every letch alike prepared, &c—*

Yon pissing-corner was her stand,
Where safe from watchman's danger
She undismayed stretched forth her hand
To each unbuttoned stranger.
She bared her buttocks as they pissed
To lure them with her notions,
Then like the Indian eel did twist
In strange electric motions,
*For every letch alike prepared, &c—*

Her voice had such a luscious force
That, serpent-like, its graces
Did make each stranger turn his course
And stand to her embraces!
The chords of sympathy did rend
With notes so soft and thrilling
That ravished misers stopped to spend
And fumble for their shilling!
*For every letch alike prepared, &c—*

Her body was a lottery fair
    To prick where'er it pleased you,
In a–se, or c—t, or mouth, or ear,
    She every way would ease you.
No qualms or scruples e'er had she,
    Whatever whim besieged you:
Still Jenny's kind assenting plea
    Was, 'Well sir, I'll oblige you.'
    *For every letch alike prepared, &c—*

A bumper let our fingers thus
    High raise to her perfection,
For Jenny's fingers oft for us
    Raised many a stout erection.
Within our bosoms let her live
    In kind retaliation, *in recompense*
Whose body did admission give
    To all the male creation:
    *For every letch alike prepared, &c—*

Now tune thy trump, immortal Fame,
    To sounds of lewd sensation!
In bursts of bawdy blast her name
    To every distant nation!
For ever let these climes resound,
    The scene of all her glory!
And Horse-Guards Jenny live renowned
    The first in bunters' story!

*For every letch alike prepared,*
    *She valued not a button,*
*And culls of every humour shared*
    *The charms of Jenny Sutton!*

CHARLES MORRIS

## The Rigs of the Times

One day as I rambled 'cross Kensington Park
On these sorrowful times I made this remark,
And sat myself down in the shade for to write
These verses to show that the world's all a bite:
    *For honesty is all out of fashion*
    *And these are the rigs of the times.* *tricks, cheats*

If you mean to thrive, you must follow my plan.
You must swagger and swear and cheat all you can.
The biggest deception for money contrive.
Palaver and cant, you are sure for to thrive,
*For honesty is, &c —*

You must mind that your neighbours don't see you do well.
They'll be very angry, the truth I do tell.
They'll backbite and slander to get you in thrall
And gladly rejoice to see your downfall,
*For honesty is, &c —*

The baker in cheating is none of the least
For his bread like a sponge is puffed up with yeast.
If he made his loaf as big as his wife does her head
I'm sure that the poor would never want bread,
*For honesty is, &c —*

The farmer's daughter has got an air-balloon crown.*
No wonder that butter's sixteen-pence a pound.
If you say, How so dear? — answers the sweet lass,
There's a French war, and the cows have no grass.*
She has learned her excuse,
She is up to the rigs of the times.

The next is a butcher — ay we must bring him in,
Asks tenpence a pound and thinks it no sin.
He cocks up his steelyards and makes them go down *scales*
And swears it is weight though it wants a full pound,
*For honesty is, &c —*

The next of the landlord's tricks you shall hear.
When he sees you have money, and calling for beer,
He'll bring you a relish to make the pot walk,
But I'd have you take care of the nick in the chalk, *his reckoning*
*For honesty is, &c —*

Though money is scarce and the times very bad,
The people are running stark air-balloon mad.
The women with pride the land do infest.
Though they have ne'er a smock, their heads must be dressed,
*For honesty is, &c —*

The best air-balloon profit that any can find
Is to send them all off in a high gale of wind.

The balloons in the air, let the clouds on them burst,
Then the lightest of rogues will break their necks first,
*For honesty is all out of fashion*
*And these are the rigs of the times . . .*

**air-balloon crown:* head-dress fashion inspired by manned balloons, which were first displayed in England in 1784 (a rig of their promoters, as the final stanzas see it)

**French war*: in the 1790s — a lean time for the poor, with much radical protest

## Molly Put the Kettle On

Molly put the kettle on, Molly put the kettle on,
Molly put the kettle on, we'll all have tea.
Sookey take it off again, Sookey take it off again,
Sookey take it off again, they have run away.

O what did Jenny do, O what did Jenny do,
O what did Jenny do for a bawbee? *a halfpenny*
She pulled up her petticoat, her blue-fringed petticoat,
She pulled up her petticoat above her knee.

In comes sailor Dick, who'd been to sea for a long trip,
Swearing he'd have some flip — shiners he had galore.*
Music now began to play, Poll and Sook jigged away,
'Two girls and a fiddler' was the play, with 'Jack capering on the shore'.

Jenny says it is no sin for girls to have a drop of gin,
Then we'll dance and figure in, by one, two, three and four.

Fetch then without delay from the shop o'er the way,
From the shop o'er the way where you have been before.

It was in St Catharine's Bay, where Jack he rolled it night
and day. *at St Catharine's Dock, Wapping*
While one shot in the locker lay he did sing, rant and roar.
'Fiddler, play up brisk, I say. Landlord, what's to pay?
The last shot shall fly today, and then to sea for more.'

So Molly put the kettle on, we shall have a drop of a dram,
Drink a health to Jack that's gone, for he shiners spent galore.
Another health to Jenny too, with her petticoat fringèd blue.
Now without any more ado, we all have had tea.

A good example of an adult song that was purified for the nursery
* *flip*: a drink made of beer, brandy and sugar; *shiners*: money
The lost rhyme for 'galore' at the end implies a saucier ending, with 'whore'

## The Pink of Clerkenwell

I am the Pink of Clerkenwell, *one in the height of fashion*
For many years I've borne the bell,
O'er all the blades I cut a swell.
I'm up to every go.
From Smithfield on a market day
A merry runt I drive away. *he steals an animal*
My pals are on the milling lay, *housebreaking*
While I sing Fal de ral tit
Tit fal de rol
Tit fal de ree,
While I sing Fal de ral tit.

When Poll and I walk though the street
We throw off slang at all we meet,
Or if lads or girls will stand the treat,
Into some *cove* we bundle.
We laugh at all who then pass by.
If Poll is *yellow* I sew up her eye *if she's jealous I hit her*
And while that she pretends to cry —
Why, I sing, &c —

At every flash-house we're known
And at Ball's Pond the *swell's* my own,*

Where I ne'er choose to go alone
    Whene'er a *rum* one's baited,    *a good bull*
But roll in a cart with my knowing flame.
If my dog's tossed I catch the same,
To bite his foot I think no shame,    *[to goad him on*
    And then sing, &c —

And when an execution's planned,
Close to the *drop* I take my stand*
To see the lads die hand-in-hand,
    Although it is a pity.
Bad luck to every *snitch*, say I,    *informer*
Afraid for himself to touch the *cly*.    *money*
God send they at the *crap* may die,    *gallows*
    While I sing, &c —

One night, as we came through the street,
A *cull* he wanted with Poll to speak —    *a man (dupe*
So I tipped her the wink on him t' be sweet
    To see what he'd be at.
Said I, 'You thief, why, that's my wife.
Against you she shall smack her life.'    *swear on the Bible*
So we both called 'Watch!' to quell the strife
    And then sung, &c —

And when Old Lantern Scout came near,    *night-watchman*
Said I, 'Here's something very *queer*.    *wrong*
I charge the fellow standing here.'
    Said he, 'We'll settle the matter,
And because you're a gentleman I know,
The *cove* shall take your word, or so.'    *magistrate*
Then while the *cull* to quod did go    *to the cells*
    We both sung, &c —

The time has been that many a week
We've lived upon the *upright sneak*,    *stealing pots from pubs*
But now for better things we seek
    And *fencing* is our *lay*.    *receiving is our game*
And though 'Old Iron' we hang out,    *their sign*
We take in pewter, *tick* or *clout*,    *watches; handkerchiefs*
Or for anything safe we make no rout,
    While we sing, &c —

All you that would be flash and fine,
Like us get in the knowing line,    *up to all the dodges*

Nor mind the Bench's *rum* design
While you can *palm* the *traps*; *bribe the police*
For while you don't quite *weigh your weight* *[see endnote*
You may defy both small and great
And row in each boat like the prigs of state,*
And then sing Fal de ral tit. *1793*

**Ball's Pond*: long the scene of bull-baiting — out beyond Islington village

**drop*: the 'new drop' at Newgate, a more efficient scaffold devised when the ride in a cart to Tyburn was abolished in 1783

* Play a double game like great ministerial thieves (echo of *The Beggar's Opera)*

## The Post Boy

I'm a Hounslow young lad, and Tidy's my name.
Full many a job have I drove,
Yet never crossed nag that was wind-galled or lame
But always had such as would move.
A tight pair of buckskins and boots jetty black, *leather breeches*
My spurs ever polished and smart,
A trim little jacket to put on my back
Was always the pride of my heart.

A good ten mile an hour in common my pace
While leaving behind every rip. *inferior horse*
They try to put by, but I lead them a chase
And tip 'em the smack of my whip.
When oft as I'm driving along in this style,
Through many a town as I go
The girls of each inn will bestow me a smile.
Their meaning I very well know.

Then I find 'em a-gig whenever I call,
And loll at my ease on return.
I laugh and I jeer, and I talk with 'em all,
But Patty's my only concern.
At an inn near to Windsor the little rogue dwells,
Well known by her nice winning air,
That all other girls of the place she excels
And is called pretty Patty the fair.

We have both made a vow, should we get the stuff,
To marry and so become one
As others have done, for 'tis common enough.

We'll set up an inn of our own,
Then she'll be called madam and I'll be called sir.
We'll stick up the sign of the Star.
'Mongst postboys and waiters I'll bustle and stir
While Pat hollows loud in the bar.

GEORGE SAVILLE CAREY

## Good Ale, thou art my Darling

The landlord he looks very big
With his high-cocked hat and powdered wig.
Methinks he looks both fair and fat,
But he may thank you and I for that.
For O good ale! thou art my darling,
Thou art my comfort night and morning.

The brewer brewed thee in his pan
And the tapster draws thee in his can,
So I with them will play my part
And lodge thee next unto my heart,
For O good ale, *&c* –

And if my wife should thee despise,
By Jove, I'll beat out both her eyes,
But if she loves me as I love thee
A happy couple we shall be,
For O good ale, *&c* –

Thou oft hast made my friends my foes,
And often made me pawn my clothes,
But since thou art so near my nose,
Come up, my friend — and down it goes,
For O good ale! thou art my darling,
Thou art my comfort night and morning.

## Deborah and Jonathan

Jonathan a-wooing went.
He was such a bonny man!
And matrimony was the bent
Of little jolly Jonathan.
Deborah, the damsel's name,
Buxom was and frisky–o!

And sure as ever Sunday came
He drove her in his whisky–o. *a light gig*
Oh, the whisky!
Fine and frisky!
What a happy maid and man,
Deborah and Jonathan!

Jonathan, a squabby elf,
Very short though strong enough,
Found his wooing, like himself,
Not half a quarter long enough.
Cries he, 'Twill be a lucky hit
With wealthy Deb to tether–o!
So dug for Deb the marriage pit
And in they fell together–o!
O the tumble,
Jolt and jumble!
What a frisky wife and man,
Deborah and Jonathan!

Deborah had money got,
Jonathan diminished it,
Drank about, nor left his pot
Till fifty times he finished it.
When tipsy, he then Deb would pout —
When sober, scratch and quarrel–o!
He bangs the door, damns, flounces out,
And soaks again his barrel–o!
O the croaking,
Scratching, soaking—
What a happy maid and man,
Deborah and Jonathan!

## Answer to Chit-Chat

The satiric song of Chit-Chat I mean now to reverse,
And offer this to you for better or for worse,
Though I have no opponent, retaliation's due
As all the ladies' foibles I have pointed out to view,
So now, my pretty ge'men, I'll have a touch at you.

Their pretty little brutus combed up so neat and spruce, *upswept hair*
Their pretty little snuffboxes they often introduce.

With dashing boots and spurs on, a natty whip beside,
A stranger would of course suppose they meant to take a ride,
But the deuce of any horse they have whereon to get astride.

Their collars and their cravats which cover all their chin,
And every foppish means devised the ladies' hearts to win.
Their coats are lined with sarsenet to cut a flaming dash.
All other sorts of lining they consider merely trash,
Though a *very, very* few have their pockets lined with cash.

Nor are those flaming blades *bon ton* now completely dressed
Without a pretty quizzing-glass suspended from their breast,
A dashing golden watch-chain to constitute the beau,
A pretty bunch of seals en suite to make a glaring show,
Though probably no watch at all, or one that will not go.

Their pretty little fingers too, all bedizened out with rings.
Almost up to their shoulders are their small-clothes fixed
with slings, *trousers, worn very high-waisted*
Their boots with military heels, and boot-tops nearly white.
At dances, fights and races they place their whole delight,
And with gaming and with rioting they turn the day to night.

These pretty dashing gentlemen, when they have lost their all,
Their credit's gone, too late they find their pride must have a fall —
Perhaps a tender loving wife and pretty children dear —
Reflection strikes that poverty's approaching very near.
With a pretty little pop-gun then he ends his life's career.

## Four in Hand

With spirits gay I mount the box, the tits up to their traces,
My elbows squared, my wrists turned down, dash off to Epsom races.
With Buxton bit, bridoon so trim, three chestnuts and a grey —
Well coupled up my leaders, then *ya hip!* we bowl away.
*Some push along with four in hand while others drive at random*
*In whisky, buggy, gig or dog-cart, curricle or tandem.*

(*Spoken*) Ya! ya! ya hip! go along wi' ye. — I say, Bill, if I hadn't turned the leader neatly over the old woman we should have dashed neck and crop into the china-shop. — Why didn't you keep on that side of the road? — Where are you coming, *Johnny Raw*? — You be d—d, who made you a coachman? Why didn't your servant take hold of the reins? — Where are you going to now? — Ya hip! had all the *Brighton flashmen* in a long trot. — D—me, that's prime!*

*Some push along with four in hand, &c —*

Prime of life to go it, where's a place like London?
Four in hand today, the next you may be undone.
Where belles as well as beaux to get the whip-hand strive,
And Mrs Snip, the tailor's wife, can teach her spouse to drive.
So Jackey Snip, his wife and all to Dobbin's back are strapped on
In one-horse shay to spend the day with neighbour Stitch at Clapton.*

> (*Spoken*) Master Snip, I desire you'll not be vulgar today. — Vell, I von't if I can help it. — Here, ostler, bring my dog a snap of hay, and the horse a glass of gin and beer. — Landlord, bring me a *thimble-full* of brandy. — Who are you? — Who learned you to drive? — What d'ye mean by that? I'm Richard Cypher, esq, attorney and solicitor, belonging to the honourable *Neck or Nothing*, have gone through all the gradations of buggy, gig, and dog-cart, tandem, curricle, unicorn and four-in-hand; neglected nothing, dashed at everything — *pegged at a jarvey* — *tooled* a mailcoach — and now have attained the credit of being *bang up*.*

*Some push along, &c* —

Thus 'tis with all who in London are thriving,
Both high life and low life at something are driving.
A peer and a prentice now dress so much the same,
You cannot tell the difference, excepting by the name.
On Epsom Downs, 'Say, Billy, zounds! that cannot be Lord Jockey.
Egad! But now I see it is — I took him for his lacquey.'

> (*Spoken*) Ya! ya hip! ya hip! prime work — kept the Bristol mail at *long-trot*. — Why, these men haven't paid the toll. — Didn't I show you the ticket? — What's the number? — 281 — Pay the man or I'll knock your chops about. — You've got no money. — That's a queer half-crown, it won't do, it's a Frenchman. You'd better give us threepenn'orth of *Brumjim* ha'pence than this French emperor's money. — That's not what I gave you. — Yes it is. — None of your smashing tricks here — Why, zounds, this is a proper *cross and jostle*! Spoonies, sawneys, come, be off, thus —*

*Some push along with four in hand while others drive at random*
*In whisky, buggy, gig or dog-cart, curricle or tandem.*

ISAAC POCOCK

* *Brighton flashmen*: young bucks trying to match his speed — by that date a mere six or seven hours London–Brighton

* The Snips have harnessed a workhorse to their shay (chaise)

* *unicorn*: three-horse carriage; *pegged at a jarvey*: taken over the reins from a coachman; *bang up*: first-rate

* *Brumjim*: Birmingham; *smashing*: passing counterfeit money

# Tantararara, Rogues All!

Come, come, my good masters, what's all this about,
Such grunting and groaning, within doors and out?
Some mountain is bursting, or will ere 'tis long,
Just to keep up the tune of the oldfashioned song.
Sing Tantararara, rogues all, rogues all!
Sing Tantararara, rogues all!

The farmers— Oh no! *Farming Gentlemen* now,
Who know nought about either pasture or plough,
Tell us plain that the clodpoles for such things were born.
'Tis enough that *they know when to lock up their corn!* *[to boost the price*
*Sing Tantararara, rogues all, &c —*

The brewers (poor creatures!), monopoly's crew,
Complain of the *hardships* they're forced to go through!
And while they buy up all they can, far and near,
Deem it hard to get *fivepence a pot* for *small beer!*
*Sing Tantararara, rogues all, &c —*

The miller (sly dog) in *his way* gets a pull,
And while the mill's going, keeps grinding John Bull!
Yet Bull tells the miller, in spite of mill-clack,
Though his *outside is whitened,* his *in* is d——d *black!*
*Sing Tantararara, rogues all, &c —*

The grazier, who seldom does business by halves,
And blood-draws the Bull breed as so many calves,
With the middle-man bargains to keep up the price,
And thus lives to bite us, as cats bleed the mice!
*Sing Tantararara, rogues all, &c —*

The butcher, while cutting his mutton and beef,
Cries, 'The trade is so starving, it kills me with grief,'
And while he is rolling with riches and fat
Exclaims, 'Why, I don't get a farthing by that!'
*Sing Tantararara, rogues all, &c —*

The grocers, sweet things! are *too sweet* in their way
To meddle with *birch-twigs,* or deal in foul play,*
So the laws and exciseman but leave them alone:
They can dish up their *tea-stuff* with *leaves* of their own!
*Sing Tantararara, rogues all, &c —*

Cant! Cant! is the order and *hum* of the day,
While honesty's kicked like a strumpet away.
Pimps, sharps and pickpockets join hands with defaulters,
Some waiting for *places*, and others for *halters!* *hangman's nooses*
Sing Tantararara, rogues all, rogues all!
Sing Tantararara, rogues all!

* *birch-twigs*: grocers were caught adulterating tea with dried leaves and other dubious stuff — a scandal of 1818, probable date of this song

## Doctor Monro

'Dear doctor, be clever, and fling off your beaver.
Come, bleed me and blister me, do not be slow.
I'm sick, I'm exhausted, my schemes they are blasted
And all driven heels-o'er-head, Doctor Monro.'
'Be patient, dear fellow, you foster your fever.
Pray, what's the misfortune that bothers you so?'
'O doctor! I'm ruined! I'm ruined for ever!
My lass has forsaken me, Doctor Monro.

'I meant to have married and tasted the pleasures,
The sweets, the enjoyments, in wedlock that flow,
But she's ta'en another, and broken my measures,
And fairly confounded me, Doctor Monro.'
'I'll bleed and I'll blister you, over and over.
I'll master your malady ere that I go.
But raise up your head from below the bed-cover
And give some attention to Doctor Monro.

'If Christy had wed you she would have misled you
And laughed at your love with some handsome young beau:
Her conduct will prove it; but how would you love it?'
'I soon would have lamed her, dear Doctor Monro.'
'Each year brings a pretty young son or a daughter;
Perhaps you're the father, but how shall you know?
You hug them — her gallant is bursting with laughter —'
'That thought's like to murder me, Doctor Monro.'

'The boys cost you many a penny and shilling.
You breed them with pleasure, with trouble and woe,
But one turns a rake and another a villain.'
'My heart could not bear it, dear Doctor Monro.'

'The lasses are comely and dear to your bosom,
  But virtue and beauty has many a foe!
O think what may happen — just nipped in their blossom —'
  'Ah, merciful heaven! Cease, Doctor Monro.

'Dear doctor, I'll thank you to hand me my breeches.
  I'm better: I'll drink with you ere that you go.
I'll never more sicken for women or riches,
  But love my relations and Doctor Monro.
I plainly perceive, were I wedded to Christy
  My peace and my pleasures I needs must forgo.'
He still lives a bachelor, drinks when he's thirsty
  And sings like a lark, and loves Doctor Monro.

## Stop the Mill

Oh, stop the mill, stop the mill, stop it, I pray, *the treadmill*
For I have been treading a good deal today.
My head is quite sore from the thumps I've received
And my bones ache so much that sorely I'm grieved.
  Then stop the mill, stop the mill, stop it, I pray,
  For I have been treading a good deal today.

Oh, stop the mill, keeper, for my feet are quite sore.
Let me out, and I swear I'll go thieving no more.
This is dev'lish hard work when I'm put to the test,

And I'm laluped and bruised if I just stop to rest.
    Then stop the mill, etc —

Oh, list! Mr Keeper, I've lost all my breath.
Oh pray let me out, or 'twill give me my death.
And once out — if I ever come here to be banged,
I'll deal in false screens first, and then I'll be hanged. *forged banknotes*
    Then stop the mill, stop the mill, stop it, I pray,
    For I have been treading a good deal today.

## The Muff

### A regular out-and-out flash ditty

Really wherever one passes,
    Induced by the winter, no doubt,
We see the wives, women and lasses
    Their hairy things showing about.
Some songs in your ears have been ringing
    And what you have thought precious stuff
Not improved by the muff who's been singing;
    But now I shall sing of a muff.

A muff! It were funny to trace it —
    Its beginnings, use, habits to mark.
Eve's, as the first we must place it,
    Red lining, and fringe very dark.
The ancients to us have been handing
    The fashions, I'll venture to say.
The colours have been of long standing,
    They're the same women wear to this day.

When Dame Eve the right path forsakèd,
    Of course her concern was great,
And Adam, when he saw her naked,
    He gave her a covering straight.
He too had not any clothes on
    And the weather was chilly and rough,
And she, seeing him stand stiff and frozen,
    Said, 'Here, just slip into my muff.'

The cold weather sorely did grieve her,
    And there is no record to tell 't
Whether Eve's muff was squirrel or beaver,
    Though I think it must have been felt.

Ladies aren't so covered at all now
    As then, when the limbs were less supple.
Full dressed they go to a ball now,
    But naked Eve went to a couple.

But muffs often change — who can doubt it?
    Miss Brown's muff, when only fifteen,
Was soft, plump, no hair scarce about it,
    And the smallest hole ever yet seen.
At thirty, tough usage so tried her
    That her muff was not worth a pin,
And the hole it got wider and wider
    And a piece she was forced to put in.

At sixty she was near to croaking,
    For from black it was turning to grey,
And her muff it had had so much stroking
    That the nap was almost rubbed away.
From its former size it was much shrunken,
    Ragged inside and out, and declined.
A yard long it was once, though now sunken,
    And no more she could now get it lined.

## A Lamentable Lamentation

O Lord, O Lord, what times are these for making alteration,
For pulling down and building up throughout this hugeous nation.
They mend, improve and alter things, and former ways all flout 'em.
There's nothing left o' th' good old times but a song they sings
    about 'em.

Unbounded steam bears sov'reign sway, and man's of no utility.
It drives a pile or makes a pin with equal great facility.
It to the fancied powers of magic rapidly approaches:
It hatches eggs, it washes clouts, impels ships and stagecoaches.

The companies that's formed of late exceed imagination, sirs,
And one in female breasts hath caused a wondrous agitation, sirs,
For children they're to get by steam, as by a late improvement, sirs,
The girls are all to be served out by a patent steamer movement,
    sirs.

. . . . . . . .

In former times a great event would serve a year to talk about.

Now wiser grown, they last a week and then no more are thought
about,
Unless some deed, terrific quite, our senses should annoy, sir,
Like Thurtell's, Kean and Mother Cox, Miss Foote or Fauntleroy, sir.*

Some short time since 'bout Mrs Cox the public all were modest-
struck
And railed at Kean for having made Cox look just like a forest-buck.
Their modesty was all my eye, though Kean they poured their ills on,
For those who hissed him daily read the Life of Harriette Wilson.*

This naughty jade's notorious life sets wedded lords a-weeping,
To think that into all their faults their spouses may be peeping.
'False man!' they cry, 'the book tells me that nastily you've kissed
her.'
And some scream out, 'You filthy wretch! You've bodkined
Harriette's sister.'

Time was, when you were muslin-struck you'd cross the bridge to
Dover-street:*
At any house you chanced to knock, a score of willing girls you'd
meet.
But now so moral are the times, they're milling sent to Brixton,*
And they've scarcely left us one at all to exercise our tricks on.

*1825*

*John Thurtell, notorious murderer; the actor Edmund Kean, sued for damages for adultery with the wife of an Alderman Cox; Maria Foote, though of dubious reputation, awarded a generous £3,000 in a breach-of-promise suit; Henry Fauntleroy, executed for forgery — all sensations of 1824

*When Harriette Wilson, an enterprising courtesan, published her memoirs in instalments in 1825, detailing her connections with the Duke of Wellington and many others, people queued week after week at the bookshops

*not in Mayfair, but Great Dover Street over the Thames in Southwark

*to the treadmill in Brixton prison

## Jerry Abershaw's Will

### Sung at the Cider Cellars

### Tune, *The twelve-inch chive*

Vhen the noted Jerry Abershaw vas cast for death
And vas sentenced to exhibit in chains O!
He inwited all his pals for to vitness his last breath,
And their legacies to take of his remains O!
Said he to Tommy Clark, 'You my 'secutor shall be,

But before upon my vill ve do begin O!
In order that my vishes you more plainerer may see,
Let us *vater* vell our *vinkers* vith some gin O!' *[wet an eye: drink*

And vhen that they had vetted both *vinkers* with the max *gin*
And viped it vell off vith some more O!
Said Tommy, 'I vill do anything vot you vill ax,
Just to score off the snitches' old score O.' *informers*

Then said Jerry, 'Take these *poppers* and this fourteen-inch chive.*
They are *bussom friends* that werry seldom fails O.
They'll keep privet all your secrets as long as you do live,
'Cause, do ye see, a dead man never tells no tales O!

'This popper cured the charley vhen ve cracked the doctor's ken*
Vith *blue boluses* he never did digest O. *pills of lead*
This *chive gammed* the captain and this gagger mummed his *hen,**
For vhich Billy Haines was forced to stand the test O!

'This belcher *ding* to Dolly to flash upon her breast, *neckerchief*
To remind her vhen she lifts it to her nose O
Vhen I am in my *everlasting suit* so tightly dressed
And no friend to wisit Jerry but the crows O!

'These garters give to Bet, and bid her bind them round her head.
They vill make her snooze as still as any mouse O —
They are vot vas used to *pacify* old vimmen in their bed,
Just to keep 'em quiet vhile we cleared the house O!

'And vhen I ride in state I vill make the svells to stare
If my pals vill come and *play a game of fives* O! *pick pockets*
A backee-stopper each from my tenter hooks I'll spare,
Vhat vill show them how to regulate their lives O!'

So vhile another dose of *pigeon's milk* went round
St George's tenor did begin to toll O — *[tolling for the hanging*
The Or'nary appeared and most thunderly he frowned, *clergyman*
And said, 'Lord-a-mercy on your vicked soul O!'

Said Jerry, 'I'm no snitch — from hypocrisy I'm free,
And I'm sartain you can't preach me a reprieve O.
If I have robbed the world, all the world has cheated me,
Then for vot have I the more than them to grieve O?

'The exciseman fleeces every vun of all that they do gain,
The bishop just for nothing takes his tithes O!
The minister sells places but the pension does retain,
And the lawyers' quills do cut as deep as scythes O!

'The doctor gives us physic just to make our sickness vorse,
Then says he can't find out our complaint O —
The physician vot he sends puts your guineas in his purse,
Writes dog Latin, takes his leave like any saint O!'

At last he vas ordered for to quit his dingy cage,
Which made his *pals* and *blowens* look so shy O, *flash girls*
And be ready to go off in the eight o'clock stage
Down to Vimbleton, the Surrey air to try O! *

He said his mother told him he would die in his shoes,
'Cause he boned his father's *tatler* from his fob O, *stole; watch*
But to prove she told a lie, while his scrag was in the noose
As a legacy he kicked them to the mob O.

. . . . . . .

'So of the vicked vorld I vill now take my leave,
For I never found a man vot I could trust O —
From the pedlar to the peer all their smiles are to deceive
And there is but vun Great Being that is just O!'

* 'Take these pistols and this fourteen-inch knife'
* 'This pistol shot the watchman when we burgled the doctor's house'
* 'This knife stabbed the captain and this gag silenced his wife'
* To be gibbeted at Wimbledon — the scene of the crime for which he is to die

## The Duo Amoroso

### Written on the marriage of an eminent Music Composer

To his bride as she blushing lay by her Adonis
Cried Quaver, 'My idol, my dear Margarette,
Take this hautboy in hand, most enchanting its tone is,
And I'll teach you, my love, a delightful duet.'
Then the pipe to her rosy lips quickly conveyed was,
While she fluttered and trembled, and crimsoned all o'er,
For the dear little novice ashamed and afraid was
As she never had played this same lesson before.
*Oh sweet is de tune of Duo Amoroso,*
*De movement how soft of de charming duet!*

Encouraged at length by the words of her lover,
She waited with patience the tune to begin.
First fingered a movement, then – volti – turned over,
Opened her mouth and the hautboy took in.

But alas! a shrill squeak was the first note she sounded,
For far troppo presto began he at first
And her poor little mouth by the hautboy was wounded,
Which too far and too forcibly in it was thrust.
*Oh sweet, &c*

Grown wise by experience, now Quaver chose largo,
For a slow movement suited his fair pupil best,
And 'My dear,' whispered he, 'we'll not now so fast go,
But stop at each pause and take breath at each rest.'
Adagio soon past, now they enter larghetto.
Crescendo, crescendo, still onward they pressed,
Till getting at length out of all moderato,
They slur o'er each pause and they slide o'er each rest.
*Oh sweet, &c*

In brisk allegretto behold now they're trilling,
In brisker allegro now shaking so sweet,
While to render the harmony ravishing! — killing! —
They the double-tongue use, and their music's complete.
Prestissimo goes the Duo Amoroso
And Margarette turns up with rapture her eyes,
Till with ecstasy pierced by the dear vigoroso,
'O dolce! O dolce!' sweet Margarette cries.
*Oh sweet, &c*

Con furia proceed they — till turning subito,
In melting cadenzas the duo descends.
Some trills and some porte-voix — beneplacito,
And the duo in tempo languiscente ends.
'Da capo!' cries Margarette, 'your duo's enchanting,
And fain, my dear Quaver, again I'd begin!'
'Assai!' replies Quaver, for breath who was panting,
'You see, my dear girl, we have come alla fin!'

## The Little Black Thing

Tune – *The Bailiffs are Coming*

A little black thing
Set on a cushion.
It opened its mouth
And had ne'er a tooth in.
A fifer and two little drummers came there,
And the quarters they found were all covered with hair.

The fifer went in
And he jigged it about.
The two little drummers
Kept thumping without.
The fifer came out and he hung down his head,
And the two little drummers made sure he was dead.

The fifer rose up
And he went in again,
And the two little drummers
Kept thumping like men.
The fifer came out and he fell in a swoon,
When the two little drummers struck up a fresh tune.

They made such a noise
That the fifer awoke.
He went in again
For the finishing stroke.
Then the fifer came out, and he went in no more,
And the quarters he left were gaping for more.

## The Transport's Complaint

### An excellent flash parody on 'The Exile of Erin'

There stood on the shores of far distant Van Dieman
An ill-fated victim of handcuffs and chains,
And sadly he thought on the country of freemen
Where the housebreaker thrives and the pickpocket reigns.
For the clog at his feet met his eye's observation,
Recalling the scenes of his late avocation,
Where once, ere the time of his sad transportation,
He sang bold defiance to the beaks and the law.

'Oh! hard is my fate,' cried the much-injured fellow.
'How I envy the fate of the gay kangaroo!
I envy the pouch where her little ones dwell O.
I envy those haunts where no Peelers pursue. *constables*
Oh never again shall I, nightly or daily,
Cut throats so genteelly, pick pockets so gaily,
Nor see my pals scragged at the ruthless Old Bailey — *hanged*
I'm nailed sure enough by the beaks and the law.

'Oh where is my woman — my flashy young Sarah,
Who nightly went out, togged so smart, on the pave.

With the slap on her cheeks, oh no blowen was fairer; *makeup*
Who when I was frisky such pleasure me gave.
Never again — no, never — not never
Shall we get gallows lushy, or slumber together. *very drunk*
No more shall I play with her bubbies so clever —
I've lost my flash woman by the beaks and the law.

'Oh where are my kinchins? All stowed in the workhouse, *children*
The poor little bastards my Sarah she bore.
The poor little kids — oh they never did irk us.
I shall ne'er kick their a—es or wollop them more.
Yet content I would be if, my Sarah, they'd let me —
Only one night, if they'd let me sleep with thee,
All that man can give woman, my Sarah, I'd give thee,
Then sing bold defiance to the beaks and the law.'

## The Doctor's Pills

Oh, mercury pills — those teasing pills,
By Dr Eady made;
Those nasty pills — those working pills,
They with my form have played!
Last veek I vith a mot did go, *whore*
A flaring gal vos she.
She warmed my tail, and Eady, oh!
Gave mercury pills to me!
*Gave mercury pills to me!*

Oh, damn the pills — those nasty pills,
They've filled my mind vith dread.

They've teased my bones and swelled my gills
    And my teeth torn from my head.
Now in the Lock I'm fixed pell-mell *the VD hospital*
    With a painful vile chordee. *genital disorder*
I feels as sore and hot as h-ll
    Vith the pills they gave to me!
    *The pills they gave to me!*

## I am a fine blowen

I am a fine blowen togged out so gay, *whore*
And down the Quadrant I take my way. *in Regent-street*
I never goes one fadge under my price: *one farthing*
They must pay for my mutton if they want a slice.
On my own bottom I walks the pave *working for myself*
For I am a girl wot knows how to behave,
And I am sure there is none on the town
What can do the thing that is right half so brown. *so thoroughly*
    Then wot lady or where in London now going
    Lives half so well as the Quadrant flash blowen?

At night in fine togs I am off to the play.
About the box-lobbies I sport it away.
I pick up a swell who has plenty of blunt *cash*
And I make him come down to get into my —. *pay cash down*
In the morning I give him a blow-out of tea,
For which I make him well pay, do you see?
And before that he leaves me, without any doubt,
His pockets they are completely turned out.
    Then wot lady or where in London now going
    Lives half so well as the Quadrant flash blowen?

## The Old Blowen's Lament

Oh! pity my sorrows — a poor old mot
    Wot can no longer pad it.
I'm out of luck. No blunt I've got, *cash*
    Though vonce indeed I had it.
Some years ago, I vos, you know,
    The rage in Cranbourne Alley,
But now the covies pass me by
    And Sarah doesn't *wallee.* *value*

I once could sport fine togs indeed
And men I had, full thirty,
But now I'm ugly and in need,
And ragged, old and dirty.
I vonce had sich a slap-up crib — *fine lodgings*
And made a pretty farden — *lots of money*
But now beneath the Pi–az–zas
I snouse in Common Garden. — *Covent Garden*

Each von as views me does me mock
And kicks me in the puddle.
I've only just come from the Lock — *VD hospital*
And I can scarcely toddle.
I'm not the lady I vonce vos,
I'm togged in vorkhouse patches
And forced to yarn my livelihood — *earn*
By selling songs and matches.

I'm not so wery ugly yet
Although my skin is yellow.
I'm not so bad as squinting Bet,
And she has got a fellow.
I'm full of life and wigour still,
And to a man a treasure:
Then some kind soul just take me home
And I will give him pleasure.

I'm only just turned sixty-four,
So, coves, vhy are you scorning?
I vants a crown and nothing more,
And breakfast in the morning.
Oh, take compassion now on me.
I'd treat ye if I had it.
*Then pity the sorrows of a poor old mot*
*Vot can no longer pad it.*

## Brighton Chain Pier

I once knowed a gemman, at Brighton last year,
His hobby was bathing close by the chain pier.
Every morning he'd go, when he felt rather sick,
To enjoy the salt water and show people his
Perfection in swimming, with grace so combined,
He was full of vigour before and behind.

He would dive like a dolphin, come up like a cod;
The ladies, astonished, exclaiming, 'How odd!'
He would float on his back, and for crabs he would hunt,
Then he'd imitate a woman washing her
Clothes out so tidy — deny it who dare,
What a beautiful figure, what rough curly hair!

After swimming one hour and doing his best,
He'd walk gently out for a few minutes rest—
Full of water and wind, oh, my eyes! how he'd start
To enjoy, sirs, the pleasure of letting a
Fresh wave roll over him and knock him bang down.
There's pleasure in country as well as in town.

Gentle Bill Richy, why stand you there
Without your breeches, exposed to the air?
The policemen are coming to stop all your frolics,
For bathing in sight here and showing your
Body all naked and covered with hair.
What a sight for a maiden, be she dark or fair!

Gentle Bill Richy, now put on your clothes.
Don't heed the police; at them turn up your nose.
See what crowds of fine women, on the cliff now they stick.
He turns round and shows, sirs, the females his
Precarious state he is in on the sands.
See how he shivers — look how he stands!

Policemen surround him, they show him no quarter.
He gives them the double by a jump in the water.
They pursue him in boats but they cannot him pass,
So he bids them goodbye, then he shows them his
Artful manoeuvres. I've told you in rhyme:
Some more I'll relate to you some other time.

## *Second Part*

Then Bill kept on swimming and diving like fun,
And floating at times with his face to the sun.
He'd open his mouth, out the water to spit,
And in doing so took in a great lump of
Seaweed and fungus that was floating hard by.
Oh, it made Billy turn up the white of his eye.

Being tired and squeamish, he swam towards the Steyne,
And got by mistake in a lady's machine. *bathing-machine*
Poor Bill looked astonished, the lady she swore,

But as good luck would have it, she turned out a
Woman of pleasure he'd known very well.
He once was her beau, sirs, and she was his belle.

He begged her to lend him her wrapper and clogs
That he might get out and look after his togs.
She lent him her bathing gown; when says he, 'Oh, you duck!
Before I leave you now I must have a
Farewell embrace, for to get off's no joke,
And then on her back, sirs, he gave her a stroke.

Bill opened the door, then out he did pop,
When he suddenly heard a voice calling out Stop!
'Twas the man, sirs, who watched the machine, and no sluggard.
Says Bill, 'I don't know you, so go and be
Boiled like a lobster!' in a voice soft as silk.
Says the man, 'What, you're trying that woman to bilk.'

Bill bolted like lightning, on towards the Steyne,
And got snug at last in his bathing-machine.
He dressed himself quick, combed his curly locks,
Went home, and found out, sirs, he had got the
Pea-jacket torn he'd just bought— Such a gap!
And very soon after he found he'd the

# SOURCES AND FURTHER NOTES

The head of each page of notes indicates the pages of text to which those notes refer. Each item is signalled by its first line in bold type.

If the location of a source is *not* stated, it is in the British Library. Sources cited in code form such as Harl.3991 or Eng.poet.e.14 are manuscripts — except for a few collections of broadsides or printed songsheets, specified when they occur. When several sources are given, each has helped to establish a text.

Collections of broadside ballads have made a relatively small contribution to the total, as a summary of the chief ones will show.

Madden (Cambridge University Library): 16,354 pieces (some of them bearing more than one item) from 1700 to the early 19th century, collected by Sir Frederic Madden, keeper of manuscripts at the British Museum, 1837–66

Pepys (Magdalene College, Cambridge): collection begun by the eminent lawyer John Selden, acquired by Samuel Pepys, and built up by him to a total of 1,775 by the 1690s (published in *The Pepys Ballad Collection Facsimile*, 5 vol, Cambridge, 1987)

Roxburghe (British Library): begun in the late 17th century by Robert Harley, Earl of Oxford; enlarged by the Duke of Roxburghe and later owners, bringing the total to 1,466

For convenience, a few recurring sources are cited by short titles:

Lawes ms: this is Add. 53723, Henry Lawes's handwritten collection of 323 of his song settings, from 1634 to about 1650

Merry D: *Merry Drollery, or a Collection of Jovial Poems, Merry Songs, Witty Drolleries, Intermix'd with Pleasant Catches*, 1661 (Bodleian)

Percy ms: Add.27879, collection found by Bishop Thomas Percy in Shropshire, 'lying dirty on the floor ... being used by the maids to light the fire' (of 190-odd items that survive, from ancient ballads to songs of the 1640s, Percy used 45 in his *Reliques of Ancient English Poetry*, 1765—but not one that is in this book)

Wilson ms: Mus.b.1 (Bodleian), song manuscript of Dr John Wilson, 'the best at the lute in all England', professor of music, University of Oxford, 1656–61, then chamber musician to Charles II

Wit&D: *Wit and Drollery, Jovial Poems*, 1656

## 1 *Love's pleasures, love's pains*

**Thirsis to die desirèd** Nicholas Yonge, *Musica Transalpina*, 1588, the first printed collection of madrigals in English
In his translation (dating from 1583) of Battista Guarini's much-loved madrigal, 'Tirsi morir volea', Yonge fits his words to the music of Luca Marenzio: lines of seven and eleven syllables, with some variation. For a later version, see page 50. One of many poets who reworked the idea was John Dryden in his song 'Whilst Alexis lay prest' in his play *Marriage à la Mode*, 1672.

**Cruel, you pull away too soon** Thomas Morley, *Canzonets or Little Short Songs to Three Voyces*, 1593 (dedicated to Mary, Countess of Pembroke)

**I go before, my darling** Morley, *The First Booke of Canzonets*, 1595

**What saith my dainty darling?** Morley, *The First Booke of Balletts*, 1595 (translation from a madrigal of Giovanni Gastoldi)

**My lovely wanton jewel** Morley, as above; from Italian, author unknown

**Lady, you think you spite me** Morley, as above
The original, a madrigal of Alfonso Ferrabosco I, an Italian who spent some years in London, was first translated by Nicholas Yonge. His version opens:

Lady, if you so spite me,
Wherefore do you so oft kiss and delight me?

**Fie, fie, fie, what a coil is here!** Robert Jones, *The Second Booke of Songs and Ayres*, 1601

**I care not for these ladies** Thomas Campion, in Philip Rosseter's *A Booke of Ayres*, 1601

**Are lovers full of fire?** Francis Davison, *A Poeticall Rapsodie*, 1602; set by Robert Jones, *The First Set of Madrigals*, 1607

**What is beauty but a breath?** Thomas Greaves's *Songes of Sundrie Kindes*, 1604

**When from my love I looked for love** John Bartlet's *A Booke of Ayres*, 1606

**Think'st thou, Kate, to put me down** Robert Jones's *Ultimum Vale, or the Third Book of Ayres*, 1605; only known copies at Royal College of Music, London, and Schlobitten Castle, East Prussia

**What if I sped where I least expected** Jones, as above
In two manuscripts of a slightly later date, Add. 24665 and Christ Church 439, the tense changes to the present, 'What if I speed... / What if I miss...'

**Though my carriage be but careless** Thomas Weelkes's *Ayeres or Phantasticke Spirites*, 1608

**Four arms, two necks, one wreathing** Weelkes, as above

**Love not me for comely grace** John Wilbye's *Second Set of Madrigales*, 1609

**Young and simple though I am** Campion's words, first published in Alfonso Ferrabosco's *Ayres*, 1609; then in Campion's *Fourth Booke of Ayres*

**Sweet Cupid, ripen her desire** William Corkine's *Ayres*, 1610

**Lais now old, that erst attempting lass** Orlando Gibbons's *First Set of Madrigals and Mottets*, 1612

**Come hither, you that love** Beaumont and Fletcher, *The Captain*, about 1612; full text of the song in Drexel 4257, New York Public Library (setting by Robert Johnson, a member of Shakespeare's company, the King's Players)

**Away, away, call back what you have said** William Corkine's *Second Booke of Ayres*, 1612

**Dear, why do you say you love** Add. 10308, Sir John Aytoun's collection of poems by his uncle Sir Robert (1570–1638), secretary to James I's and Charles I's queens (lines 9–10, missing from Add. 10308, supplied from Add. 25707)

**I do confess th'art smooth and fair** Lawes ms; John Playford's *Select Ayres and Dialogues*, 1659
In a collection of Robert Aytoun's poems in the *Bannatyne Miscellany*, 1827, the third line from the end is harsher: 'And thou shalt sigh when I shall smile.'

**Have I found her? O rich finding!** Francis Pilkington's *First Set of Madrigals and Pastorals*, 1613; also set by Thomas Bateson, *Second Set of Madrigales*, 1618

**O when I think what a paltry thing** Add. 18936

**See the building** Add. 24665 and Percy ms; expanded broadside version entitled 'A Well-wishing to a Place of Pleasure' is in Roxburghe ballads, I, 454

**Art thou that she than whom no fairer is?** Add. 24665; ms 439, Christ Church, Oxford

**As on a day Sabina fell asleep** Add. 24665; Bodleian ms Rawl. poet. 172
A popular theme. The origin seems to be a Campion song (*A Booke of Ayres*, 1601), 'It fell on a summer day'. Jamy has found Bessie in her bower:

> Jamy then began to play.
> Bessie as one buried lay,
> Gladly still, through this sleight,
> Deceivèd in her own deceit.
> And since this trance begun
> She sleeps every afternoon.

Someone got hold of 'As on a day Sabina fell asleep' and swelled it to a 96-line broadside version, 'Cupid's Courtesie in the wooing of fair Sabina', still current about 1670, with successive stanzas ending '...but would not hear / ... not know / ... not feel / ... not lie / ... not have', etc, and concluding:

> With kisses, kindly from her I did part.
> She took my love, and gave to me her heart,
>     Which I will keep,
> Which I will keep tied up in chains of gold,
> For what Sabina had she could not hold.

This was reworked yet again as a briefer, more sophisticated song, 'Sabina in the dead of night', published in Henry Playford's *Banquet of Musick*, 1689, whose closing stanza ends, 'she did hear, see, feel, sigh, kiss, and do'.

**Down lay the shepherd swain** Percy ms; Dyce 25.F.39, Victoria & Albert Museum Library; ms PwV41, Nottingham University Library

**Why were we maids made wives** Add. 24665, Egerton 2026
Such wives inspired many songs. One of the 1680s, 'The Scolding Wife's Vindication, or An Answer to the Cuckold's Complaint', takes 64 lines. A sample:

> Sure never was wife so fooled
> As I, for a year or two.
> I did for him whate'er I could,
> Yet nothing at all he'll do.

I feasted him every day
With lamb-stones and cock-broth too,
Yet all this cost was thrown away.
He nothing at all will do.

Foods as stimulants – 'oyster pies and rhubarb too' – are also mentioned in a slip-song that appeared in various versions well into the 19th century, 'O dear O' or 'My Husband has no Courage in Him'. A few extracts:

Seven long years I've made his bed,
Six of them I've lain beside him.
This morning I rose with my maidenhead.
That shows he's got no courage in him. *O dear O.*

I wish that he was dead and gone.
In the grave I quick would lay him,
And I would try another man
That's got a little courage in him. *O dear O.*

Come all fair maids where'er you be,
Don't take a man before you try him.
Don't have to sing a song like me,
My husband's got no courage in him. *O dear O.*

This, like many other broadside songs, survived in muddled form as a 'folksong', to be collected by Cecil Sharp in the early 1900s.

**Lovers, rejoice, your pains shall be rewarded** John Fletcher, *Cupid's Revenge*, 1615 (for a revival of the play, 1637, William Lawes set the song)

**Beauty, since you so much desire** Campion, *Third and Fourth Booke of Ayres* (printed about 1617; but the refrain is quoted in the play *Eastward Ho*, 1605)

**Cupid is Venus' only joy** Thomas Middleton, *More Dissemblers Besides Women*, about 1615 (second stanza missing from first printing of the play, 1657, but in Add. 29481, with music)

**Hark, ye virgins that so prize** Bodleian ms Eng. poet. c. 50

**When meadow grounds are fresh and gay** ms 325, Corpus Christi College, Oxford; Add. 30982 (both are manuscript collections of Oxford dons)

**When Phoebus addressed his course to the west** Percy ms; ms in British Library volume C.39.a.37; Wit&D; Merry D
A Dutch translation is in an Amsterdam song collection of 1621, *Boertigheden* (refrain: *O dood my, dood my, dood my niet,/Ick heb my noch niet bereyd).*

**Walking in a meadow green** Percy ms; Add. 22582

**Is it true I am derided** Add. 25707, Add. 33998; *Le Prince d'Amour*, 1660

**Men that more to the yard nor the church** Percy ms
A mystery song: sophisticated work, but no hint of it has been seen elsewhere.

**Great and proud, if she deride me** Stowe 962
The Percy ms has another version, ending like this:

Man by reason should be guided
And not love where he's disdained.
If that once he be derided,
Others' love may be obtained
  Hold you not one maid so rare:
  There's none that lives without compare.

**A man and a young maid that loved a long time** Percy ms
Bishop Thomas Percy marked with three big Xs every item in his manuscript that he could not think of printing in his *Reliques*. This of course was one. The poetry of its ending was silenced for too long.

**'Once and no more,' so said my love** ms 327, Corpus Christi College, Oxford

**When I was young, unapt for use of man** Add. 25303, Add. 33998, Wilson ms

**How great delight from those sweet lips I taste** Thomas Tomkins, *Songs of 3, 4, 5 and 6 Parts*, 1622

**My days, my months, my years I spend** John Attey, *First Booke of Ayres*, 1622

**Why should passion lead thee blind** Egerton 2421, Add. 30982; Bodleian mss Don. c.57 and Eng. poet. e.14; *Poems of Pembroke and Ruddier*, 1660 (which attributes it to William Herbert, Earl of Pembroke); many variant readings

**Stay, lovely wanton, stay** Stowe 962

**Young Thirsis lay in Phillis' lap** Walter Porter, *Madrigals and Ayres*, 1632; Wilson ms and Wilson's *Cheerfull Ayres or Ballads*, 1659 (different setting)
See notes, p 322, to 'Thirsis to die desirèd'

**Come, lovers, all to me** Porter, as above; John Playford's *Select Musicall Ayres and Dialogues*, 1652, set by Henry Lawes

**Since all things love, why should not we** Porter, as above

**Ladies whose marble hearts despise** Add. 11811, Add. 22118; Wit&D
The manuscripts (time of Charles I) credit 'Will Munsey' – probably the one who became a fellow of Trinity, Cambridge, in 1632.

**Be not thou so foolish-nice** Add. 10309, Harl. 6917; *The Academy of Complements*, 1650; John Wilson's *Cheerfull Ayres or Ballads*, 1659

**Now in the sad declension of thy time** Add. 31432 (William Lawes's manuscript of 63 songs)

**Faith, be no longer coy** Add. 31432 (see above); printed in John Playford's *Select Musicall Ayres and Dialogues*, 1652

**Disdain me not, sweet love, though I am old** Add. 22582, Harl. 7332, Lawes ms (first two stanzas)

**Fond lovers, what d'ye mean** *Poems by John Cleaveland*, 1661; *J. Cleaveland Revived*, 1662; *Oxford Drollery*, 1671
This was dropped from a later collection of verse by Cleveland (died 1658); but he certainly wrote another poem mocking the fashion of platonic love at Charles I's court in the 1630s ('For shame, thou everlasting wooer! / Still saying grace, and ne'er falling to her'). The fashion, inspired by followers of Charles's French queen, produced a series of poems entitled 'Against Fruition'. A poem in several manuscripts of the time begins:

> When I do love, I would not wish to speed
> Nor plead fruition rather than desire,
> But one sweet lingering expectation feed,
> And gently would protract, not quench, my fire.

To go back further, see Ben Jonson's 'Doing a filthy pleasure is, and short', based on a fragment attributed to the first-century poet Petronius Arbiter.

**Do not delay me** Lawes ms (in his *Third Book of Ayres and Dialogues*, 1658, Lawes gives 'Henry Harrington, son of Sir Henry Harrington' as the author)

**Cupid is an idle toy** Wilson ms; *Wits Interpreter,* 1655; ms 327, Corpus Christi College, Oxford, with an extra stanza:

Wonder not at virtue now
Though she keep a single vow.
To be poor is to be chaste:
Venus hath a golden waist.
Love and gold far wars do wage
For ever, since the Golden Age.
Money, cunny are the things
That make a god and conquer kings.

**I swear by muscadell** Bodleian ms Don. c. 57; John Wilson's *Cheerfull Ayres or Ballads,* 1659
A version of this is sung in *The Variety,* a play of 1639 by William Cavendish, Duke of Newcastle — the song presumably by Wilson, not the duke.

**'Tis not your virtues make you to refuse me** Wit&D; Add. 22582 with a less pointed ending:

She spoils her market that sets too high a price
On her device.

**I am confirmed a woman can** Lawes ms; *The Academy of Complements,* 1650; John Playford's *Select Musicall Ayres and Dialogues,* 1652
Very popular; it has been attributed to Sir John Suckling.

**All the materials are the same** Add. 29396 and many other mss; *Wits Interpreter,* 1655
A setting in the Wilson ms has a more singable refrain: 'Then tell me where those creatures are / That can at once be chaste and fair'. It adds a stanza:

Then be not nice, for that (alas)
Belies thy thoughts and thee.
Thou lovest, I know, and not one grace
Bedecks thy body or thy face
But pleads within for me.

**Ill tide the cruel peace that hath gained a war on me** Add. 11811
The manuscript is pre-Civil-War. In 1671 *Westminster Drollery* gives the song with a topical twist, 'A Scotch Girl's Complaint for an Englishman's going away when my Lord Monk came for England', referring to General Monk's role in restoring Charles II. Its lines 3–4 come nearer to the triple rhyme with 'O methought he was the blithest one / That e'er I set mine eyes upon'.

**Fine young folly, though you were** William Habington's play *The Queen of Aragon,* performed 1640
Frequently found in mss and in print. Rawl. poet. 84 has a good example of corruption: 'Fine, young, jolly though you were'. Playford 1653 has a setting by William Tompkins; its line 27 reads, 'Courteous soul, when next I court'.

**I can love for an hour** Add. 29396 ; John Playford's *Select Musicall Ayres and Dialogues,* 1653; and many others
Set by William Lawes; I follow the Playford text except for its bungled line 12, 'They can live for ever'.

**Though Cupid be a god** Lawes ms

**O smother me to death** Lawes ms

**If thou dost love me as thou say'st** Lawes ms; Drexel 4257, New York Public Library (Lawes did not put this irreligious song into print)

**Whenas I do record** Percy ms; Add. 29396
The second source is later and poorer, but helps to amend some faults in the first. It is much more Scottish. In stanza 3 it has 'She'll give you twea for eane', reminding one of the woman's plaint in Robert Burns's bawdy version of 'John Anderson, my jo': 'I've twa gae-ups for ae gae-down / John Anderson, my jo'.

**I love thee for thy fickleness** Lawes ms; John Playford's *Select Ayres and Dialogues*, 1659
Also in Drexel 4257, where it ends, 'I'll mortgage all the land I have / To play with thee, my honey'.

**What could any man desire?** John Wilson's *Cheerfull Ayres or Ballads*, 1659; *The Academy of Complements*, 1650 (poorer version)

**Note of me was never took** *The Marrow of Complements*, 1654

**If my lady bid begin** Wilson ms; Wilson's *Cheerfull Ayres or Ballads; The Academy of Complements*, 1650
In the ms, line 7 begins 'Pinch my lips'; line 13 is 'Quit their hard fortune, mine is free'.

**Prethee die and set me free** Drexel 4041, New York Public Library
In this manuscript, of about 1650, the poem differs widely from the version printed in Sir John Denham's *Poems and Translations*, 1668, which lacks stanza 4 and has a new one placed as stanza 2:

'Tis not cheeks nor lips nor eyes
That I prize,
Quick conceits or sharp replies.
If wise thou wilt appear and knowing,
Repartee,
Repartee to what I'm doing.

The book has various misreadings, such as 'Nakedness itself were naked' for line 12. When it was published, a year before Denham died, he was ill and having fits of madness, so will not have seen it through the press. The song is derived from a Martial epigram (XI, 104), '*Uxor, vade foras aut moribus utere nostris. . .*' Herrick also used it in his 'What kind of Mistress he would have':

...Let her Lucrece all day be,
Thais in the night, to me.

**Oh that I durst but thread your needle, lady** *Sportive Wit: The Muses Merriment*, 1656 (Bodleian)

**Maids they are grown so coy of late** *Cupid's Masterpiece*, about 1656, Bodleian; also in *The Marrow of Complements*, 1655, but eight lines longer

**If thou wilt love me, I'll love again** Add. 11608 (stanzas 1 and 2); Drexel 4257, New York Public Library

**Thy love is yet asleep, cannot be waked** Add. 32339
This and the next eight songs are in two manuscript collections of the work of John Gamble, who was a musician and composer in Cromwell's time and then employed at court throughout Charles II's reign. They are notable for their darting, quirky personal style, free of the fashions of the time.

**Prithee, oh prithee, prithee— 'Tis not well** Harl. 6947 and Add. 32339

**Great sums of love now thou dost owe me** as above

**Love is a sickness and a strange disease** as above

**As thou dost look in love of me** as above

**What a thin, fine, cool, airy love at first** as above

**Love should be gentle sweet delight** as above

**Love's actual sins I did commit** as above

**I saw myself on shipboard lie** Add. 32339

**I loved a maid, she loved not me** Merry D

**Poor Jenny and I, we toiled** *The New Academy of Complements, erected for Ladies, Gentlewomen, Courtiers, Gentlemen, Scholars, Souldiers, Citizens, Countrey-men, and all persons, of what degree soever, of both sexes*, 1671

**As I walked in the woods one evening of late** *Westminster Drollery*, 1672; Playford's *Choice Ayres*, 1676
A less earthy version, without 'A little of that which Harry gave Doll', is sung in Thomas Shadwell's *The Miser*, 1672, an adaptation of Molière's *L'Avare.*

**Of all the brisk dames, my Selina for me** *Westminster Drollery*, 1672; John Playford's *Choice Songs and Ayres*, 1673

**Since to restrain our joy, that ill-bred, rude** Bodleian mss Rawl. poet. 159 and Eng. poet. d. 152; ms PwV45, Nottingham University Library

**I am so deep in love** broadsides, Pepys III, 220; Roxburghe III, 483
I have refrained from making cuts in this heartfelt ballad (surely by a woman), even though its 96 lines show some of the prolixity encouraged by the large broadside sheet. It was evidently a big seller: its tune, though borrowed from another ballad, 'Cupid's Courtesy', came to be known as 'I am so deep in love'. And it inspired a reply, 'The Young Man's Vindication Against The Virgin's Complaint'. A few glimpses of this:

Men are not half so bad
    As you would make them...
Maidens false-hearted are,
    I can report it...
'Tis but a pettish strain
    For to love no man.

**Sawney was tall and of noble race** Playford's *Choice Ayres and Songs*, 1680/1

**Once did I love a bonny bonny bird** broadside, Pepys III, 107
This was printed about 1681. Variants evolved in the 18th century, as usual retaining the more memorable lines. A good example is 'The Young Maid's Fancy to Her Sweetheart in the Similitude of a Bird' (*The Highland Lasses Garland*, PP 161, Douce collection, Bodleian):

Once I had a bonny bonny bird,
Flew in and out at my request.
And I put on my robe so fine;
In my bosom he did build his nest, *brave boys.*

He builded without and he builded within,
And my bonny bird flew out anon.
But my bonny bird has taken his flight
And to the green forest is flown, *brave boys.*

It's up the green forest and down the green forest
Like one quite distracted in mind
Thinking to catch my bonny bonny bird,
But my bonny bonny bird I could not find, *brave boys.*

I caused a bell to be tied to his foot,
And I thought he'd been all my own,
But my bonny bird has taken his flight
And the devil knows where he's gone, *brave boys.*

He set me upon his dissembling knee
And he looked me steadfast in the face.
He gave unto me a dissembling kiss
But his heart was in another place, *brave boys.*

But she that has catched my bonny bonny bird,
Let her make the best of him she can.
Let her catch him or want him, or find who will,
I will lie with him now and then, *brave boys.*

In *Beautiful Fanny's Garland,* also 18th century, it has become a man's ballad for his lost girl. There is the same closing idea:

He that hath gotten my bonny bonny bird,
  Let him keep her in the best manner he can.
I swear by my bow, whether I have her or no,
  I'll hawk with her now and then.

**Of late did I hear a young damsel complain** broadside of about 1681 (broadside collection C.22.f.6)
This young man's talk of girls giving him money is not mere boasting, for there are other songs in which loving girls speak of making such gifts. Girls had opportunities to acquire spare cash as street vendors, etc.

**When the kine had given a pailful** D'Urfey's *Choice New Songs,* 1684
In D'Urfey's final collection in 1719, he titled this 'Tom and Doll, or the Modest Maid's Delight', made minor changes and dropped the last stanza.

**Oh mother! Roger with his kisses** Henry Playford's *The Theater of Music,* Third Book, 1686

**When first I began to court** broadside, Pepys V, 250, 'Printed and Sold by J Millet, next door to the Flower-de-Luce, in Little-Brittain [London], 1689'
Further to this ballad's descent into the puzzleheaded 'Foggy Dew' fragments collected from village singers by Cecil Sharp and others: the 17th-century ballad evidently continued in circulation for some time, for there are direct descendants of it in eight-page songsters of the late 18th century. Here is one printed in Limerick, 'The Bug-a-Boo':

'Twas when I was a bachelor,
  I was a roving blade,
But yet my chief delight it was
  In courting one fair maid.
I courted her on winter nights
  And in summer days also,
But still her answer was to me,
  O no, O no, sir, no.

I being grievèd at the same
  Then bid my love adieu,
But did perceive she was inclined
  That I should still pursue.
Farewell, I cried, my dearest dear.
  No longer will I stay,
But soon as morning light appears
  I shall go hence away.

My love came to my chamber door
  As I lay fast asleep,
And there my love did mourn, sir,
  And there my love did weep.
She wrung her hands and tore her hair,
  Crying, What shall I do?
Then into bed to me she came,
  For fear of the Bug-a-Boo.

The first part of that happy night
  We did both sport and play,
And then my love lay in my arms
  Until that it was day.
But when daylight it did appear,
  She cries, I am undone!
I said, My love, be not afraid,
  For the Bug-a-Boo is gone.

The very next day I married her.
  She proves a virtuous wife.
I nourish her, I cherish her,
  I love her as my life.
I ne'er upbraid her with the same,
  Nor e'er intend to do;
But when she looks and smiles on me
  I think on the Bug-a-Boo.

Here, the implication seems to be that she *pretends* to be in terror of a bug-a-boo; and it can represent fear of being left an old maid.

A version printed at Kilmarnock, 'The Roving Bachelor', has some extra lines that go with his having set up the Bug-a-boo:

I rose from bed and softly crept
  My chamber door unto,
And said, My dearest dear, come in
  For fear of Bug-a-boo.
I clasped my arms around her waist,
  Led her my bed unto,
And still she cried, Oh I'm afraid
  Of that ugly Bug-a-Boo...

Bug-a-boo may have been corrupted into 'foggy dew'; or might a Scots variant have had 'bogy dhu' (black bogy), pronounced 'boggy doo'?

**I gave her cakes, I gave her ale** *The Banquet of Musick*, 1689; set by Purcell

**Phillis at first seemed much afraid** *The Banquet of Musick*; set by Samuel Ackroyde

**Celemena, pray tell me** Henry Playford's *Deliciae Musicae*, Book IV, 1696 Erotic boy-and-girl dialogues had a vogue. This songbook has another , set by John Eccles for Pierre Motteux's play *Love's a Jest*. Here is most of it:

*He* Come then, let us kiss, let us kiss and hug,
Let's kiss and hug, let's kiss and hug each other
Like my father and my mother...
Are thy bubbies a-coming?
Are thy bubbies, thy bubbies, thy bubbies a-coming, child?
Let me see, let me see, let me see, I must kiss, I must kiss.

*She* Oh no no! Oh pray! Fie, fie, fie!
No no no, no no no, you shan't.
*He* There's nobody sees us, then why do you fear?
Now a little more, good Betty. (*Kisses her*)
*She* Fie, fie, you make me blush, I swear,
Yet methinks 'tis very pretty.
*He* Well, we'll marry ere 'tis long.
*She* You're too little. *He* You're too young.

**Young Coridon and Phillis** Harl. 7315, headed 'Song by a Lady, 1698'
This charming song was first published in 1707, attributed to Sir Charles Sedley. In 1712 it appeared in *Wit and Mirth: or Pills to Purge Melancholy* with a setting by Jeremiah Clarke.

**Peggy in devotion** *Wit and Mirth: or Pills to Purge Melancholy*, Vol II, 1700

**Last night a dream came into my head** *Wit and Mirth: or Pills to Purge Melancholy*,Vol V, 1714

**'Tis I have seven braw new gowns** *The Tea-Table Miscellany*, 1724
A song collected by Allan Ramsay and 'brush'd up', as he put it, for his miscellany. Reprinted in song-sheets, in time it became a garbled folksong.

**Ungrateful Robin, to complain!** broadside collection LR. 271. a. 2 (No184)
For a pitcher joke, Robin could recall Kitty of Coleraine, who drops her pitcher of milk when she meets Barney M'Leary. He consoles her with a kiss, perhaps more, for 'she vowed for such pleasure she'd break it again'. And soon after, 'the devil a pitcher was whole in Coleraine'.
It may seem perverse not to print the 'Robin's Complaint' to which Nanny is replying. It is a justifiable economy, for her reply deals point-by-point with his complaint, as the following lines from it show:

Did ever Nanny's heifers fast
If Robin in his barn had hay?
Though to my fields they welcome were,
I ne'er was welcome yet to her...

Within this week her pigeons have
Eat up a peck of peas at least.
Her little pigeons kiss; but she
Will never take a kiss from me...

Alas, poor wretch, what shall I do
If Nanny does not love me soon?
If no relief to me she'll bring
I'll hang me in her apron-string.

'Robin's Complaint' is no hack ballad but is by a Scottish earl's son, Charles Hamilton, Lord Binning (1697–1732). It was printed in *The Gentleman's Magazine*, 1741, but was also popular as a broadside, as was the reply.

**I laid my head on a lonesome pillow** *The Wandering Lover's Garland*, no date, perhaps 1730
In the plaints of betrayed pregnant girls, certain images recur. The leaves marking the passing months are also in the old Scottish song 'Waly Waly":

O Martinmas wind, when wilt thou blaw
And shake the green leaves off the tree?
O gentle death, when wilt thou come
And take a life that wearies me?

A 16th-century fragment has this:

Oaken leaves in the merry wood so wild,
  When will you grow green-a?
Fairest maid, and thou be with child,
  Lullaby mayst thou sing-a.

Stanza 2 of 'I laid my head on a lonesome pillow' digests a couplet from an earlier broadside song, 'No Creature is so False as Man': *To think that I so silly be / To love that man that loves not me.* That song has other passages that entered folksong, such as this early glimpse of 'There is a tavern in the town':

There is a house in Chatham town
My love went to and set him down
And took a stranger on his knee...

Another is a stanza that turns up, with variations, endlessly:

I wish I were some silly fly,
Then on his bosom would I lie
That all the world may plainly see
I love him though he loves not me.

**Hey ho! Who's there?** printed songsheet, collection H.1601 (sung in *The Boarding-School, or The Sham Captain*, 1733, based on D'Urfey's *Love for Money*)

**I am as brown as brown can be** *The Tom Tit*, Part 2; *The Brown Girl's Garland* (Harding collection, Bodleian) – both chapbook songsters of about 1750
This is descended from a 64-line ballad printed in Francis Child's *The English and Scottish Popular Ballads*, Part IX, 1894, 'taken down lately by the Rev S Baring-Gould from a blacksmith in Devon', which fills out the narrative.

He sent for me, the brown, brown girl
  Who once his wife should be.
O ne'er a bit the doctor-man
  His sufferings could relieve.
O ne'er an one but the brown, brown girl
  Who could his life reprieve.

She takes all day going... she cannot stand for laughing... and then:

'You flouted me, you scouted me
  And many another one.
Now the reward is come at last
  For all that you have done...'

She had a white wand in her hand,
  She strake him on the breast.
'My faith and troth I give back to thee,
  So may thy soul have rest.'

'Prithee,' said he, 'forget, forget.
  Prithee, forget, forgive.
O grant me yet a little space
  That I may be well and live.'

No: she will dance on his grave... Her white wand and power of life and death are witch-like. She has cast a fatal spell on him for flouting her love.

This powerful brown girl is quite distinct from the one in the ballad 'Lord Thomas and Fair Eleanor' or 'The Nut-Brown Bride'. There, Lord Thomas casts aside the beautiful Eleanor and marries the brown girl because she is rich — a choice that leads to the violent deaths of all three.

**My fiddle and Flora** *An Antidote Against Melancholy*, 1749

**By that mole on your bosom so soft and so white** printed songsheet, collection B.316.d (by a minor composer, 'the ingenious Mr Samuel Jarvis', says *The Bacchanalian Magazine*)

**A loving couple met one day** *The Shepherd's Son's Garland*, Sheffield, 1753, Douce collection, PP 161, Bodleian
The song probably began in Scotland. A version, 'Dainty Davie', collected in the mid-18th century by David Herd, has parallel passages such as:

> It was down amang my daddy's pease,
> And underneath the cherry trees:
> O there he kist me as he pleas'd
> For he was mine ain dear Davie.

Burns often heard it sung, and polished up a version. The song also evolved in London: it is recorded by Francis Place (see page 14). His lines 4–6 are:

> Both together to sport and play,
> And for to pass the time away
> He showed her little Davy.

Davy takes Kate to, among various places, her father's barn —

> There he pulled out his long consarn,
> And it was as long —— as this my arm
> And he called it little Davy...
>
> When forty weeks were come and gone,
> Bonny Kate and Davy,
> When forty weeks were come and gone, etc,
> She was delivered of a son,
> And she called it little Davy.

**I made love to Kate** *The Gentleman's Concert*, songster, published in Aldermary Church Yard, Bow Lane, 1750?; and various others

**As I was a-walking to Chelsea one day** *The Entertaining Companion, or Merry Songster's Delight*, 1766

**I am a poor black, 'tis true** street-ballad collection 1875.d.16
Though on an uncommon theme, this was popular enough to be reprinted for decades (the campaign against the slave-trade touched hearts at all levels). Is the ballad by one of the literate blacks whose existence in London is now recognized? The man is named as George Sighbus in 'The Chamber-Maid's unkind Answer'. She pities him but cannot overcome her prejudice:

> I wish he a white man were;
> I soon would ease his care
> And be his only dear,
> No longer cruel...
>
> Was I with him to wed,
> Be he never so civil,
> I should think within my bed
> I had the devil...

**When jolly Dick and Jane were wedded** country chapbook (title missing), collection 11622.c.22

**At sixteen years old you could get little good of me** slip-song, J Evans, 42 Long Lane, 1794 (Madden collection, Cambridge)
It is hard to say whether this is the original song to the well-loved tune. The 'Johnny's so long at the fair' version was being sung in the 1790s ('The Favourite Duett of O! Dear what can the Matter be'). At the time of William

Pitt's disastrous campaigns of 1793–4 against the revolutionary French, the songwriter Charles Morris had a great success with a satirical parody, 'Billy's Undone us by War': *Oh dear, what will become of us,/ Dear, dear, what will become of us,/ Oh dear, what will become of us? / Billy's so fond of the wars!*

**When we went out a-shooting** *The Rambler's Flash Songster*, 1830?

# *Rakes and wantons*

**John, you're my husband's man, you know** ms 439, Christ Church, Oxford

**My mistress loves no woodcocks** ms 439, Christ Church; ms 176, Corpus Christi College, Oxford; Bodleian ms Rawl. poet.26

**The man that hath a handsome wife** Percy ms

**My mistress is in music passing skilful** Add. 29481; Merry D

**The birds flew over the green, boys** Harl. 6057

**Nay pish, nay phew, in faith and will you? Fie!** Egerton 2421, Add. 30982 and many other British Library mss; eight mss in the Bodleian; *Sportive Wit*, 1656 (Bodleian)

A great favourite of Charles I's time. The variant readings and obvious errors in many copies suggest that gentlemen were eager to acquire word-of-mouth versions. My careful conflation can claim to be better than some of theirs.

'A Maid's Denial' inspired a song. Three of five stanzas from ms Drexel 4257, New York Public Library:

> Now out upon this fooling, for shame!
> Nay pish, nay fie, in faith you're to blame.
> Nay come, this fooling must not be.
> Nay pish, nay fie, you tickle me...
>
> Your buttons do scratch, you ruffle my band,
> You hurt my thigh. Pray take away your hand.
> The door stands ope that all may see.
> Fie, pish, away! You tickle me...
>
> But now I see my words are but vain,
> For you 'a' done and why should I complain?
> Nay, to't again, the way is free.
> Since 'tis no more, pray tickle me.

There is a precursor too, in a manuscript songbook of about 1500 (Add. 5665). In a tavern buttery a gentleman is fondling a barmaid (spelling modernized):

> 'Be peace! Ye make me spill my ale...
> Let go, I say. Straw for your tail!'

Soon it comes to this:

> 'Come, kiss me.' 'Nay!' 'By God, ye shall!'
> 'By Christ, I nill. What says the man?
> Ye hurt my leg against the wall.'

And at last to this:

> 'Now have ye laid me on the floor.
> But had I wist when ye began,
> By Christ, I would have shut the door.'

**Sweet, do not stay, but come away, come away, come away** Add. 29492; Bodleian ms Rawl. B. 35; Pepys V, 195

This seems to have been circulating for more than 60 years before Pepys bought his broadside in 1691 (Add. 29492 dates from 1623–30, Rawl. B. 35 from a little later). The Pepys broadside, entitled 'The Helpless Maiden's Call to the Bachelors', has many variant readings. Here are a few:

Stanza 1, 'Sweet, if thou lov'st me... / And dearest, thy assistance lend / To stand a helpless maiden's friend, / Or else I shall be forced to spend.'
Stanza 2, 'What men are they, but lazy drones / That stay till maidens make their moans.'
Stanza 3, 'For if by chance I should fall sick / He would not fail me in the nick.'
Stanza 4, 'For if I am too young you fear, / I can resolve you, look you here.'
Stanza 5, 'I'm a right woman up and down... / ...to dance the wedding jig.'
Stanza 6, 'I know a younger girl has done't.'
Stanza 7, 'Few maids have met with so good luck / As to encounter, the first pluck. / Oh this would tempt young girls to —'

Pepys's next broadside is 'The Bachelor's Answer', in the same style:

Love, I am ready at your call.
At your call, at your call,
Love, I am ready at your call.
For I attend at your command,
And here is both my heart and hand,
With something else I know will ——
*At your call, at your call,*
With something else I know will please you...

**Fie, away, fie, what mean you by this?** Lawes ms (he did not print it)

**I am a knight's lady and lately decayed** Harl. 6057 (about 1630)
Years later, in 1675, the ballad publisher Philip Brooksby issued 'The Modern Whore, or We'll raise up our honour again' (Douce collection, Bodleian). It begins much the same but then takes its own line. A few of its 20 stanzas:

Let a girl of a dozen run over to France,
'Tis the readiest way herself to advance.
Return when she will, she may practise her dance
And raise up her honour again.

The nobles and gallants about her do flock.
One gives her a gown and the other a smock,
And she, pretty heart, snatches every man's cock / To, etc...

The miss-à-la-mode lives the happiest life.
The pleasure is hers, but the care and the strife
She honestly leaves to the husband and wife / To, etc...

A bankrupt may set up this trade if he please.
Be he pimp or gallant, he may live at his ease,
So he keeps himself free from the modish disease, / To, etc...

For a maidenhead lost, there's no cure like this.
She may then by authority wantonly kiss.
She's as good as a wife, if she be but a miss / And may, etc.

So search the exchanges, the Old and the New,
And what I have told you you'll find to be true.
'What d'ee lack? what d'ee buy?' They are of the crew
That raise up their honour again.

If you buy but a cravat, sleeves, stockings or socks,
She must wait on you home forsooth, she and her box.
You pay her with money; she you with the pox,
And we raise up our honour again.

**Her for a mistress would I fain enjoy** Egerton 2421, Egerton 2725; *Wits Interpreter*, 1655; *Wit Restored*, 1658 (with minor variations)
This is a translation of epigram 78 of the fourth-century poet Ausonius. It is attributed to William Strode (1602-45), canon of Christ Church, Oxford.

**Thou dost deny me 'cause thou art a wife** Wit&D; *Musarum Deliciae, or The Muses Recreation*, 1656

**Full forty times over I have strived to win** Harl. 3991; Bodleian msAshmole 36; Wit&D, Merry D ; *Oxford Drollery*, 1671
Samuel Pepys, years after his student days at Cambridge in the early 1650s, remembered being taught this song by a woman 'whom I knew better than they think for' (she was banished by the university authorities for immorality). All the surviving versions of this much-circulated song are faulty at some point. I hope the author (Suckling?) would accept my conflation. An example of the slips that occur in casual transmission is line 30. Harl. 3991 has 'If you man them discreeetly'; the printed versions have 'mind'. The siege metaphor and 'working about' call for 'mine'. As Helena says in *All's Well that Ends Well*, 'Bless our poor virginity from underminers and blowers-up!'

**Though Oxford be yielded and Reading be taken** Alex Brome, *Songs and Other Poems*, 1661

**He that will court a wench that is coy** Ashmole 36, Bodleian, and many other manuscripts; *The Academy of Complements*, 1650; John Playford's *The Treasury of Musick*, 1669
An early inspiration for this song is in John Fletcher's play *The Beggars' Bush*, 1615. A man asks, 'Canst tell me a way now, how to cut off my wife's concupiscence?' The reply is: 'I'll sing ye a song for't.

'Take her and hug her
And turn her and tug her
And turn her again, boy, again.
Then if she mumble
Or if her tail tumble,
Kiss her amain, boy, amain.'

**Now farewell to St Giles's** broadside (credited to L.P., probably Laurence Price, chief rival to the balladeer Martin Parker) , collection C.20.f.14

**Farewell Three Kings, where I have spent** *The Mysteries of Love and Eloquence*, 1658 (edited by one of John Milton's nephews, Edward Phillips)

**O that I could by any chemic art** Merry D

**Soldiers fight and hectors rant on** Thomas Jordan, *A Royal Arbour of Loyal Poesie*, 1664 (written for one of Jordan's shows for the sheriffs of London)

**Oh, fie upon care!** Roxburghe III, 252 (with note, '1662–3'); Pepys III, 138
A later Pepys broadside, 'The Poor Whore's Lamentation', is not so cheerful:

My price it was a guinea
Not long before last Easter,
But now there is so many
I'm glad to take a tester *sixpence*
For why? The trade is spoiled of late:
There's little Nancy, Bridget, Prue and Kate,
They'll play at you know what
For twopence and a pot…

**Pox on 'um all! These mistresses must be** Bodleian ms Rawl. poet. 84

**O had you been there to have seen it!** Bodleian ms Eng. poet. d. 152

**The cocks may crow in the day** Eng. poet. d. 152

**I'll have no serving-man, footman or cooks** *A Jovial Garland*, 1670

**I'd have you, quoth he** *Windsor Drollery*, 1672
In *Oxford Drollery*, 1671, there is a longer version, in which she spurns him:

> I'd hug thee, quoth he.
> Would you hug me? quoth she.
> How much, sir?
>
> Why, a little, quoth he.
> 'Tis a little, quoth she.
> Not a touch, sir!
>
> I am sickish, quoth he.
> Are you sickish? quoth she.
> But why, sir? *etc.*

**A maid, I dare not tell her name** *The New Academy of Complements*, 1671

**Was ever mortal man like me** Sloane 655; *The Cabinet of Love* (published with *The Works of the Earls of Rochester, Roscommon and Dorset*, 1735), where it is entitled 'Lord Rochester against his Whore-Pipe'
Rochester's editors do not accept this as his. It certainly belongs to someone who matches him in attitude, if not in poetic style. Each of the sources helps to correct the other. The manuscript lacks 'mortal' in line 1, for example, but it supplies lines 4–6. In the book, c--t and fucking are censored to dashes.

**Whitehall c—ts are grown so common** Harl. 7312, a collection with many Rochester items; also in Nottingham University Library ms PwV32, a collection entitled 'A Suplement to some of my Lord Rochesters Poems'
The 10 lines I print make a self-contained poem (which I feel they originally were), much the best part of a piece beginning 'Fucksters you that would be happy / Have a care that c—t don't clap ye'. It warns against 'City c—ts' and 'Country c—ts' as well as those of the court at Whitehall, and then gives this dubious advice:

> But follow me and you shall prove
> Safe in the variety of love.
> Every tarse-indulgent spark
> Shall enjoy at Whetstone Park
> A drunken, sound, obedient whore.
> What can mortals wish for more?

Whetstone Park was a noted bawdy-house neighbourhood convenient to the lawyers of Lincoln's Inn (the name lives on in a shabby lane).

**There's ne'er a lad in our town that's worth an ounce of powder** broadside published by Philip Brooksby, 1682
The catchy Daniel Cooper tune was used for many ballads; moved up in society owing to its inclusion in *The Dancing Master*, 1695; and travelled far — it even figures in Tolstoy's *War and Peace*.

**Dear pickaninny** Thomas D'Urfey, *The Comical History of Don Quixote*, Part 3, 1696
In his 1719 collection D'Urfey drops the last four stanzas. He makes line 10 read 'King's money so slowly', a jibe at George I, the only sovereign in his long career to show him no favour.

**The old wife she sent to the miller her daughter** D'Urfey, as above (sung by Mary the Buxom)
D'Urfey borrowed the idea from 'The Lusty Miller', published as a broadside a few years earlier by Philip Brooksby, which begins:

The good-wife her daughter did send to the miller
To grind her grist neatly, and for to come back.

When the first daughter, Peggy, comes back, all she can say is, *Ay! marry sir, there's a brave miller indeed!* Sister Betty is next: she comes back and stands 'like an image both senseless and dumb'. Jenny too is overwhelmed. So the mother hurries off to investigate this miller, with equally potent results — a touch that D'Urfey did not have room for in his 40 lines, against the broadside's 108.

**What life can compare with the jolly town rake's** *The Younger Brother, or The Amorous Jilt*, 1696 (the play by Aphra Behn, but the song by Peter Motteux); ms Mus.Sch.C.95, Bodleian, set by Daniel Purcell

**'Tis sultry weather, pretty maid** *The Words of a new Interlude...in the New Opera called The Island Princess*, 1699; ms Mus.Sch.C.95, Bodleian, set by Jeremiah Clarke
Peter Motteux's *The Island Princess* (after a play by John Fletcher) was first performed 1698, with the great bass Richard Leveridge as the gentleman. The song was later borrowed for *The Recruiting Officer*, 1715, and other plays.

**The sun was just setting, the reaping was done** *Wit and Mirth: or Pills to Purge Melancholy*, 1699

**Now all my friends are laid in grave** *Wit and Mirth...The Second Part*, 1700
Another example of an old ballad reworked and cut down to convenient length for a play and songbook. This is derived from 'A Fair Portion for a Fair Maid', published in the 1630s by the great ballad-writer Martin Parker, which begins 'Now all my friends are dead and gone' and has the refrain, 'Yet I have but a mark a year,/And that my mother gave me'. Here are a few of the 120 lines Parker gave to this enterprising girl from 'Wostersheere':

My fashions with the moon I change
As though I were a lady...
French gowns with sleeves like pudding-pies
I have at my requesting.

My coach drawn with four Flanders mares
Each day attends my pleasure.
The water-men will leave their fares
To wait upon my leisure.
Two lackeys labour everywhere
And at my word run far and near
*Though I have but a mark a year*
*And that my mother gave me*

I would my sister Sue at home
Knew how I live in fashion,
That she might up to London come
To learn this occupation...

**A lusty young smith at his vice stood a-filing** *Wit and Mirth*, 1700; set by Richard Leveridge, composer as well as star bass singer

**Early in the dawning of a winter's morn** *Wit and Mirth*, 1700, set by Leveridge

**In our country, and in your country** *Wit and Mirth ... The Second Part*, 1700; additional stanzas from 'The Merry Haymakers, or Pleasant Pastime between the Young Men and Maids in the Pleasant Meadows', broadside published by Charles Bates about 1700–15 (Euing collection, University of Glasgow)

**Pillycock came to my lady's toe** *Wit and Mirth ... Volume III*, 1707
A hundred years after *King Lear* was first performed, here is an echo of the Fool's song, 'Pillycock sat upon Pillycock hill'.

**All in the land of cider** *Political Merriment*, Part II, 1714
The knight scandalized by John and Susan's fornication seems to have been Sir Edward Harley (1624–1700), who was born and died at Brampton Bryan, an estate of the eminent Harley family. A devout man, in the Civil War he fought on the parliamentary side, and he wrote on the theme of Christian redemption. The song (to the tune of 'All in the land of Essex') thus probably dates from before 1700.

**Would you have a young virgin of fifteen years?** songsheet,, 'Mr Durfeys Song in the Modern Prophets' (play performed 1709), collection H.1601
The same collection has another song, 'The Way to Gain Her', with a similar routine (seamstress, Quaker, country lass, widow). A sample stanza:

> Do you fancy a seamstress brisk and gay,
>     Her age about fifteen, sir?
> You must walk in her shop like a finical fop
>     With your snuffbox and your cane, sir.
> You must compliment fine and kiss with a smack.
> If her heels fly up and she fall on her back,
> Be sure you be ready to give what she'll lack,
>     And I warrant you, boys, you gain her,
>         You gain her,
>     I warrant you, boys, you gain her.

**I owed my hostess thirty pound** songsheet, collection H.1601

**Oh Jenny, Jenny, where hast thou been?** *Wit and Mirth: or Pills to Purge Melancholy*, Vol I, 1719
Thomas D'Urfey reassembled and added to the *Wit and Mirth* series in 1719–20, making six volumes with a total of 1,144 songs and poems, of which 350 of his own made volumes I and II. He seems to have derived 'Oh Jenny, Jenny' from an old Scottish song. Allan Ramsay in his *Tea Table Miscellany* prints a different version among his 'auld sangs brush'd up'. Yet another is in a cheap songster, *The Female Garland* (Douce PP 161, Bodleian). Its refrain goes:

> O Joan, Joan, where hast thou been?
> Thy father and mother has been seeking thee.
>   *I have been ranting, bravely talking,*
>   *Keeping of Jockey's company.*

Three of the incidents are similar:

> My mother sent me to the hedge
>     To dry the clothes so speedily.
> I fell over the bramble bush
>     And Jockey fell on top of me.
>
> My mother sent me to the mill
>     To grind the corn so hastily.
> She had better have gone herself
>     For the miller has took his toll of me.

My mother sent me to the church,
There some fine person for to see,
And there I was pushed both by priest and clerk
And other fellows two or three.

But Joan does not count on Jockey taking care of her in spite of all:

Alas, alas, what must I do?
My belly I find begins for to swell.
But who got my belly up,
The devil knows who, I can't tell.

**A fisherman took a fair maid in his boat** broadside, Firth b. 33, Bodleian

**A young man and a maid, put in all, put in all** *Wit and Mirth: or Pills to Purge Melancholy*, Volume VI, 1720
This uses the rhyme-scheme and tune of the ballad 'Jack Hall', whose great vogue began in 1707 when a chimneysweep of that name was hanged. Soon after 1720 additional stanzas were created for the 'put in all' song, and then a new refrain, *bowl away*. Francis Place heard two women singing it to a large crowd opposite Somerset House in the 1780s. He recalled two stanzas:

My smock's above my knee, she did say, she did say,
My smock's above my knee, she did say.
My smock's above my knee
And you may plainly see
You may have a smack at me, *bowl away*.

A guinea to a crown I will lay, I will lay,
A guinea to a crown I will lay,
A guinea to a crown
That I beat you up and down
With any girl in town, *bowl away*.

Those stanzas appear almost verbatim in a small broadside of about that time, 'The Bowling Match', with four other stanzas not worth quoting. The song was still current in the 19th century. A Preston slip-song of about 1840, 'Bowl Away!', has the 'guinea to a crown' bet, and still ends with the man's defeat:

Why, the devil's in the man, she did say.
Why, the devil's in the man, she did say.
Why, the devil's in the man,
For his p—k it will not stand
Though I rolled it in my hand, *bowl away*.

When he'd spent his store, bowl away,
When he'd spent his store, bowl away,
When he had spent all his store
Then a man can do no more.
Then he damned her for a whore, *bowl away*.

**Come all you roving blades** broadsides, Madden 6, 1617; Roxburghe III, 386
Another version, 'Bobbing John', is in Robert Jamieson's *Popular Ballads and Songs*, Edinburgh, 1806. John is a piper whose back is 'as braid's a door'.

Hey for Bobbing John!
Kittle up the chanter! — *tickle*
Queans are a' gane gyte — *gone mad*
To fling wi' John the Ranter...

**Jolly Tom and Clever-legged Dick** songsheet, collection H.1601; 'the words by Mr A[rthur] Bradley'

**You rakes that are jolly and never will marry** *The Gentleman's Concert*, songster, Aldermary Church Yard, 1750?; slip-song, Madden collection, vol 5, 1329

The song may be from the 1730s. Dr W H Grattan Flood's *Story of the Bagpipe*, New York, 1911, says the most remarkable player of the Uillean (Irish) pipes in the 1720s 'was Lawrence Grogan, Esq, of Johnstown Castle, County Wexford [born 1701], better known among his fellows as Larry Grogan, who shone as a composer as well as a performer' (he wrote 'Ally Croker' in 1725).

On the subject of the landlady's twitcher (line 20): it is strange that this article of clothing has escaped the *Oxford English Dictionary*. A theatre song of 1721, 'The Maid's Twitcher', was a great hit. It opens like this:

> A damsel, I'm told, of delicate mould
> (Whose father was dead, to enrich her),
> Of all her fine things, lace, ribbons and rings,
> Prized nothing so much as her twitcher.
> Poor girl, prized nothing so much as her twitcher.
>
> The youths all around, with courtship profound,
> Tried every art to bewitch her,
> But she was so chaste she'd not be embraced
> By anything else but her twitcher...

But brisk Strephon undoes 'the mystical knot of her twitcher'. The song's tune, originally 'Cupid's Trapan', became known as 'The Twitcher' and is so named in many ballad operas. Twitchers were not a brief fashion: a poem of 1736 by the noted Lord Chesterfield, 'Advice to a Young Lady', has this: 'Your pinners set right, your twitcher tied on...' A dialect meaning of 'to twitch' was 'to fasten or draw tightly'; evidently a twitcher went round the waist.

**Come boys, let's be jolly and drown melancholy** engraved songsheet, collection I.530

**As I was driving my wagon one day** *The Gentleman's Concert*, songster, Aldermary Church Yard, 1750?

**Belinda has such wondrous charms** *The Merry Medley*, about 1750
A reworking of a song set by Purcell, 'Celia has a thousand charms', which has a touch more realism, ending 'She's false as well as fair'.

**A hearty, buxom young girl am I** *The Delights of the Chace*, songster

**I dressed myself both fine and gay** *The Marybone Concert*, songster

**How happy a state doth the damsel possess** broadside, collection C.116.i.4

**When Venus and Bacchus by turns did delight** songsheet, collection G.313

**Chloe's the wonder of her sex** *The Buck's Bottle Companion*, 1775

**Through nations ranging, raking elements** *The Rakes Frolick*, one of a collection of 38 Irish-printed songsters, 11622.df.34
This was published in the 1780s by W Goggin, Limerick, 'Book-seller and Stationer, Corner of Bridge-street, where Country Chapmen may be supplied with Histories, Manuals, Penny-books, Primmers [Primers], Spelling-books, large & small Pictures plain or painted, a large assortment of Ballads, and every other Article in the Bookselling and Stationery Business, on cheaper Terms than at any other Shop'. The tune for 'Stauka an Varaga' survives in Ireland, sung to other words but still with 'Oro' refrains.

**I am a fair maid that loves good company** *An Answer to Stauka an Vauraga*, songster published, 1780s, by John Brown, Monaghan; collection 11622.df.34

**You jolly young rakes who love for to freak** *Hush Cat from under the Table*, songster, published 1787, Monaghan; collection 11622.df.34
The tune for this is No 49 in Brendán Breathnach's *Ceol Rince na hÉireann* (Dance Music of Ireland), Dublin 1976. It has been variously known as 'Whip the Cat from under the Table', 'Huish the Cat', 'Foxy Mary', 'Peas on the Hearth' – and in Irish, *Bimid ag Ól*.

**Great boasting of late we have heard of the feat** Madden collection, vol 5; *Darby O'Gallagher, or the answer to Morgan Rattler*, songster, W Goggin, Limerick; Francis Place collection, Add. 27825
The sources are so imperfect that I have had to print a conflation. As for 'Morgan Rattler' himself, Goggin printed a muddled version that begins:

I'm a jolly young blade, a weaver by trade.
Among the young girls I'm a noted frolicker.
At every wake the young girls do speak,
Here comes the young blade they call Morgan Rattler.

He sings at his loom like a thrush in the bloom.
At night with the girls he still is a flatterer.
They never seem coy, but tremble for joy
When they get a taste of his Morgan Rattler.

It's late in the night I met my delight.
I brought her down street and gave her a bottle…

This is the only survivor I have seen, though 'Morgan Rattler' must have been often reprinted (see Introduction, page 15, for its popularity in London, and for a further stanza). Francis Place's friend Hayward records four stanzas of Darby O'Golicker, which also 'had an immense run'. O'Golicker was not Morgan Rattler's only virile challenger. In 1788 a Newry printer promoted Manus M'Allister, a mason by trade:

…Then with a stout blow of two stones below
He made her to scream like a cat in a factory…

Goggin himself offered Paddy O'Slattery, and then Paddy O'Rafferty —

As I went up to the fair of Drogheda,
Who should I meet but Dolly-come-straddle-me…

By this and by that and the leaves of an ivy tree,
As sure as you're there she loved this young Rafferty.
She pulled out her purse and that very handsomely.
Oh, you are my darling! says Paddy O'Rafferty.

Here we begin at the top of our wickedness,
*Shou sheen a rean a nenought a guaghty,*
She fell down and I fell on top of her…

But Morgan Rattler was the man with staying-power. The name became a term for anything first-rate. It was also slang for a weapon favoured especially by sailors ashore, a club short enough to be carried concealed up a man's sleeve, but made potent with a knob of lead at the end – and thus of phallic appearance. In the British forces, men named Morgan were nicknamed Rattler even in recent times. Yet the song itself has nearly vanished from the record.

**As I was going along the road** *A Garland of New Songs*, Newcastle upon Tyne
This song (otherwise 'Moll in the Wad') has many variant verses. It gave its name to a dance tune of the 1790s.

**A lusty young coachman his horses was whipping** collection of broadsides, 1876.e.20 (with some emendations from *The Flash Casket* of about 1820)

**My mither built a wee, wee house** Charles Kirkpatrick Sharpe, *A Ballad Book*, published 1824, but a collection of 18th-century work
In *The Merry Muses of Caledonia* (see bibliography), among the songs classified as collected by Burns there is another version that matches three stanzas out of six, though in different order, and lacks the first two and the final one.

**O wat ye what my minny did** manuscript at end of *The Merry Muses: A Choice Collection of Favourite Songs* (Cup. 805. aa. 8), printed about 1820–25. A note says 'the free songs at the end' were transcribed from a manuscript of Burns by Peter Cunningham, son of Allan Cunningham, the editor of Burns.

**The Dey of Algiers, when afraid of his ears** *A Complete Collection of Songs by Captain Morris*, 1788 (9th edition)
Captain Charles Morris (Life Guards) entertained George Prince of Wales and his cronies with the Plenipo. And its fame travelled far. Burns valued it: in 1788 he sent a friend a copy. In 1799 its publishers were prosecuted by the Proclamation Society (named after the prince's father's proclamation of 1787 'for preventing and punishing vice'), but the society failed to get a conviction.
In his old age Morris issued a collection of his songs, *Lyra Urbanica*, stripped of anything 'that might pain the pure and gentle eye of Innocence'. He died at 93, in the first year of Victoria's reign.

**I'm saucy, rolling, leering Bett** *The Festival of Anacreon. Containing a Collection of Modern Songs written for the Anacreontic Society, the Beef-Steak and Humbug Clubs*, 1788, Bodleian

**I am a young dairy-maid, buxom and tight** slip-song, C Paul, Seven Dials

**Oh, do it, dear charmer, again** *The Flash Minstrel!*, 1830?

**My name is Sam Swipes, and Sal is my dear** *The Cuckold's Nest of Choice, Flash, Smutty and Delicious Songs . . . ADAPTED FOR GENTLEMEN ONLY*, 1830?

**Oh, I'm getting still more hot for you, my charming Mrs Bond** *The Ri-Tum Ti-Fum Songster: A Slashing, Dashing, Leary, Frisky and Delicious Collection of GENTLEMEN'S SONGS, never before printed, and now Singing with immense Applause at all Select Concerts*, 1830?

## *Merriments, mockings, miseries*

**What hap had I to marry a shrew** Sloane 1489; Thomas Ravenscroft's *Pammelia* (songbook), 1609
The first stanza of this is in a music manuscript, dated 1580, at King's College, Cambridge (Rowe ms 1). Of the 57 rounds and canons in that collection, all but nine are also in Ravenscroft's songbooks. 'What hap had I' is sung by a shepherd in Robert Greene's play *The Tragical Reign of Selimus*, 1594.
Husbands' plaints go back a long way. In a 15th-century ms, Sloane 2593, a song warns young men not to marry older women. An extract (modernized):

When I come from the plow at noon
In a riven dish my meat is done.
I dare not ask our dame a spoon.
  I dare not say, when she says 'peace'.

If I ask our dame bread
She takes a staff and breaks mine head
And doth me run in under the bed.
  I dare not say, when she says 'peace'.

**Let Lobcock leave his wife at home** Ravenscroft, as above
At line 2 the Rowe ms (see above) has 'That roisters may ruffle his lusty Joan'.

**When Francus comes to solace with his whore** Sir John Davies, in *Epigrammes and Elegies*, ?1596

**Faith, wench, I cannot court your sprightly eyes** *Epigrammes and Elegies*, but not by Davies (many variant versions over the next 60 years)

**Come drink to me and I will drink to thee, to thee** Ravenscroft, *Pammelia*
A canon for four voices, as is the next.

**Of all reckonings I love good cheer** Ravenscroft's *A Briefe Discourse ... Charactering the Degrees*, 1614

**O love whose power and might** Add. 24665 and various other manuscripts; *The Marrow of Complements*, 1654; Wit&D
A Bodleian manuscript, Rawl.poet.26, heads this 'Mr Lawson of St Johns Colledge his verses to his mistresse' – perhaps Peter Lawson of St John's, Oxford (died 1619). Jibes such as 'I take no ease for sleeping' go far back. For example, in a 15th-century manuscript at Gonville & Caius, Cambridge:

When I sleep I may not wake,
So much on her I think...

I am brought in such a pine,
Y-brought in such a bale, *grief*
When I have right good wine
Me list drink none ale. *I want to*

**Beware, fair maids, of musky courtiers' oaths** William Corkine's *The Second Booke of Ayres*, 1612.
In Add. 10309 the author is given as J Sylvester: Josuah Sylvester, Groom of the Chamber to James I's first son, Prince Henry, who died in 1612. One might speculate that Sylvester then lost his post — and felt free to see this published.

**Away with sickly wenches, whitely faced** William Goddard, *A Neaste of Waspes*, 1615

**Franciscus swears he'll be no more forsworn** Henry Parrot, *The Mastive, or Young-Whelpe of the Olde-Dogge*, 1615

**In a Jùly moister than December** Add. 10309, Add. 30982 and various other donnish collections; *Witt's Recreations*, 1640
Bodleian ms Ashmole 38 contributes an extra opening couplet: 'Apollo, help me to rehearse/A prick too long to stand in verse.'

**Here six foot deep** Sloane 1792; Ashmole 38, Bodleian; and many others
A collection used by an 18th-century catch club, ms Add. 31463, has a variant with an example of the sort of bawdy trick played in catch-singing. It ends:

His fate I envy, and shall think it hard
When I die to be buried in a count– in a count– in a count– in a
count– in a count– in a count– in a count– in a count–
in a country churchyard.

**I prethee, sweetheart, grant me my desire** Harl. 3889; Wit&D
This song, playing on at least 30 proverbs and catch-phrases, delighted Samuel Pepys. April 11, 1661: 'We did some business; and then ... sung a song or two, and among others, took great pleasure in *Goe and be hanged; that's twice god b'w'y.*' Six days later he met the man who had sung it, bought him a drink, 'and did get of him the song that pleased me so well ... of *Shitten come Shits, the beginning of love*'. It goes back at least to 1623, when a broadside version

was entered in the Stationers' Register. It underwent many changes. Harl.3889 begins at 'Alas, what rejoicing' and is my only source for stanza 6. A broadside in British Library collection C.22.f.6 (from which I take the title) lacks stanzas 5–8 but offers 'The Witty Maid's Answer'. Her best stanza:

> Thou may'st go follow thy sweetheart to Norwich.
> She is a lass that's fit for your tooth.
> A slut's good enough to make sloven's porridge
> And that was the reason ye left me, forsooth.
> But this I say, and will do so still:
> 'Tis a good Jack makes a good Jill.

She ends with a pithy phrase: 'And this shall be my last reply,/Go walk up out, knave. What care I?'

**It is a kind of pleasing thing** Egerton 923 and many others, with variants and additions
An ancient bit of fun. A 15th-century manuscript, Sloane 2593, has the lines:

> Withouten feet it can stand.
> It can smite and has no hand.
> Rid [riddle] yourself what it may be...

*Wit and Mirth: or Pills to Purge Melancholy* of 1707 has a musical setting (refrain: 'With a humbledum, grumbledum, humbledum, grumbledum, hey!')

**A ballad, a ballad, let every poet** *Musarum Deliciae: or The Muses Recreation*, 1656, W&D 1656, *Wit Restor'd*, 1658
This dates from 1620. The monstrous women are the chief topic of a London gentleman, John Chamberlain, in a letter of January 1620 (*The Chamberlain Letters*, ed. Elizabeth McClure Thomson, 1966):

> Yesterday the Bishop of London called together all his clergy about this town and told them he had express commandment from the king [James I] to will them to inveigh vehemently and bitterly in their sermons against the insolency of our women and their wearing of broad-brimmed hats, pointed doublets, their hair cut short or shorn, and some of them stilettos or poignards and such other trinkets of like moment... The world is very far out of order.

Soon Chamberlain reports the pulpits ringing with denunciations of these women. 'The players [in the theatres] have likewise taken them to task, and so do the ballads and ballad-singers, so that they can come nowhere but their ears tingle.' They were attacked too in a little book, *Hic Mulier or the Man-Woman*, over their broad-brimmed hats, and for 'exchanging ... the modest upper parts of a concealing straight gown to the loose, lascivious open embracement of a French doublet, being all unbutton'd to entyce ... and extreme short wasted to give a most easy way to every luxurious action; the glory of a faire large hayre, to the shame of most ruffianly short lockes.'

**'Tis late and cold, stir up the fire** John Fletcher, *The Lovers' Progress*, performed about 1623

**I came unto a Puritan to woo** Merry D; *Rump: or an Exact Collection of the Choycest Poems and Songs Relating to the Late Times*, 1662 (source of title)
This is in three Bodleian manuscripts of the 1630s, with many variant readings. In Rawl.poet.199 the last eight lines read:

> 'O do not swear,' quoth she, 'yet put it out,
> Because I would not have you break your oath.'
> I felt a bed there as I groped about.
> 'Introth,' quoth I, 'here will we rest us both.'

'Swear ye introth?' quoth she. 'Had you not sworn
I had not done't, but took it in foul scorn.'
'Then will you come?' quoth I. 'Though I be loath
I'll come,' quoth she, 'be't but to keep your oath.'

**Bacchus, Iacchus, fill our brains** Lawes ms
The masque for which Lawes set Aurelian Townshend's song appears to have been performed at Hampton Court with William Cartwright's play *The Royal Slave* — two years after Lawes set Milton's *Comus.*

**Hang sorrow and cast away care** John Hilton's *Catch that Catch Can*, 1652
This and the next song were set by William Lawes, who was killed in 1645; and all the songs in these catch books no doubt date from before the 1650s

**The pot, the pipe, the quart, the can** Hilton's *Catch that Catch Can*, 1658

**If any so wise is** *Catch that Catch Can*, 1652; set by Dr William Child (1606–97), a Gentleman of the Chapel Royal from 1660

**A pox on the jailer and on his fat jowls** *Catch that Catch Can*, 1652

**Have you observed the wench in the street?** *Catch that Catch Can*, 1652

**Wilt thou be fat? I'll tell thee how** *Catch that Catch Can*, 1658

**She lay all naked in her bed** Harl.3991; Wit&D; Wilson ms
Wit&D has a sort of parody of this, even more freely descriptive, beginning 'She lay up to the navel bare'. It has this vivid stanza:

Her hand beneath my waistband slips
To grope in busy wise:
Which caused a trembling in her lips
And a shivering in her eyes.

This time, though, it is no dream ... unfortunately. It ends:

But a pox upon true jests and dreams,
I had better have lain without her.

**Yes, I could love, could I but find** Add.10337; *The Academy of Complements*, 1650; John Playford's *The Treasury of Musick*, 1669
Several manuscripts record other thoughts on their ideal. Stowe 962 ends:

Not sullen silent, nor all tongue;
Not puling weak nor manlike strong;
Modest, yet full of pleasing mirth,
And close as centre of the earth;
That calls to bed with melting eyes,
And sweet and fresh as morn doth rise,
If such a mistress I could find, etc —

**A justice walking o'er the frozen Thames** *Witt's Recreations*, 1640

**Love thee! Good faith, not I** Lawes ms (and Lawes's *Third Book of Ayres and Dialogues*, 1658)

**When John Cornutus doth his wife reprove** *Witt's Recreations*, 1645

**I blame not lusty Doll that strives so much** *Witt's Recreations*, 1645

**He who would write an epitaph** *Witt's Recreations* 1645

**She was so exquisite a whore** Add.22582
James Howell, traveller and letter-writer, wrote to a friend from Madrid in 1622: 'Hereunto I will adde a strong and deepe fetcht character, as I think you

will confesse when you have read it, that one made in this Court of a Courtesane.' Here it is in Spanish:

*Eres puta tan artera*
*Qu'en el vientre de tu madre*
*Tu tunistas de manera*
*Que te cavalgue el padre.*

Much later, in the time of Charles II, the English version was applied to at least two of his mistresses, Barbara Villiers and Nell Gwynn.

**As I was riding on a day** Harl.3991

**I sing the praises of a fart** *Witt's Recreations*, 1645 (*Westminster Drollery*, 1672, has a version with 22 new lines)

**If any man doth want a house** *Sportive Wit*, 1656, Bodleian; Merry D; *The New Academy of Complements*, 1671
Various hands worked on this over the years. The first four stanzas are chiefly according to *Sportive Wit*; the fifth is from Merry D. After 'You cannot miss your way', Merry D has:

None ever yet within my house
Did ever weep or wail.
You need not fear the tenure of it
For it is held in tail.

*New Academy*'s fifth stanza has these lines:

But though my house be deep and dark
'Thas many a man made merry,
And in't much liquor has been spent
More precious far than sherry.

**What though I were not pewed, but stood in yoke** *Wits Interpreter*, 1655

**To be a whore, despite of grace** Charles Cotton's *Poems on Several Occasions*, 1689

**In this cold monument lies one** Wit&D
In a collection of Charles Cotton's verse, *Poems on Several Occasions*, published two years after his death, this poem differs at many points from Wit&D of 1656. The main variants are: after line 6, an extra couplet, 'As soft and snowy as that down / Adorns the blow-ball's frizzled crown'; the next couplet reads, 'Pleasant as th'odorous month of May; / As glorious and as light as day'; lines 17–18, 'For so she was, and since there are / Such whores, I could wish them all as fair.' I think the Wit&D compiler got hold of the better manuscript.

**Will women's vanities never have end?** Harl.3991; *Musarum Deliciae: or The Muses Recreation*, 1656
The Rev Dr James Smith (1605–67), who was for a time a navy chaplain, was Sir John Mennes's friend. Of his 16 stanzas I have dropped 7, 8 and 10–16.

**When I see the young men play** John Gamble's *Ayres and Dialogues*, 1656 (translation by Thomas Stanley from the *Anacreontea*)

**A boat, a boat, bring to the ferry** Bodleian ms Rawl.poet.152
This is an expansion of a catch in *Catch that Catch Can*, 1652:

A boat, a boat, haste to the ferry,
For we'll go over to be merry,
To laugh and sing and drink old sherry.

**But now for rules before we eat** Wit&D

**All in the land of Essex** broadside of 1659 in collection 669.f.21; Sir John Denham, *Poems and Translations*, 1668
Ralph Green's backsliding seems to have been in 1653. Cavaliers revelled in stories about erring sectarians: Sir John Birkenhead wrote another Colchester lampoon, 'The Four-Legg'd Quaker', and also 'The Four-Legged Elder, or a Horrible Relation of a Dog and an Elder's Maid'.

**This dog may kiss your hand, your lip** *Wits Interpreter*, 1655

**A silly poor shepherd** *Sportive Wit*, 1656 (Bodleian); *The New Academy of Complements*, 1671; *Windsor Drollery*, 1672
A broadside piracy of this makes it twice as long. A taste of its dialogue:

'O fie! my dear husband, you sure are in jest.
You see how I labour to get you the best.
I card and I spin, both above and below,
To clothe you till you no cuc-colder can grow.'

'You say you plucked wool from hedge, bush and tree
To make a warm coat and a nightcap for me,
But you reel at a rate, with a spindle so free,
That I fear when they're done the cuc-colder to be...'

**Are you grown so melancholy** Merry D
In *Choyce Poems by the Wits of Both Universities*, 1661, a song entitled 'The Lash' uses the same clever rhyme-scheme. A sample:

Come, you divines that live so pure
And keep another to serve your cure,
  You will preach, not to teach, but to show
  Phrases fine, scarce divine, how they flow.
The benefice you'll keep, whilst another starves the sheep.
  Come, I must lash you.

Come, you physicians that do kill
More than you cure, to try your skill:
  Our disease does you please, and we see
  Our relief is our grief. For the fee
You'll cure us of our purse, when our bodies are far worse.
  Come, I must lash you.

**It was my chance to pass by** *A Jovial Garland*, 1670

**You courtiers scorn us country clowns** *Oxford Drollery*, 1671

**I went to the tavern, and then** *Westminster Drollery*, 1672

**And I have a mind to be married** *Westminster Drollery*, 1672

**Let us drink and be merry, dance, joke and rejoice** *Choice Ayres, Songs & Dialogues*, John Playford, 1676
This song, written for a Lord Mayor's entertainment in 1675, became a popular classic and acquired many new stanzas. For example, in a broadside, 'The Careless Gallant' (Roxburghe collection), published before 1680:

I never could gain satisfaction upon
Your dreams of a bliss when we're cold as a stone.
The sages call us drunkards, gluttons and wenchers,
But we find such morsels upon their own trenchers.
  For Abigail, Hannah and Sister Prudènce   *[Puritan girls*
  Will simper to nothing a hundred years hence.

Or the following, in a cheap 'garland' of about 1750:

The plush-coated quack, whose fees to enlarge
Kills people by licence and at their own charge,
He builds up fine structures by ill-gotten wealth,
By his doses of opium and packets for pelf.
Thus health and long life he pretends to dispense.
Himself will be mouldy a hundred years hence.

**A chambermaid was got with child** *Mock Songs and Joking Poems*, 'By the Author of Westminster Drollery', 1675

**What 'a devil ails our poets all** *Wit and Drollery*, 1682

**Since the pox or the plague of inconstancy reigns** *Choice Ayres and Songs ...The Second Book*, John Playford, 1679

**Religion's a politic law** Harl.7315; Portland PwV44, Nottingham University Library; ms Firth c.16, Bodleian
Gentlemen of libertine views had this and other irreverent verses professionally copied by 'scriptoria' for private circulation. The Harleian manuscript copy is annotated 'By the Ld Dorset or Cha: Blount', meaning Charles Sackville, Earl of Dorset, and Charles Blount, a deist who wrote against superstition. Both were friends of the poet Rochester, a scorner of churchly orthodoxies. His 'Satire Against Mankind' (1674–5) hits at the cleric who

...frames deep mysteries, then finds 'em out,
Filling with frantic crowds of thinking fools
Those reverend bedlams, colleges and schools.

This is clearly echoed in 'Religion's a politic law'. The song got into print. Vol 26 of the Madden collection has a broadside version, perhaps circulated privately. A version even reached the lower orders: St Bride Printing Library has a 48-line street ballad, 'The Politick Law'. Neither gives a printer's name.

**I'll tell my mother, Jenny cries** *New Ayres and Dialogues*, 1678
**Fie, nay, prithee John** *Wit & Mirth, An Antidote Against Melancholy*, 1682
A revised version, entitled 'A Chiding Catch', set by Dr John Blow, is in *The Second Book of the Pleasant Musical Companion*, 1701:

Fie! nay, prithee John!
Do not quarrel, man!
Let's be merry and drink about.

You're a rogue, you've cheated me,
I'll prove before this company.
I caren't a farthing, sir, for all you are so stout.

Sir, you lie, I scorn your word
Or any man that wears a sword.
For all you huff, who cares a t—
Or who cares for you?

**To thee, to thee and to a maid** *Catch that Catch Can*, John Playford, 1685

**Sir Walter enjoying his damsel one night** Add.29397 (1682–90); *The Second Book of the Pleasant Musical Companion*, 1701
According to the memoirist John Aubrey, when Sir Walter Raleigh got a maid of honour 'up against a tree in a wood', her 'sweet Sir Walter!' protests ended, 'in the ecstasy', as 'Swisser Swatter Swisser Swatter'.

**'Tis woman makes us love** *Catch that Catch Can*, 1685

**Full bags, a brisk bottle and a beautiful face** *The Pleasant Musical Companion, Second Book*, 1686

**Once, twice, thrice I Julia tried** *The Pleasant Musical Companion, Second Book*

**In a cellar at Sodom at the sign of the T—** *New Poems . . . All Written by Mr D'Urfey*, 1690

This may have inspired the refrain of a ballad published in the 1690s by Philip Brooksby — 'And show me how my daddy got me'.

**Say, good Master Bacchus, astride on your butt** *Apollo's Banquet*, 1691

**Phillis, the fairest of love's foes** *The Merry Musician*, 1716

This dates from long before 1716: in a manuscript of Charles II's time, Rawl. poet.173, Bodleian, it is found among songs by Rochester, Sedley, etc, and is entitled 'A Catch by Ld Dorset', that is Charles Sackville, Earl of Dorset.

**Love is now become a trade** *The Theater of Music*, Henry Playford, 1685

**Corinna, I excuse thy face** *The Banquet of Musick*, 1692

**Young women and damsels that love to go fine** broadside in collection C.22.f.6, not later than 1696

The topknot-calf alluded to is in a broadside (Pepys V, 412) that begins:

> In Somersetshire as it happened one day,
> Down in a meadow where my cattle did play,
> Whilst Colly took bull there, a lady came by
> *With topknots of ribbands full six storeys high.*
>
> You'd wonder to see how my cow she did stare,
> And bull at the topknot drew backward his ware.
> They frighted were both when this lady came by
> *With towers and topknots full six storeys high. . .*

This shock at a critical moment produces a monstrous calf — with topknot.

**Do not rumple my topknot** songsheet, collection K. 5. b. 15, 1690s (with false titlepage from *Joyful Cuckoldom*, 1671)

A Pepys broadside, 'The Kind Lad and Scornful Lass', lifts this song and pads it out by making it a dialogue.

**Should I not lead a happy life (*hick*)** *Deliciae Musicae*, Second Book of the Second Volume, Henry Playford, 1696

**Hey ho! hey ho! hey ho! hey ho!** Add. 29378, collection of theatre songs set by John Eccles, who became Master of the Musick to Queen Anne

The song was for a play of 1697, *The Intrigues at Versailles*.

**Hark, the cock crowed. 'Tis day all abroad** *Wit and Mirth: or Pills to Purge Melancholy*, 1699

**Lady, sweet now, do not frown** *Wit and Mirth ... The Second Part*, 1700 (set by Samuel Akeroyde, a leading theatre composer)

**Doff with your clogs and ceckers** broadsides, Roxburghe III, 424, and Madden collection, vol 26; no date, no printer

Each broadside has stanzas lacking in the other. I have deleted a few. The song evidently has a long ancestry. *Sportive Wit*, published 1656 but mainly dating from years earlier, has a song with one very similar stanza:

> The first beginning was Sellenger's Round,
> Where the cow leapt over the moon,
> And the goodwife shit in the pisspot
> And the cream ran into her shoon.

'Wigan' suggests a Lancashire origin. The madcap improvization resembles that of the 'dreg-songs' noted by David Herd, the 18th-century Scottish collector, which workmen devised competitively in their lunch-break. Here is a taste ('white-breek' and 'steel-pike' are a foot-soldier and a lancer):

Kenned ye nae white-breek?
White-breek and steel-pike
Kissed the lass behind the dyke
And she whelped a bairnie…
Tell me a true note,
True note, true song!
I've dregged o'er long,
O'er lang, o'er late,
Quo' the haddock to the skate.
Quo' the skate to the eel,
Cock nae I my tail weel?

Early nonsense-spinning can be found in *Christmas carolles newely Inprynted* of about 1550 (spelling modernized):

Nine mile to Michaelmas
  Our dame began to brew.
Michael set his mare to grass.
  Lord, so fast it snew!
The cow broke loose, the rope ran home,
  Sir, God give you good-morrow… *etc*

**Good-morrow, Gossip Joan** *Wit and Mirth: or Pills to Purge Melancholy*, 1714; songsheet collection G.305
In its long life, 'Gossip Joan' was added to, reshaped, and corrupted. In a 19th-century broadside collection, 11630.f.7, chiefly Irish and American, she becomes Gossip Jones. The duck stanza emerges like this:

My duck has swallowed a snail,
And is not that a wonder?
The horns grew out of her tay-hay-hail,
Of her tay-hay-hail, her tay-hay-hail,
And split her rump asunder, Gossip Jones.

Village singers gave Cecil Sharp their versions in 1903 and 1908. Here is one of their less inept stanzas:

Old zow she eat the trough
And was not that a wonder?
Instead of her little che wee wee
She brought forth nothing but timber.
    God save Joan!

**Being drunk last night, I found** *A New Academy of Complements*, 1715
This piece with its over-tricky rhyme-play was digested into a 24-line song 'to a tune of the late Mr Henry Purcell's' for the 1719 edition of *Wit and Mirth: or Pills to Purge Melancholy*. It begins:

Drunk I was last night, that's poss. *[positive]*
    My wife began to scold.
Say what I could for my heart's blood,
    Her clack she would not hold.

**What a fine thing have I seen today!** songsheet collection H.1601
Hoop skirts remained a satirical topic for years. A song printed a little later in York, 'The Wonderful Virtues and Comical Conveniences of the New-Fashion Hooped Petticoats', laments that they are even being worn by girls of the lower classes. And it detects reasons for the hoops' appeal:

So strange and fantastic young ladies are grown,
Not only Miss Madam, but Gillian and Joan,
They must have such petticoats never was known,
    Large hooped petticoats, monstrous petticoats,
    Bouncing hooped petticoats, maids...

I tell you they was not invented for pride,
For when a young miss has a chub by her side, *young man*
Should there come a search, straight her spark she can hide
    In large petticoats, monstrous petticoats,
    Bouncing hooped petticoats, maids...

One faculty more I had like to've forgot.
You know in the summer when weather is hot
The air may blow under and cool you know what.
    Oh! brave petticoats, monstrous petticoats,
    Bouncing hooped petticoats, maids.

**Our grannums of old were so piously nice** broadside, collection 1872.a.1

**There was a buxom lass and she had a velvet a——** songsheet, collection H.1601

**Ye circum– and uncircumcised** songsheet, collection H.1601; broadside, collection 1876.f.1

**Cloe, a coquet in her prime** *A Collection of Songs ... by Mr Leveridge,* 1727
Richard Leveridge was a noted bass singer in the theatres and other entertainments of the early 18th century,and proprietor of a Covent Garden tavern.

**You find from the beginning** songsheet, collection H.1601

**What though I am a London dame** *The Robin*, songbook of 1749 (but the song is of about 1727)

**What though they call me country lass** songsheet, collection G.315; broadside, collection TC.6.a.8

**Fair Venus, the goddess of beauty and love** Roxburghe III, 421

*AUGUSTAN GRAFFITI*: 12 items from *The Merry-Thought: or, The Glass-Window and Bog-House Miscellany*, 1730–32:

**Clarinda lay here; No hero looks so fierce in fight; Because they cannot eat, some authors write; Drunk at Comb-alley, horrid drunk; Hither I came in haste to sh–t; Whilst Lady Mary slept at ease; Good Lord! Who could think; Within this place two ways I've been delighted; Have you not in a chimney seen; The cook, confound her, boiled no roots; Such places as these; The nicest maid, with the whitest rump; From costive stools and hidebound wit**

**O you merry, merry souls** *The Hop Garland*, undated (64 lines cut)

**My bunch of rods, for flogging cull** *The Harlot's Progress: Being the Life of the Noted Moll Hackabout*, 1732
Condoms made of gut were said to have been invented by a 17th-century Colonel Condon or Cundum, but had been in use long before. Edmund Curll, the publisher named in this Hackabout poem, announced in the *Daily Journal* in 1723, *Armour. A Poem. An imitation of Milton.* This panegyric, by the Rev White Kennet, son of a bishop, commended the condom to young men:

...Stay a while, till fitly arm'd
With *Cundum* Shield, at *Rummer* best supply'd
Or never-failing *Rose*; so may you thrum

Th'exstatic Harlot, and each joyous Night
Crown with fresh Raptures...

(*Rummer, Rose*: 'Two famous taverns of intrigue near Covent-Garden')

Twenty years later came a similar panegyric, *The Machine: or, Love's Preservative*, now in rhyming couplets:

By this Machine secure, the willing Maid
Can taste Love's Joys, nor is she more afraid
Her swelling Belly should, or squalling Brat,
Betray the luscious Pastime she has been at...
Happy the Man in whose close Pocket's found,
Whether with Green or Scarlet Ribbon bound,
A well-made Cundum...
By trusty Mother Lewis* best supplied,
Nor at the Rose or Fountain e'er deny'd.

'* *At her Cundum Warehouse in St Martin's Lane'*

As for poems on dying bawds, in 1718 Allan Ramsay wrote 102 robust lines on a noted Edinburgh one, 'Lucky Spence's Last Advice'. A sample:

My benison come on good doers
Who spend their cash on bawds and whoors.
May they never want the wale of cures — *the best*
For a fair snout.
Foul fa' the quacks that fire smoors — *smothers*
And puts na out.

My malison light ilky day — *every*
On them that drinks and disna pay
But takes a snack and rins away.
May't be their hap
Never to want a gonorrhoea
Or rotten clap.

**How happy a state doth the damsel possess** broadside, collection C.116.i.4

**The maltman comes on Monday** *The Tea-Table Miscellany*, 1733

**Now husband, the day is a-coming** *The Horn-Fair Garland*
The quaint ceremony of Horn Fair flourished at least from the 16th century. A broadside of the 1680s, 'A General Summons for those belonging to the Hen-Peck'd Frigate', gives the essentials: 'You are hereby lawfully summoned...to appear at *Cuckolds-Point* (being the antient Place of our Rendezvous) on the 18th of this Instant October, precisely by Seven of the Clock in the Morning, well fitted with a *Basket, Pit-Axe* and *Shovel*, there to give your Attendance, till the list of your Brethren, the Knights of the *Forked Order*, is called over, and then at the Word of Command to march in good order to the Gravel-Pits, there to dig Sand and Gravel for Repairing the Foot-Ways, that your Wives with their Friends may have pleasure and delight in walking to *Horn-Fair*...'

The procession was from Cuckold's Point, Deptford, to Charlton village, where a riotous three-day fair was held. The surprisingly cooperative cuckolds wore horns on their heads, and sometimes women's clothes. Lewdly decorated horns were sold at the fair, and even gingerbread men had horns.

**Of honest malt liquor let English boys sing** *The Catch Club*, 1733

**I the other night was drunk** Roxburghe III, 489

**Young Morgan was a lusty blade** *Young Morgan's Garland*, in collection 11621.c.7; slip-songs, Madden collection, vol 2, 625 and 626

The Madden versions have an introductory stanza:

Come all ye bold and swaggering blades
That go in search of plunder —
With pistols cocked and courage bold
Have voices loud as thunder.

They also add four lines that spoil the stoical ending by having the king pardon Morgan (though he has ridden in the cart to Tyburn!).

**Come all ye bucks and lads of fire** songsheet, collection G.307
*The Buck's Delight*, reprinting this about 1765, makes the title 'The Modern Lass Undressed from Top to Toe'.

**Ye brimstones of Drury and Exeter-street** *The Musical Miscellany*, 1760

**Though I sweep to and fro, old iron to find** *The Kennel-Raker's Garland*, Harding A.2, 55, Bodleian; *The Comic Songster*, 1789

**Upon the march it was my lot** *The Nightingale*, Part I, Aldermary Church Yard songster, and various others

**Near to Temple Bar lived two trading women** broadside, Madden collection, vol 26
This song is another of those heard in the London streets by Francis Place in the late 18th century. He quotes almost identical first and fourth stanzas. The verse form follows that of an early 17th-century song, 'A Puritan of late / And eke a holy sister / A-catechizing sat / And fain he would have kissed her' (I give its music). The form is used too in a song of the 1620s about whores that begins, 'Panders come away, / Bring forth your whores by clusters'. It may be that 'The Whores' Downfall' dates from the 17th century.

**To the hundreds of Drury I write** songsheet, collection I.600; *The Honest Fellow, or Reveller's Memorandum-Book*, 1790; *A New Flash Song-book, or the Bowman Priggs Delight*, Bodleian
It is not surprising that hanging ballads became popular in George III's reign, when the number of hanging offences, chiefly to do with property, passed 200. This longlived song has many variants. The *Honest Fellow* version describes the procession in carts from Newgate to Tyburn:

Through the streets our slow wheels do move.
The tolls of the death-bell dismay us.
With nosegays we're decked and clean gloves,
So trim and so gay they array us.
The passage all crowded we see
With maidens that view us with pity.
Our air all admiring agree
Such lads are not left in the city.

And its four closing lines are:

By the gullet we're tied very tight.
We beg all the spectators, pray for us.
Our peepers are hid from the light,
The tumbril shoves off and we morris.

Francis Place in his reminiscences writes (ms Add. 27826): 'The streets from Newgate to Tyburn were thronged with people, and all the windows of the houses filled… People used to wait the coming of the carts… some holding a pot of beer in their hands, others a measure of gin, to treat the criminals… Others threw oranges and apples to them… Songs were sung and the ballads sold at the corners of the streets, all along Holborn, St Giles's and Oxford

Street. These songs were either bawdy songs or songs commending the acts and deeds of highwaymen and other thieves.' The riotous processions were ended by means of an order of 1783 establishing the scaffold outside Newgate jail. But still huge crowds gathered, and were worked by the ballad-vendors.

The phrase in the song about 'birth, education and parents' echoes the patter of hawkers selling Last Dying Speech broadsides. Place quotes them: 'Here's all the right and true last dying speech and confession, birth, parentage and education, life, character and behaviour of the three (or six or ten) unfortunate malefactors who was executed this morning at Tyburn.'

**De night before Larry was stretched** songster printed at Monaghan, 1788, *Young Squire Reynolds's welcome home to Ireland* (and many later songsters, broadsides, etc, both Irish and British)
Various Irish gentlemen of the 1780s have been credited with this. A note on a Madden broadside says it was by 'William Maher of Waterford a linen draper & called from a club foot Hurlfoot Bill'. Others credit Kane O'Hara, 'poet laureat' of the convivial Kingdom of Dalkey, Dublin. Larry was one Laurence Coffey. A sequel, 'Larry's Stiff' (printer, W Goggin, Limerick), begins:

As soon as poor Larry was stretched
  De boys dey soon cut him down proper.
We did every ting dat we cud
  In hopes to cheat Jack the breth-stopper, *Jack Ketch, hangman*
But all we cud do it was fudge
  For Jacky is seldom mistaken...

Note that in Larry's time hanging was by strangulation, not by a neck-breaking long drop. Another song published by Goggin, about the hanging of one Luke Caffrey, tells of the belief that a hanged man might be revived by 'a snig in de jugler' (snick in the jugular). Luke tells his friends:

'Oh, you know dat it is me last hope,
As de surgints of 'otomy tell us,
Dat when I'm cut down from de rope
You'll bring back de puff to me bellows
    And set me once more on me pins...'
Wid de stiff to the shebeen we hied,
But det had shut fast ev'ry grinder.
His brain-box hung all on one side
And no distiller's pig could be blinder...
We lent him a snig, as he said,
On de jugler, 'tis here dat de mark is.
But soon as we found him quite ded
In de dust-case we bundled his carcase,
*And gave him a bloody long lease of de sanctified sod in de*
    *Ospital-fields, your soul!*

**Come all ye country yea-and-noes** songsheet, collection G.307

**Oh the other day as Sandman Joe** songsheet, collection G.312; Francis Place collection (Add. 27825)

**Come list awhile, I'll tell you how, to Joe the sandman's joy, sir** *The Festival of Anacreon*, 1788, Bodleian

**Ye scamps, ye pads, ye divers and all upon the lay** *The Choice of Harlequin* (published text of the pantomime), 1782
This was such a hit that it inspired parodies. In 1787 *Parsley's Fashionable Lyric Companion* has a song sung 'in the Character of a Jew Broker':

Ye jobbers, underwriters, ye all of pen and ink,
Who in the Alley's gay parterres your tea and coffee drink,
Rattling up your yellow-boys, come hither at my call:
I'm buyer, or I'm seller, and I can sherve you all.
Ye bulls, ye bears, ye lame ducks and all ye waddling crew,
If 'twas not for us smoutchers I don't know what ye'd do...

In 1794 John Devonshire's *Songs Political, Satyrical and Convivial* has 'The Duck and Apollo Blades'— meaning the bad characters who haunted the Dog and Duck (closed by order, 1799) and Apollo Gardens in St George's Fields, Lambeth. A sample:

*Ye bucks, ye rolling kiddies and all upon the lay,*
*In this gay town of London you frolic, sport and play.*
*Flashing of your plumage, with nappers decked so fine,*
*At the Apollo, Duck and Pup, with your mots you cut a shine.*

At jelly-house and bagnios the flats they oft take in.
The queans they flash the milky-way to lure you to their ken.
First your bit they hobble ere they to snooze will go,
Then deaf to sage experience, you stroke some rotten frow...

My peepers! Who've we here now? Why sure it is poor Tom,
Who with many a rolling quean his length has oft-times gone;
But p–x, that dire usurper, has proved poor Tom's o'erthrow
And now no more with demi-reps poor Tom his length can go.

Besides 'Duck and Pup', popular jokey variations on pub names were 'Fist and Five Shillings' for The Hand and Crown, and 'The Scarcity' for The Maidenhead. 'Flash the milky-way': the women bare their breasts to lure men in; 'your bit they hobble': they demand advance payment.

**Dinner o'er, and grace said, we'll for bus'ness prepare** songsheet, collection G.307; *The Comic Songster*, 1789

**A flaxen-headed milkmaid** songsheet, collection G.377

**Come, charge your glasses! Let us raise** *A Complete Collection of Songs by Captain [Charles] Morris*, 1788 (9th edition)

**One day as I rambled 'cross Kensington Park** broadside (L Lund, York), collection 1870.c.2; songster (G Swindells, Manchester ), collection 11621.b.14
New versions of this heartfelt piece keep appearing into the 19th century.

**Molly put the kettle on, Molly put the kettle on** *The Vocal Museum* and *The London Songster*, collection 1077.g.47

**I am the Pink of Clerkenwell** *The Bacchanalian Magazine and Cyprian Enchantress*, 1793
In the last stanza, 'weigh your weight' means to have so many crimes to your name that a police informer who got you convicted would win the maximum reward, £40, rich pickings (if you were a highwayman, the informer would also get your horse and money). Constables got their cut — so had a motive to let criminals go on offending till they 'weighed their weight'. This sheds light on a teasing footnote by Lord Byron to *Don Juan*, Canto 11, in which he quotes some lines on a highwayman and his girl: 'She'll surely turn snitch for the forty, / That her Jack may be regular weight.' He is quoting a street-song, 'The Dog and Duck Rig', which he seems to have carried abroad with him.

**I'm a Hounslow young lad, and Tidy's my name** *One Thousand Eight Hundred*, collection of verse published by George Saville Carey (son of Henry Carey) in 1800 but dating from some years earlier

**The landlord he looks very big** broadside, collection 1870.c.2

**Jonathan a-wooing went** *The Buck's Delight*, Dublin, 1795?, Harding collection, Bodleian

**The satiric song of Chit-Chat I mean now to reverse** *The Universal Songster*, 1825 (but dating from years earlier, like other songs in this collection)

**With spirits gay I mount the box, the tits up to their traces** *Tegg's Prime Song Book, Bang Up to the Mark!*, 1810
The song was 'sung with unbounded applause' by the noted comic actor Charles Mathews, playing Dick Cypher of the Four-in-Hand Club in a hit of 1810 at the Lyceum Theatre, the musical farce *Hit or Miss!* by Isaac Pocock.

To have a vehicle of any sort was a step up socially. Of those named in the refrain, only the curricle and tandem rise to two-horse quality. A 'four in hand' was either a stagecoach or a rich man's carriage, the Rolls of its day.

**Come, come, my good masters, what's all this about** *The Universal Songster*

**Dear doctor, be clever, and fling off your beaver** *The Universal Songster*

**Oh stop the mill, stop the mill, stop it, I pray** *The Songster's Companion*, about 1820

**Really wherever one passes** broadside, collection 11621.k.5

**O Lord, O Lord, what times are these for making alteration** *The Rumcodger's Collection of Prime New Flash & Amatory Songs*, 1825–30

**Vhen the noted Jerry Abershaw vas cast for death** *The Fal-Lal Songster*, 1830?

**To his bride as she blushing lay by her Adonis** *The Fancy!*, songster, 1830?

**A little black thing** *The Flash Chaunter*, one of many flash songsters sold, about 1830 onwards, by William West, a leader in this field

**There stood on the shores of far distant Van Dieman** *The Knowing Chaunter, or Kiddy's Cabinet!* (West)

**Oh, mercury pills — those teasing pills** *The Delicious Chaunter* (West)
A parody on 'My Native Hills'.

**I am a fine blowen** *The Flare-up Songster, or Flash Kiddys' Fancy*, 1830?

**Oh! pity my sorrows — a poor old mot** *The Flash Olio*, 1830?
To the tune of 'Pity the sorrows of a poor old man'. Another songster, *The Flash Minstrel*, has a rival parody:

> ...I vonce upon Coventry-street so gay
> Could pick up many a couter. *a pound*
> Then pity the sorrows of a poor old mot
> That can't get a kid to suit her...
>
> So all you coves vot vants a gal,
> Speed up – I'll be your sleeper.
> For sixpence sleep with me you shall,
> And you'll not find one that's cheaper.

**I once knowed a gemman, at Brighton last year** broadside (Green, Birmingham), collection LR.271.a.2
To the tune of 'Love's Ritornella', popular from 1829. Although the broadside is my only sighting of Bill Richy, his exploits evidently went on being celebrated: Alan Bold's *Bawdy Beautiful*, 1979, has an enfeebled 20th-century version. ...Seekers of wholesome seasides will note that as early as 1830 bathers could encounter 'a great lump of '.

# BIBLIOGRAPHY

*Sources for all the items, and much else besides, are given in the endnotes. Here are just a few books for readers who would like to explore the field further. Many of those of recent date have useful bibliographies.*


ANTHOLOGIES & REPRINTS

Ault, Norman, *Elizabethan Lyrics from the Original Texts*, 1966; *Seventeenth Century Lyrics from the Original Texts*, 1950 (pioneering; first published in the 1920s)

Barke, James, and Sydney Goodsir Smith, *The Merry Muses of Caledonia*, Edinburgh, 1965/1982

Beal, Peter, general editor, *J. Cleaveland Revived, Parnassus Biceps, Wits Recreations*, etc, 17th-century verse miscellanies in facsimile, Aldershot (Scolar), 1990

Burford, Ephraim John, *Bawdy Verse: A Pleasant Collection*, Penguin, 1982; from 1400 to 1786

Chambers, Edmund, and Frank Sidgwick, *Early English Lyrics*, 1907, 1966; to early 16th century

Crawford, Thomas, *Love, Labour and Liberty: the eighteenth-century Scottish lyric*, Cheadle, Cheshire, 1976

Davis, Walter, *The Works of Thomas Campion*, 1969

Doughtie, Edward, *Lyrics from English Airs, 1596–1622*, Harvard University Press, 1970; full texts from 27 songbooks

Ebsworth, the Rev J Woodfall, *Merry Drollery Compleat*, 1875; *Westminster Drolleries*, 1875; *Choyce Drollery* plus *An Antidote Against Melancholy*, 1876: pioneering reprints with commentary, by unstuffy Victorian clergyman

Farmer, John S, *National Ballad and Song: Merry Songs and Ballads*, 5 vol, 1897; uncensored (facsimile reprint, New York , 1964)

Herd, David, *Ancient and Modern Scottish Songs*, 2 vol, Edinburgh, 1973; reprint of 1776 edition

Holloway, John, and Joan Black, *Later English Broadside Ballads*, vol I, 1975; vol II, 1979; selections from Madden collection, Cambridge

Johnson, James, and Robert Burns, *The Scots Musical Museum*, facsimile of 1787–1803 edition, 2 vol, Aldershot (Scolar), 1990

Legman, Gershon, *The Merry Muses of Caledonia*, New York, 1965

Parker, Derek, *An Anthology of Erotic Verse*, 1982

Pinto, V de Sola, and A E Rodway, *The Common Muse*, 1957/1965; 450 years of ballad poetry, chiefly from broadsides

Randall, Eric Lemuel, *The Merry Muses and Other Burnsian Frolics*, 1966

Robbins, Rossell H, *Secular Lyrics of the XIVth and XVth Centuries*, Oxford, 1956

Speaight, George, *Bawdy Songs of the Early Music Hall*, 1977

Sternfeld, Frederick, and David Greer, *English Madrigal Verse, 1588–1632*, Oxford, 1967; revision of Edmund Fellowes's 1920 edition; 1,700 texts, including lute-songs

Stevens, John, *Music and Poetry of the Early Tudor Court*, Cambridge, 1961

Walker, Keith, *The Poems of John Wilmot Earl of Rochester*, Oxford, 1985

Wardroper, John, *Love and Drollery*, 1969

*Wit and Mirth, or Pills to Purge Melancholy*, New York, 1959, reprint of 1876 edition of the songbooks of 1719–20

MUSIC

Chappell, William, *Popular Music of the Olden Time*, 1855–9: pioneer study (reprint, New York, 1965)

Dart, Thurston, et al, *The English Madrigalists*, 1956—, revised edition of Edmund Fellowes's *The English Madrigal School*, 1914–24; *The English Lute-Songs*, 1975—, revised edition of Fellowes's *The English School of Lutenist Song-Writers*, 1920–32; reprints of early 17th-century songbooks

Day, Cyrus, and Eleanore Murrie, *English Song-Books 1651–1702*, Oxford, 1940; guide to 252 song-books containing 4,150 songs

Fiske, Roger, *English Theatre Music in the Eighteenth Century*, Oxford, 1986

Folk Music Society of Ireland, *Popular Music in Eighteenth-Century Dublin*, Dublin, 1985

Maynard, Winifred, *Elizabethan Lyric Poetry and its Music*, Oxford, 1986

Nyman, Michael, *Come Let Us Drink*, Great Yarmouth and New York, 1972; 57 catches by Henry Purcell

Pilkington, Michael, *Campion, Dowland and the Lutenist Songwriters*, 1989; for singers, detailed repertoire of more than 400 songs

Simpson, Claude, *The British Broadside Ballad and Its Music*, Rutgers University Press, New Brunswick, New Jersey, 1966; 540 examples

Spink, Ian, *English Song: Dowland to Purcell*, 1974/1986

Sternfeld, Frederick, general editor, *English Lute Songs*, 9 vol, Scolar Press, Menston, Yorks, 1967–71, facsimile reprints of songbooks, including Thomas Campion, William Corkine, John Dowland, Robert Jones, Thomas Morley, Francis Pilkington, Walter Porter, Philip Rosseter

BACKGROUND STUDIES

Crawford, Thomas, *Society and the Lyric: A Study of the Song Culture of Eighteenth-Century Scotland*, Edinburgh, 1979

Hobbs, Mary, *Early Seventeenth-Century Verse Miscellany Manuscripts*, Aldershot (Scolar), 1992

Legman, Gershon, *The Horn Book: Studies in Erotic Folklore and Bibliography*, 1970; assertive study, valuable on bawdy song

Livingston, Carole Rose, *British Broadside Ballads of the Sixteenth Century*, New York/London, 1991

Palmer, Roy, *The Sound of History: Songs of Social Comment*, Oxford, 1988; balladry through the centuries; good bibliography

Shepard, Leslie, *The Broadside Ballad, a Study in Origins and Meaning*, 1962; *The History of Street Literature*, Newton Abbot, 1973

Shields, Hugh, *Narrative Singing in Ireland*, Dublin, 1993

Spufford, Margaret, *Small Books and Pleasant Histories: Popular Fiction and its Readership in Seventeenth-Century England*, Cambridge, 1985

Watt, Tessa, *Cheap Print and Popular Piety 1550–1640*, Cambridge, 1991

# FIRST-LINE INDEX

# AUTHOR INDEX

*(These men contribute no more than 19 per cent of the total)*